# the Infidelity Cure

# Advance Praise for The Infidelity Cure

———————— ■ ————————

*"As a psychotherapist specializing in working with men over the past 35 years, I have witnessed the devastating impact of affairs. The Infidelity Cure: How to Rebuild Your Life & Relationship after Your Affair by Dr. Jeanne Michele provides a comprehensive roadmap for men to face, heal, and recover from trauma caused by betrayal. While the author explores the shifting landscape of masculinity, she explores the underlying dynamics of infidelity and identifies ways to rebuild trust, make amends, honor commitments, and live a life of integrity—all in service to creating a deep, loving relationship with yourself and your partner. The assessments, stories, and reflecting questions throughout the book will save you years of therapy. I highly recommend this excellent book!"*

— **LEONARD SZYMCZAK, award-winning coauthor of**
***Power Tools for Men: A Blueprint for Healthy Masculinity***

*"As a former crisis counselor, and executive leader, I've seen all sides of infidelity. I've witnessed many affairs born at work—often by men, but some by women as well. What I haven't seen is such a comprehensive resource for navigating this complex topic. Dr. Michele's book delves into the internal and external motivations behind affair behavior and offers simple research-based strategies to help partners heal and rebuild trust. And despite the topic being heavy, this book inspires hope and joy while engaging readers through real-life, relatable examples. I believe it will help anyone regardless of whether or not infidelity has touched their lives, given its universal lessons on emotional and psychological growth."*

—**SCOTT CARBONARA, author, leadership speaker,**
**and CEO of Spiritus Communications**

*"The Infidelity Cure boldly invites you to ask yourself: Who am I now? Who do I want to be? And then shows you, step by step, how to navigate your way into true and lasting intimacy, one brave question and communication at a time."*

—**ANNA HUCKABEE TULL, Author of Living the Deeper YES**

"Finally, a book that offers men who have betrayed a road back...not to where the marriage was when they strayed from it, but to a new place that embraces the pain that caused them to stray, and uses it as a beacon of light to show them a new way forward, humbled but also empowered to become the profound and thoughtful, honest and caring communicator they always had the potential to be. The Infidelity Cure has not only helpful answers, but beautiful, rightful questions that lead back to love."

— **JOANNE MEDNICK, LMFT, PsyD, Founder of Serenity Trauma Center**

"After being in the Reactive Stage of life and losing what's most meaningful, Dr. Michele gently led me to a place of self-discovery and helped me discover a value system that I can hold myself accountable to. We found a place of comfort that focuses on being honest with myself first, which caused me to realize that anything short of honesty with those around me is senseless.

Dr Jeanne Michele is a blessing, someone who not only aids in the management of discomfort without judgement but also gently prods so that one can find the answers from within. Her new book The Infidelity Cure is a testament to her unwavering commitment to helping people rebuild their lives and realign their focus on what truly matters."

— **CHASE C.**

A GUIDEBOOK *for* MEN
*and the* WOMEN WHO LOVE THEM

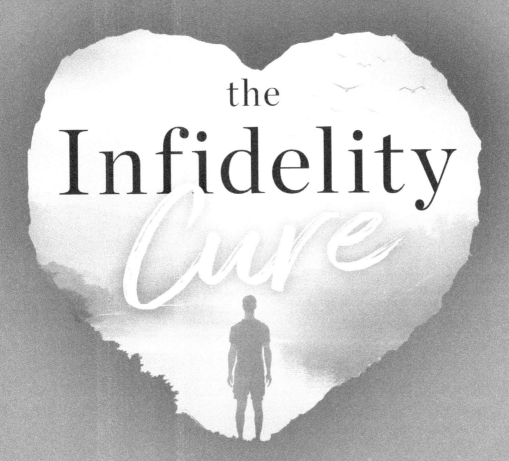

# the
# Infidelity
## *Cure*

How to Rebuild
Your Life & Relationship
After Your Affair

# Jeanne Michele, PhD

Cataloging-in-Publication Data

Names: Michele, Jeanne, author.

Title: The infidelity cure : how to rebuild your life & relationship after your affair, a guidebook for men and the women who love them / Dr. Jeanne Michele, PhD.

Description: Newport Beach, CA : Sacred Journeys Publishing, 2024. | Summary: Provides compassionate and straightforward guidance for men recovering from affairs. Narratives and practical strategies help readers explore affair behavior, relationship rebuilding, and how to best support their partner's healing. Offers insights and techniques for men, their partners, and counseling professionals.

Identifiers: LCCN 2024915246 | ISBN 9798991084338 (hardcover) | ISBN 9798991084307 (pbk.) | ISBN 9798991084314 (ebook) | ISBN 9798991084321 (audiobook)

Subjects: LCSH: Adultery. | Man-woman relationships – Psychology. | Masculinity. | Men – Psychology. | Husbands. | Marriage. | BISAC: FAMILY & RELATIONSHIPS / Marriage & Long-Term Relationships. | SELF-HELP / Gender & Sexuality. | SOCIAL SCIENCE / Men's Studies.

Classification: LCC HQ806.M53 2024 | DDC 306.736 M--dc23

LC record available at https://lccn.loc.gov/2024915246

First Edition
ISBN: 979-8-9910843-0-7 (print)      ISBN: 979-8-9910843-3-8 (hardcover)
ISBN: 979-8-9910843-1-4 (ebook)      ISBN: 979-8-9910843-2-1(audiobook)

# Dedication

■

**To the men who have enriched
and challenged my life:**

**To My Father Eugene,**
who taught me that how a person presents
themselves on the outside can be vastly different
from how they feel on the inside.

**To My Brother Michael, and My Dear Friend Gary,**
whose courage in the face of daunting obstacles, taught me
the value of finding the gift hidden in the challenge,
the power of walking through your fears, and the
importance of cherishing every precious moment of life.

**To Wilson, Devynn, and Mason,**
may you embrace the richness of the life you've
been given. May you make wise choices, value learning
and personal growth, extend kindness and respect to
others, believe in the power of your dreams,
and know how much you are loved.

**To Bill,**
I miss you.

# Contents

—————————————————■—————————————————

INSPIRATION FOR THE BOOK . . . . . . . . . . . . . . . . . . . . . . . . . . . . xviii

IS THIS BOOK FOR YOU? . . . . . . . . . . . . . . . . . . . . . . . . . . . . . . . xx
    Others Who May Benefit . . . . . . . . . . . . . . . . . . . . . . . . . . . xxii
    Who this Book Is Not For . . . . . . . . . . . . . . . . . . . . . . . . . . xxiii
    If You Are Not Sure What You Want . . . . . . . . . . . . . . . . . . . . xxiv
    The Types of Relationships this Book Addresses . . . . . . . . . . . . .xxv
    Word Usage . . . . . . . . . . . . . . . . . . . . . . . . . . . . . . . . xxvi
    How to Use This Book . . . . . . . . . . . . . . . . . . . . . . . . . . . xxvii

INTRODUCTION . . . . . . . . . . . . . . . . . . . . . . . . . . . . . . . . . . . . 1

## Part One
Exploring the motivation, drivers, and vulnerabilities
that set the stage for affairs and affair recovery. . . . . . . . . . . . . . . . . . . . 3

CHAPTER 1: Affair Questions, Statistics, and Drivers . . . . . . . . . . . . . . . . 7
    Affair Statistics . . . . . . . . . . . . . . . . . . . . . . . . . . . . . . . . . 8
    Why Men Stray . . . . . . . . . . . . . . . . . . . . . . . . . . . . . . . . 10
    What Men Want . . . . . . . . . . . . . . . . . . . . . . . . . . . . . . . 11

CHAPTER 2: The Mechanics of Motivation:
Understanding the Driving Forces Behind Human Behavior . . . . . . . . . . . . 13
    The Motivation Assessment . . . . . . . . . . . . . . . . . . . . . . . . . 16

CHAPTER 3: Affair Vulnerability Factors (AVFs) . . . . . . . . . . . . . . . . . . 23
    Internal Affair Vulnerability Factors: Feeding the Need for Connection . . . . . . . . . 24
    External Affair Vulnerability Factors: Situational Influences . . . . . . . . . . . . . 29
    Affair Vulnerabilities and the Impact of Affair Engagement . . . . . . . . . . . . . 32

# Part Two

Meeting your challenges head on: critical steps in recovery . . . . . . . . . . . . . 37

**CHAPTER 4: Emergency Dos and Don'ts** . . . . . . . . . . . . . . . . . . . . 39

    Roadblocks to Repair . . . . . . . . . . . . . . . . . . . . . . . . . . . 41

**CHAPTER 5: Recovery Process Timeline** . . . . . . . . . . . . . . . . . . . 45

**CHAPTER 6: You've Been Caught. Now What?** . . . . . . . . . . . . . . 49

    The Power of Stories . . . . . . . . . . . . . . . . . . . . . . . . . . . 50

    Facing Your Choices: The Story of Jim, Liz, and Shelly . . . . . . . . . 50

    To Tell or Not to Tell? That Is the Question . . . . . . . . . . . . . . . 55

# Part Three

Unpacking the past: how our needs, desires, and family
shape our self-perception and relationships . . . . . . . . . . . . . . . . . . . . 59

**CHAPTER 7: The Quest for Completion** . . . . . . . . . . . . . . . . . . . 61

    The Missing Piece . . . . . . . . . . . . . . . . . . . . . . . . . . . . 62

    Three Core Needs . . . . . . . . . . . . . . . . . . . . . . . . . . . . 63

    Pain and Pleasure . . . . . . . . . . . . . . . . . . . . . . . . . . . . 67

**CHAPTER 8: Influences of Your Family of Origin on Who and How You Love** . . . . . . . 71

    The Impact of the Past Upon the Present . . . . . . . . . . . . . . . . 72

    Psychosocial Development . . . . . . . . . . . . . . . . . . . . . . . 75

    The Impact of Adolescence . . . . . . . . . . . . . . . . . . . . . . . 76

# Part Four

The anatomy of an affair: how affairs begin, evolve,
and the best way to end them . . . . . . . . . . . . . . . . . . . . . . . . . . . 93

**CHAPTER 9: Affairs Phase One: In the Beginning** . . . . . . . . . . . . . 95

    Defining Infidelity . . . . . . . . . . . . . . . . . . . . . . . . . . . 96

    Types of Infidelity . . . . . . . . . . . . . . . . . . . . . . . . . . . . 99

    Physical Affairs . . . . . . . . . . . . . . . . . . . . . . . . . . . . . 99

    Emotional Affairs . . . . . . . . . . . . . . . . . . . . . . . . . . . . 100

    Online Affairs . . . . . . . . . . . . . . . . . . . . . . . . . . . . . 101

Pornographic Affairs . . . . . . . . . . . . . . . . . . . . . . . . . . . . . . . . . . . . . 102

Contributing Factors . . . . . . . . . . . . . . . . . . . . . . . . . . . . . . . . . . . . . 105

**CHAPTER 10: Affairs Phase Two: Stuck in the Middle with You** . . . . . . . . . . . . . . 107

The Addictive Properties of an Affair . . . . . . . . . . . . . . . . . . . . . . . . . . . 108

The Power of Secret-Keeping . . . . . . . . . . . . . . . . . . . . . . . . . . . . . . . . 112

Navigating Uncertainty: The Story of Joe, Carol, and Jessica . . . . . . . . . . . . . . . 113

**CHAPTER 11: Affairs Phase Three: Closing the Door— How to Clearly**
**and Respectfully End Your Affair** . . . . . . . . . . . . . . . . . . . . . . . . . . . . . 119

Unwinding Your Affair . . . . . . . . . . . . . . . . . . . . . . . . . . . . . . . . . . . 119

Ending Things with Clarity and Compassion: George, Kelly, and Katie . . . . . . . . 122

If You Think YOU are Bulletproof, Think Again . . . . . . . . . . . . . . . . . . . . . 125

# Part Five

Expanding recovery: the power of commitment,
establishing boundaries, and honoring promises . . . . . . . . . . . . . . . . . . . . . 127

**CHAPTER 12: Paths to Recovery: Putting the Pieces Back Together** . . . . . . . . . . . . 129

Five A's of Recovery: Acknowledge. Admit. Apologize. Ask. Adapt. . . . . . . . . . 132

The Recovery Process . . . . . . . . . . . . . . . . . . . . . . . . . . . . . . . . . . . . 135

How to Deal with Powerful Connections to Ensure You Don't Cross the Line. . . . . 138

**CHAPTER 13: The Impact of Making, Breaking, and Keeping Promises** . . . . . . . . . . 141

For Better or for Worse . . . . . . . . . . . . . . . . . . . . . . . . . . . . . . . . . . . 145

Working Through a Repeat Offense: Justin, Sophia, and Jen . . . . . . . . . . . . . . 145

Preparing for a Fresh Start . . . . . . . . . . . . . . . . . . . . . . . . . . . . . . . . . 155

# Part Six

Understanding things from her point of view:
supporting your partner's recovery . . . . . . . . . . . . . . . . . . . . . . . . . . . . . 159

**CHAPTER 14: The Recovery Process for Her** . . . . . . . . . . . . . . . . . . . . . . . . . 161

From Her Perspective . . . . . . . . . . . . . . . . . . . . . . . . . . . . . . . . . . . . 162

Working Through Grief and Trauma . . . . . . . . . . . . . . . . . . . . . . . . . . . . 163

The Hardest Parts for Her . . . . . . . . . . . . . . . . . . . . . . . . . . . . . . . . . 166

Some Additional Dos and Don'ts with Your Partner . . . . . . . . . . . . . . . . . . 168

Secrets, Lies, and the Fear of Discovery . . . . . . . . . . . . . . . . . . . . . . . . . . 170

Denial: Laura and John's Story . . . . . . . . . . . . . . . . . . . . . . . . . . . . . . . 170

**CHAPTER 15: For Your Spouse/Significant Other** . . . . . . . . . . . . . . . . . . . . . . . **175**

Don't Get Stuck in Regret . . . . . . . . . . . . . . . . . . . . . . . . . . . . . . . . 177

Feelings . . . . . . . . . . . . . . . . . . . . . . . . . . . . . . . . . . . . . . . . . . . . . 180

Cultivating Self-Trust . . . . . . . . . . . . . . . . . . . . . . . . . . . . . . . . . . 188

**CHAPTER 16: For the AP (Affair Partner)** . . . . . . . . . . . . . . . . . . . . . . . . . **191**

To the Affair Partner . . . . . . . . . . . . . . . . . . . . . . . . . . . . . . . . . . . 191

So, What Do You Do Now? . . . . . . . . . . . . . . . . . . . . . . . . . . . . . . . 195

One Last Reminder for Everyone . . . . . . . . . . . . . . . . . . . . . . . . . . . 198

# Part Seven

Rebuilding your foundation: the healing power of love, like, and learning . . . . **201**

**CHAPTER 17: The Need for Love and Connection** . . . . . . . . . . . . . . . . . . . . **203**

What's Love Got to Do with It? . . . . . . . . . . . . . . . . . . . . . . . . . . . . 203

How Do Couples Lose Sight of Each Other's Needs? . . . . . . . . . . . . . . 204

Love and Shadow . . . . . . . . . . . . . . . . . . . . . . . . . . . . . . . . . . . . . . 205

Expanding the Definition of Love . . . . . . . . . . . . . . . . . . . . . . . . . . 207

The Four S's: Self-Acceptance, Self-Trust, Self-Confidence, Self-Respect . . . . . . . 209

Don't Underestimate the Power of *Like* . . . . . . . . . . . . . . . . . . . . . . .210

**CHAPTER 18: Relationship Stages** . . . . . . . . . . . . . . . . . . . . . . . . . . . . . . . **213**

The Three Primary Relationship Stages . . . . . . . . . . . . . . . . . . . . . . .214

**CHAPTER 19: Sex and Intimacy** . . . . . . . . . . . . . . . . . . . . . . . . . . . . . . . . **221**

**Intimacy** . . . . . . . . . . . . . . . . . . . . . . . . . . . . . . . . . . . . . . . . . . . . . . . **222**

So, what is intimacy anyway? . . . . . . . . . . . . . . . . . . . . . . . . . . . . . . 222

**Sex** . . . . . . . . . . . . . . . . . . . . . . . . . . . . . . . . . . . . . . . . . . . . . . . . . . **228**

What *really* counts as sex? . . . . . . . . . . . . . . . . . . . . . . . . . . . . . . . 229

Everything Begins with a Conversation . . . . . . . . . . . . . . . . . . . . . . 232

The Impact of Sexual Trauma and Shame on Sexual Connection . . . . . . 238

The Importance of Consent . . . . . . . . . . . . . . . . . . . . . . . . . . . . . . . 239

Desire Discrepancies . . . . . . . . . . . . . . . . . . . . . . . . . . . . . . . . . . . . 240

A Different Happily Ever After: Chase and Clara's Story . . . . . . . . . . . . 241

Communicating with your children about the affair . . . . . . . . . . . . . . 246

# Part Eight

Embracing transformation: cultivating positive change
and strengthening your masculine core . . . . . . . . . . . . . . . . . . . . . . . 249

CHAPTER 20: The Neurobiology of Change . . . . . . . . . . . . . . . . . . . . . . . . . . . . 251

The Change Process: The Role of Desire and Fear  . . . . . . . . . . . . . . . . . . 252

The Science of Change . . . . . . . . . . . . . . . . . . . . . . . . . . . . . . . . . . . . . . . 254

How Personal Change Impacts Your Relationship  . . . . . . . . . . . . . . . . . 255

Making an Ally of Your Mind . . . . . . . . . . . . . . . . . . . . . . . . . . . . . . . . . .258

CHAPTER 21: Defining and Navigating Emotions . . . . . . . . . . . . . . . . . . . . 263

The Pursuit-Withdrawal Dance . . . . . . . . . . . . . . . . . . . . . . . . . . . . . . . . 267

Cultivating Emotional Awareness . . . . . . . . . . . . . . . . . . . . . . . . . . . . . . 268

Anticipatory Fear . . . . . . . . . . . . . . . . . . . . . . . . . . . . . . . . . . . . . . . . . . . 269

CHAPTER 22: Exploring Masculinity: Embracing Your Power, Passion,

and Purpose as a Man . . . . . . . . . . . . . . . . . . . . . . . . . . . . . . . . . . . . . . . . . . 271

The Shifting Landscape of Masculinity . . . . . . . . . . . . . . . . . . . . . . . . . . 272

Men: Careers, Leadership, and Vulnerability . . . . . . . . . . . . . . . . . . . . . 273

Shadow and Pain . . . . . . . . . . . . . . . . . . . . . . . . . . . . . . . . . . . . . . . . . . . 276

The Masks of Masculinity . . . . . . . . . . . . . . . . . . . . . . . . . . . . . . . . . . . . 277

Using Your Affair as a Catalyst for Personal Change:

The Story of Rick, Carla, and Gracie . . . . . . . . . . . . . . . . . . . . . . . . . . . . 278

CHAPTER 23: Growing and Changing as a Couple . . . . . . . . . . . . . . . . . . . . 287

The Change Process in Action . . . . . . . . . . . . . . . . . . . . . . . . . . . . . . . . . 288

Supporting Your Partner's Desire for Change . . . . . . . . . . . . . . . . . . . . . 289

# Part Nine

Bridging differences, rebuilding trust: the power of apologies, forgiveness
and authentic communication . . . . . . . . . . . . . . . . . . . . . . . . . . . . . . . . . . . 293

CHAPTER 24: Courageous Conversations . . . . . . . . . . . . . . . . . . . . . . . . . . . 295

Principles for Engaging in a Courageous Conversation . . . . . . . . . . . . . . 296

Conflict Resolution Styles . . . . . . . . . . . . . . . . . . . . . . . . . . . . . . . . . . . . 297

Processing Speed . . . . . . . . . . . . . . . . . . . . . . . . . . . . . . . . . . . . . . . . . . . 301

Regulate Your State of Mind . . . . . . . . . . . . . . . . . . . . . . . . . . . . . . . . . . 304

Courageous Conversations Framework . . . . . . . . . . . . . . . . . . . . . . . . . . 307

CHAPTER 25: Making Amends . . . . . . . . . . . . . . . . . . . . . . . . . . . . . . . . . . . 317

The Art of Designing and Delivering a Heartfelt Apology . . . . . . . . . . . . 317

Wholehearted Apology Making . . . . . . . . . . . . . . . . . . . . . . . . . . . . . . . . 320

**CHAPTER 26: Forgiveness** . . . . . . . . . . . . . . . . . . . . . . . . . . . . . . . . . . . . . . . . **329**

    Forgiveness Occurs in Layers . . . . . . . . . . . . . . . . . . . . . . . . . . . . . . . 330

    Self-Forgiveness. . . . . . . . . . . . . . . . . . . . . . . . . . . . . . . . . . . . . . 331

**CHAPTER 27: Rebuilding Trust.** . . . . . . . . . . . . . . . . . . . . . . . . . . . . . . . **335**

**CHAPTER 28: When It May be Time to Leave** . . . . . . . . . . . . . . . . . . **339**

    If you are the one choosing to leave . . . . . . . . . . . . . . . . . . . . . . . 340

    When Your Spouse Chooses to Leave . . . . . . . . . . . . . . . . . . . . . 341

    When Leaving Is a Mutual Decision . . . . . . . . . . . . . . . . . . . . . . 342

# Part Ten

Designing your future: elevate your standards.
Align with your purpose. Choose mindfully. . . . . . . . . . . . . . . . . . . . . . . 345

**CHAPTER 29: The Power of Commitment, Courage, and Trust** . . . . . . . . . . . . . . . 347

**CHAPTER 30: The Keys to the Castle: Making and Honoring Commitments.** . . . . . . 351

**CHAPTER 31: Loving Courageously: The End. The Beginning..** . . . . . . . . . . . . . . 363

Endnotes. . . . . . . . . . . . . . . . . . . . . . . . . . . . . . . . . . . . . . . . . . . . . . . . . 367

Bibliography. . . . . . . . . . . . . . . . . . . . . . . . . . . . . . . . . . . . . . . . . . . . . 371

Acknowledgements and Heartfelt Thanks . . . . . . . . . . . . . . . . . . . . . . . 380

# Inspiration *for the* Book

———————————— ■ ————————————

*"Success is never final. Failure is never fatal.*
*It's courage that counts."*
—*They Call Me Coach*, John Wooden, basketball coach, author

**This work has been inspired by the many courageous men who have come to my office wanting to be better men. It has been my honor to walk beside these men as they courageously faced their defeats, triumphs, fears, desires, and choices. I have witnessed their fierce determination to make things right at home and to become stronger leaders, better role models, and men whose integrity could no longer be called into question.**

Often driven by crisis, these men come to realize that instead of facing the challenges of life head on, they have been engaging in behaviors that are out of alignment with their own core values and beliefs. For many, this behavior included the betrayal of someone they love.

I sat with these men through their anguish, grief, shame, and search for greater meaning and purpose. I listened to their stories and helped them put their lives back together, and, in most cases, recover their relationship. I witnessed the hard work, dedication, and commitment these determined men put into making the changes necessary to support their own growth and healing, and into helping their relationships recover, heal, rebuild trust, and forge a deeper and more meaningful connection with those they love.

**I would be remiss to not also include the amazing women I have worked with— women who chose to stand face-to-face with the men they love and walk through the burning embers of their own fears, longings, and discontents.** Engaging in transformational work of this nature necessitates shoring up the edges of your own boundaries and cultivating a deeper intimacy with life itself. Your willingness to authentically engage in the work, honor your own needs, and keep your heart open enough to walk through the fire of transformation and healing, sets the stage for rebuilding your life and relationship in ways you might never have imagined. I applaud your strength and courage.

**It is to these men, and the women who love them that I dedicate this work. I am honored by your faith and trust in me. It has been my privilege to guide you and learn from you.** I wish you beauty, grace, continued self-awareness, and healing. I wish you the courage to continue to kindly and directly ask for what you want, to choose love even when it scares you to do so, to set self-supportive boundaries, to offer apologies and forgiveness for missteps, and to continue to listen to the callings of your own heart and those of your beloved's. May you know the experience of being fully alive and deeply loved exactly as you are, and may you continue to learn, grow, and expand in loving yourselves and each other.

And to you, my reader, I also commend your courage and willingness to take a deep dive into your own healing and recovery. The information on these pages has been designed to educate and offer you the opportunity to take a deeper look at who you are, the factors that set the stage for your choices, and determine who you want to be walking forward. I am honored to serve as your guide.

*Dr. Jeanne Michele*

# Is this Book *for* You?

———————————■———————————

*"Not everything that is faced can be changed,
but nothing can be changed until we face it."*
—James Baldwin, writer and activist

One of my male clients suggested I begin this book by saying, *"Face it; you f\*ck\*d up!"* He told me, *"Guys know when they screw up and need to face their mistakes."*

**This book is for you if you've realized that you are that guy—the one who f\*ck\*d up.** Never in a million years did you think you would be that guy: *the cheater.* And you keep wondering, *How did I get here?*

**This book is for you if you've been living a lie.** You risked it all but are now wondering how to repair the damage. You've given into temptation, but now you want to reclaim your relationship, your family, and your life.

**This book is for you if you don't know where to begin.** It's natural for you to have questions about how to best navigate affair recovery. And it's not always easy to find a helpful, robust, and readily available sources of support for such a complex and often-private topic.

**This book is for you if you're looking for answers and are willing to commit to learning more about yourself and your partner.** Will it take work? Yes. Lots of it. But if you do the work, I can assure you that you will emerge from the experience a better man—more connected with your core values, and with an increased capacity to effectively communicate with those most important to you.

**This book is also for you if you've been tempted to engage in an affair but haven't yet acted on that feeling.** If you're finding yourself connecting with someone outside your primary relationship and you've been tempted to take it further, you will encounter information that can help you avoid a full-blown affair. You can use this time to seriously consider the potential consequences of engaging in an affair *before* stepping into a situation that will permanently alter the trajectory of your life and your relationship.

Here are some thoughts from other men who have stood right where you are now. I invite you to check any of these boxes that apply to you:

☐ I want to save my relationship but am not sure where to begin.

☐ I'm not sure if I can make my marriage work, but I'm not ready to let it go either.

☐ I feel guilty about letting down the people I love.

☐ I'm not sure how to help my spouse/partner recover.

☐ I'm not sure how or even if I can recover.

☐ I'm not sure how much to share with my partner about my affair, or if I should tell her if she doesn't already know it happened.

☐ I don't know how I can convince my partner that the affair is really over and that I'm truly committed to making our relationship work.

☐ I'm confused by my partner's shifting moods; one minute I feel her love, the next minute her rage…or sometimes I discover her crying uncontrollably.

☐ I'm growing tired of my partner's relentless questioning. I just want to put this behind us and move on.

☐ I don't know what to say to others—my kids, my community, or my friends.

☐ I'm not sure if I'm ready to let go of my affair partner just yet.

☐ My affair partner doesn't want to let me go.

☐ I know I want to end it with my affair partner but am not sure how to do it.

☐ If I end my affair, I fear I may lose a part of myself that has been revitalized.

☐ If I recommit to my marriage, I'm afraid I'll have another affair later.

☐ I don't want to lose my spouse, but don't know if my marriage can ever be what I want it to be.

If you've selected even one of these statements, rest assured that the material in this book can serve as a valuable resource to help you work through your specific concerns, learn about the nature of relationships, and start rebuilding yours.

# Others Who May Benefit

**While this book is written directly to any man who has engaged in affair behavior or been seriously tempted to do so, it can also help your partner better understand how affairs happen, and that your affair doesn't mean that you don't love her.**

The material can be helpful for anyone who has been involved in an Affair Triangle—which includes you, your primary partner/spouse, as well as the affair partner. Since the most effective recovery occurs when everyone involved heals, a chapter has been written for each of the women affected by your behavior. In addition, there are designated exercises for you and your partner to engage in as a couple when you are ready.

***The Infidelity Cure* can also be useful if you're currently working with a coach, counselor, or mentor, as it provides a framework and tools designed to guide you through the recovery process and offer greater understanding about affairs and relationships. It's a resource that can be used by you, as well as the professional who is helping you navigate the often turbulent waters of affair recovery.**

## TO THE WOMAN WHOSE SPOUSE/PARTNER HAS HAD AN AFFAIR

If you have picked up this book because your partner has had an affair, or you suspect he may be engaging with someone else, there are insights you can gain from exploring the material.

It is not the intention of these writings to defend or justify affair behavior. Rather, it is hoped that this work offers deeper insights into how the stage can be set for affairs in general, and for your man's specific affair. A chapter has been written directly to you to help you better understand your emotional responses, heal, and recover as you work through the aftermath of your man's affair.

A key element of any recovery is self-recovery. This is true whether or not you choose to re-engage with your spouse. While you will probably never completely understand what happened, hopefully these writings will shed enough light on relationships and affairs that you can come to greater peace inside your heart and soul.

Sections throughout this book discuss ways for you and your partner to work toward creating a healthy, thriving relationship, if you decide to work through things with him. The specific couples' exercises are designed to help you both dive in a little deeper when you are ready.

### TO THE WOMAN WHO HAS FALLEN FOR AN UNAVAILABLE MAN

While this book primarily focuses on personal and partnership recovery, it can also be beneficial if you are seeking to gain a better understanding of your involvement in an affair or multiple affairs with someone who is married or deeply committed to another relationship.

Reading this book can assist you in comprehending affair dynamics and support your journey in moving on from a man who is ready to move on, or who is not fully available to you. It can also aid in your personal recovery process.

## Who this Book Is Not For

**This book is not for you if you are looking for a quick fix and are not willing to put in the work.** The road to healing is in working through what happened, not sweeping it under the rug. It takes time to heal and courage to engage in difficult discussions, rebuild trust, and forgive.

Learning how to listen and authentically engage with one another is a crucial aspect of recovery. Enhancing your ability to do so will be key to your success.

While saying you're sorry is important, it takes more to recover your marriage than just a few *I'm sorrys*. The more thoroughly you engage in the work, the greater your opportunity for creating a successful relationship. Without doing so, you won't resolve the underlying conditions that made you more susceptible to connecting with someone outside your marriage in the first place.

# If You Are Not Sure What You Want

**If you're uncertain whether you are ready to fully commit to your primary relationship,** give yourself some breathing room to decide. Full engagement in this work requires dedication and commitment. If you aren't yet ready to dive into reconciliation, be honest—first with yourself, then talk with your significant other. If you need time, ask for it. She may not agree, but that is better than continuing the deception. Your objective is to rebuild trust. You cannot do that if you begin by misleading her. If you need some space to decide, kindly and directly let her know. (You may want to review Chapter 24, as it offers a model for engaging in a courageous conversation about a difficult topic.)

**If you aren't yet willing or ready to give up the affair partner, don't pretend.** If you're not sure you're ready to give up your affair partner, it may be for a number of reasons. Maybe you aren't sure how. Maybe you aren't sure how giving up that person will affect you. Maybe you just aren't ready. This book will help you gain clarity on who and what you want.

**If you are considering ending your marriage to be with the affair partner,** I encourage you to take some time to think about what you're gaining and potentially giving up in choosing to be with her. Here are some questions to consider:

- What would your life be like if your primary relationship ended? How would that choice impact your relationship with your kids? Your friends? Your extended family? Your co-workers? What would things look like for you financially if you and your wife split? While money isn't the sole reason to stay, the financial ramifications of a divorce are important to consider.

- Is your connection with your affair partner strong enough and important enough to you that you are prepared to lose your primary partnership and create a life with her? What would that life look like on a day-to-day basis? Does she have kids? If so, are you willing to be a stepfather to them (even if they are young adult children)?

Do some soul-searching. Take time to genuinely consider what life with this person—and without your current partner—would entail.

If being with your affair partner is what you ultimately decide, I strongly advise the two of you to get some outside help to work through the upcoming challenges you will encounter as you build a life together.

**If you and your primary partner are uncertain, or even if you're taking some time apart,** this book can be used as a discernment tool to help you both decide if you want to work on your relationship. The work begins with you taking a look at you. This inner work helps to set the stage for engaging with your partner—whoever that may turn out to be—and yourself.

## The Types of Relationships this Book Addresses

Note that this book has been written from the perspective of heterosexual male infidelity with a female partner. While I am hopeful that there are some pearls of wisdom for anyone in a committed relationship who is struggling with infidelity, it is important for you to know that the language and stories reflect this dynamic.

I am by no means suggesting that heterosexual monogamy is the *right* or only way to engage in coupling. Each couple needs to discuss and agree upon what works best for them.

Betrayal is not exclusive to heterosexual, monogamous partners. **Betrayal occurs any time you act outside of what you have agreed upon as a couple.**

### AFFAIRS WITH SAME-SEX PARTNERS

While many aspects of the recovery process are similar, there are additional layers of complexity and decisions that need to be addressed when the affair partner is another man. It could be that the parties involved have been keeping aspects of their sexual preferences secret. Some men believe same-sex relationships don't count as being unfaithful.[1] While this material doesn't deal directly deal with all the nuances of a same-sex affair, it can help you work through many aspects of your betrayal. If you are navigating this, you may want to reach for some additional assistance to help you decide as a couple the best way to create new agreements for your partnership.[2]

# Word Usage

The people who show up on my couch know that I am a stickler for how we use and define words. That is because we interpret things through our own language filters, which frequently means two people may assign very different meanings to the same word. Clarifying meaning helps avoid misinterpretation, which can lead to hurt feelings, overreactions, and arguments.

There are specific words you will not hear me use. I avoid using the word *cheating* throughout most of this book due to the intense judgment it triggers. Referring to someone who has engaged in affair behavior as a *cheater* labels the person, not the behavior. Instead of *cheating,* you will hear words like *infidelity, affair, indiscretion,* or *betrayal.*

Since you will hear the word *betrayal* used frequently in this work, let's begin with my working definition of betrayal.

---

## Betrayal occurs whenever someone acts outside of an agreement made with a partner and intentionally misleads or lies to cover up their indiscretion.

---

Betrayal is not linked to any specific gender, sexual orientation, preference, or identification.

### A COUPLE OF ADDITIONAL LANGUAGE DISTINCTIONS:

- **Spouse/Partner/SO (Significant Other)** – This work is designed for people in deeply committed relationships. You may be married. You may be engaged. You may have been together for a long time. Even if the pronoun used doesn't exactly fit your particular situation, such as when I use the word *spouse* and you are not officially married, this word is used to represent the depth of your connection, which may not necessarily reflect its formal status.

- **Affair Partner (AP)** – You will periodically see me use the initials AP to refer to the affair partner.

# How to Use This Book

This book serves as both a reference guide and tool for personal and relational healing. While its primary focus is affair recovery, it delves into topics that can benefit anyone looking to strengthen their relationship.

Each individual has an optimal learning style. The information provided is designed to address varying styles through sharing stories and providing in-depth information to facilitate learning, and hands-on experiences to deepen personal and relational connection and transformation.

There are several ways you can make the best use of this book:

1. **Read the book cover to cover.** This will maximize your ability to create transformational change by gaining a better understanding of the nature of relationships, as well as the slippery slope of affairs and the emotional upheaval they create.

2. **Jump straight to "Emergency Dos and Don'ts."** If you're in a crisis because you've just been *caught,* or because you just told her and she's freaking out, there are some critical things that are important for you to both *do* and *not do* right from the start. This is a critical time. The way you respond and communicate can make your lives together significantly better or alarmingly worse. After working through the initial crisis, go back and read the rest of the book.

3. **You can scan the table of contents and highlight sections that seem the most interesting and begin with those.** I suggest that you begin by reading at least the first three chapters before jumping into other segments. If this is how you work, I still suggest you work through the exercises, particularly those that pertain to the specifics of your affair.

*The Infidelity Cure* has been designed to provide you with the clarity you need to understand where things went sideways and assist you in designing a path forward. If your spouse isn't ready to engage in recovery, or if the two of you are taking some time apart, that's okay. Your work begins with YOU. This is personal discovery work that helps you realign your behavior with your values and beliefs.

Specifically, this work has been designed to help you:

1) Determine the best course of action for your particular situation.

2) Rebuild trust and reestablish your connection with your partner should she want to engage in the trust-rebuilding process.

3) Establish more effective communication interactions, including: disclosure versus boundary setting, conflict resolution, and authenticity in speaking and listening.

4) Construct a heartfelt apology and set the stage for forgiveness.

As part of that plan, you will learn how to:

1) Effectively and skillfully end your affair (even if you have been unsuccessful in past attempts).

2) Identify internal and external factors that create more vulnerability for affair engagement to help ensure you don't inadvertently set the stage for a repeat offense.

3) Better understand the inner workings and flow of relationships.

4) Identify and recover from ineffective patterns of behavior that hinder your ability to create and sustain healthy relationships.

5) Better understand what your primary partner is experiencing.

6) Develop more constructive and conscious ways of engaging with life and your partner.

**Regardless of how you walk in the world, I hope that this book opens your heart to greater wisdom, healing, transformation, compassion, and self-awareness.** Recovery is possible for you and your relationship. Reconciliation is possible. The information and lessons in this book are based on the many men and couples I've helped heal from relational conflict, rebuild trust, and chart a stronger course forward.

Will this process take work? Yes. Lots of it. But if you do the work, I promise that you will come out of this with greater insight and clarity on what you stand for as a man. And you may just get your partner back in the process.

# Introduction

---■---

*"Your soul print is etched with the lines of your pathologies and fears, your hopes and your dreams, your memories, angers, and all of those irreplaceable, fully special pieces that make up in a unique combination the woven fabric of your story."*
—Marc Gafni, *Soul Prints, Your Path to Fulfillment*

The unique tapestry of who we are is woven from all of our experiences, challenges, and choices, including those we struggle with and regret. Part of our journey as human beings is to more fully awaken into the power and passion that resides within, embrace the unique expression of who we are, and experience the healing and transformative power of loving and being deeply loved.

When we can make peace with our past and view our missteps as lessons that lead us towards more mindful ways of living and loving, we are able to be more fully present with our loved ones and more consistently make choices that reflect our core values, beliefs, and commitments. Mastering this way of thinking requires focused attention, patience, and a willingness to release the judgments we hold against ourselves and others and recover from whatever takes us out of alignment with ourselves and those we love.

Any form of deep recovery work serves as a kind of personal soul retrieval offering opportunities to cultivate a greater depth of understanding, self-discovery, forgiveness, and reclamation. Affair recovery is no different. As cliché as it sounds, the more you are able to love, value, understand, accept, and forgive yourself, the greater your capacity to do the same for others. Infidelity recovery does have its unique challenges in that successful recovery also necessitates working directly with someone who has been impacted and hurt by choices they did not make.

The work you are embarking upon is designed to help you gain insight into yourself, your partner and the nature of relationships and affairs. If offers you the opportunity to increase your ability as Socrates is reported to have said to, "Know Thyself." In addition to expanding your self-awareness, you will also be learning how to best help both you and your partner recover and create a more solid connection moving forward, whether or not you ultimately choose to stay together.

**My journey into infidelity recovery** began to take root as more and more men began showing up in my practice who were devastated at the possibility of losing their wives and families after *their* affair. This inspired me to explore the intricacies of affairs and affair recovery, uncover their commonalities, embrace the unique journey of each person and situation, and fine-tune ways to help these men and their partners heal, gain the clarity they needed to make wise choices, and reignite their connection, or clearly and amicably honor each other's choice to go in another direction.

In *The State of Affairs*, psychotherapist and author, Esther Perel writes, "Affairs have a lot to teach us about relationships. They open the door to a deep examination of values, human nature, and the power of eros. They force us to grapple with some of the most unsettling questions: What draws people outside the lines they worked so hard to establish? Why does sexual betrayal hurt so much? … For me these conversations are part and parcel of any adult relationship."

Well managed infidelity recovery between willing partners can enhance relational authenticity, foster greater understanding, improve a couple's ability to actively listen and engage, and help promote healing from previous relational trauma. It offers the opportunity to look at ways in which your life and relationship had bumped up against obstacles, both internal and external, that became more difficult to successfully sort through.

I am by no means suggesting that infidelity is an exclusively male tendency. But in my practice, there have simply been more men knocking on my door seeking reconciliation, so I set out to write the first book for and about men, male affair behavior, relationships, and recovery.

The truth is infidelity, in its many forms, occurs more often than people think. But since there is a hidden shame associated with it, personal affair behavior isn't typically a voluntary topic of social conversation. In fact, it is even difficult to quantify infidelity statistics, since participants are presumed to be hesitant to report affairs. Estimates of lifetime infidelity amongst heterosexual Americans have varied wildly—for men, from 12 to 72 percent, and for women, 7 to 54 percent.[3]

Rumors of affair engagement by *other people* make tabloid headlines and serve as tasty food for neighborhood gossip. When judgments turn personal, however, they take on a whole new meaning. Being the subject of speculation, rumors, and gossip opens up an unimaginable world of pain and suffering for all involved.

So, why do we judge so harshly? Perhaps we judge to measure where we stand in comparison to others. Maybe seeing someone else falter helps us feel better about ourselves or judge our own failings less harshly. Sometimes judgments yield a sense of moral superiority.

**"It's easy to judge. It's more difficult to understand. Understanding requires compassion, patience, and a willingness to believe that good hearts sometimes choose poor methods."**
—Doe Zantamata, *Happiness in Your Life – Book One: Karma*

The men who have shown up in my office have been earnest in their desire to figure out what happened and why, learn how to rebuild their relationship and their lives, recover their dignity, help their partner heal, be forgiven, and forgive themselves. The work I share in this book is based upon my direct experience helping these men courageously face their choices, regain their self-respect, and rebuild their relationships and their lives.

Throughout this book, you will be introduced to these men. You will hear their stories, gain insight into what they wrestled with, and learn how they put their lives back together after their affairs. While the details have been changed to protect the privacy of all involved, each story represents a journey in and through an affair.

Whether you are the man who has had an affair, or a woman affected by an affair, I hope you can find yourself in some of these stories, and that they offer you a ray of hope and let you know that you are not alone.

# PART ONE

———————————————— ■ ————————————————

# Exploring *the* Motivation, Drivers, *and* Vulnerabilities That Set *the* Stage *for* Affairs *and* Affair Recovery

Every single man I have worked with has told me he wishes he could change what happened. Turn back time. Have another opportunity to talk to his partner about things *before* engaging in his affair. While an affair may provide a temporary respite from the pressures of life and its various challenges, it also leaves much pain and devastation in its wake.

Even men who have chosen to create a life with their affair partner, and whose marriages end, have regrets about the lies and deceit. They own that there were much better ways to deal with life and relational challenges that didn't include engaging in affair behavior. One man who ended up leaving his marriage, but continued working on himself, said, *"All the problems I had have followed me into this next relationship. I just wasn't ready to face them before. It was easier to blame them on the relationship."*

The desire to rewrite the past may be high, but in truth, the only place you can begin creating the life you desire is in the present moment. While life doesn't offer many true do-overs, it does offer opportunities for greater understanding, healing, and the cultivation of stronger relational connections.

In your affair recovery process, it is important to look at what motivated your affair engagement. What did the affair provide that may have been missing or grown dormant over time in your life and/or your relationship? Examining the underlying conditions that were in play prior to an affair can deepen your understanding of how the stage was set for your affair. Addressing this can help fortify your relationship against the possibility of repeat engagements.

In this section, we explore:

**Affair questions, statistics, and drivers:** An overview of key questions men ask when jumping into recovery, affair statistics, and a review of what tends to drive male affair behavior

**The mechanics behind human behavior:** An exploration of the internal and external motivations that contribute to choices made

**Motivation Assessment:** A tool designed to assess your motivation for engaging in recovery work

**Affair Vulnerability Factors:** An exploration of specific vulnerability factors that help set the stage for affairs in general and *your* affair(s) specifically

For the exercises, I suggest you either write in your book or a separate notebook specifically reserved for your thoughts and discoveries. If it is helpful, you can picture me walking by your side as you embark upon this journey of self and relational discovery and healing.

# 1

# Affair Questions, Statistics, *and* Drivers

———————— ■ ————————

*"The greatest challenges we face in life should be the ones we decide to take on because we have a bold vision for ourselves. This is how you know you are consciously designing your life."*
—Brendon Burchard, motivational speaker

If you are a man who has engaged in any type of affair behavior, you're likely picking up this book because infidelity has turned your world upside down. You realize that if you don't make some serious changes in your behavior and thinking, you risk losing your partner, your family, the respect of your friends, community, and yourself.

You may have all sorts of questions running around inside your head right now.

**You may be asking yourself:** *How can I prove to my wife that the affair is really over? Will she ever trust me again? Can our marriage be saved? How in the world did this even happen?*

**If this is a workplace affair, you may be wondering:** *What happens if or when my friends and colleagues find out? Have my actions jeopardized my career? My reputation?*

**If you have children, you may want to know:** *What happens if/when my kids find out? What will they think of me? How will the news of my indiscretions impact my relationship with them? Will it affect the future decisions they make about their own relationship(s)?*

**If you haven't yet broken things off with the affair partner (AP), you may be asking:** *How will I break the news to her that I am ending things to work on repairing my primary relationship?*

You may be ruminating about the answers to these questions and many others as you work through the rebuilding process with yourself and your spouse. But right now, the two most important questions you need to ask yourself are: *1) How willing am I to make the changes necessary to repair my relationship? 2) How motivated am I—really—to do this work?*

Before we dive into your personal situation and motivation, let's take a look at overall affair statistics.

# Affair Statistics

Statistics on affair behavior are difficult to nail down. This is in great measure due to the judgment, secrecy, and shame associated with an affair. Statistics are only as reliable as the integrity and willingness of people driven to complete them.

Still, there is a wide range of information about affairs cited in various publications and news outlets. To offer an overview of statistical ranges, I have chosen stats from a couple of different sources.

**According to the LA Detective Agency,**[4] 30 to 60 percent of married individuals will engage in some type of infidelity during their marriage. Keep in mind, these statistics reflect those people who are willing to admit they engaged in affair behavior **as they define it**.

Definitions of affair behavior can range from a kiss to a deep emotional connection, to various types of physical engagements that violate a fidelity agreement. For the purposes of this book:

**An affair is defined as connecting with another in ways that violate the agreements, both stated and implied, that you have made with your partner.**

Each partnership and the individuals within it may have a different idea of what constitutes an affair. That is why it is critical to clarify your agreements on which behaviors constitute a breach of fidelity within your specific partnership.

Here are some additional infidelity statistics from the *Journal of Marital and Family Therapy*[5]:

- The average affair lasts about two years.
- The percentage of marriages where one or both spouses admit to infidelity, either physical or emotional, is 41 percent.
- 57 percent of men admit to engaging in infidelity (in any relationship they have had).
- 36 percent of men and women admit to having an affair with a co-worker, and 35 percent admit to having an affair on a business trip.
- 69 percent of married couples who experience infidelity breakup up as a result of the infidelity.
- 74 percent of men and 68 percent of women say they would have an affair *if* they knew they would never get caught.
- Between 3 and 12 percent of men having affairs end up leaving their spouse and marrying the other person; 75 percent of those marriages end in divorce.
- 70 percent of couples who divorce due to an affair later admit regretting their decision.

Did those statistics surprise you? People make lots of assumptions about affairs and the people who engage in them. The typical assumption about male affair behavior is that the driving force is sexual connection. Is sex the primary reason men stray? I invite you to consider your own affair as we take a deeper look.

# Why Men Stray

*Most people stray because they're paying more attention to what they're missing than what they have.*

## WHAT'S SEX GOT TO DO WITH IT?

Sexual engagement is one form of personal and relational expression. Sex doesn't begin and end with a sex act. Sex includes thoughts, fantasies, feelings, as well as physical sensations.

Feeling sexually desired fuels more than just physical satisfaction. It can boost confidence while increasing a person's stamina and feelings of well-being. The sense of allure when someone identifies a potential sexual partner can activate these responses as well.

While sex can be a powerful driving force, contrary to some stereotypes, the sex act is not typically the sole driving factor in male affairs. There are various internal and external drivers that can lead ordinarily good men into affair engagement.

Affairs are driven by a combination of emotional, psychological, and situational factors that go beyond the mere physical aspect of sex. Unmet emotional needs, a desire for validation or excitement, childhood exposure to abuse, marital discord, infidelity and trauma, dissatisfaction in the primary relationship, and the longing for emotional connection and understanding are just some of the complex factors that can contribute to affair engagement. Recognizing and understanding these deeper motivational factors is crucial in order to address root needs and work towards healing and rebuilding trust in your primary connection.

---

**Part of the powerful pull of an affair is that it can re-awaken places inside that you haven't been attending to, or even realized had gone dormant.**

---

# What Men Want

Let's take a deeper look at some of the underlying wants, needs, and desires that can fuel affair behavior and see which ones apply to you.

Check any that apply to your situation. Place an asterisk (*) next to those that are most important to you. Double asterisk (**) any that may have been fulfilled through your affair.

☐ To feel connected

☐ To feel vital/alive

☐ To recapture lost youth

☐ To feel like someone's hero

☐ To feel wanted and desired

☐ To engage in a new adventure

☐ To explore sex with someone new/someone you are attracted to

☐ To satisfy an emerging hunger/desire/chemistry

☐ To feel honored and respected

☐ To boost confidence or know you've still "got it"

☐ To calm feelings of restlessness or to relieve stress

☐ To feel understood

☐ To escape the pressures of day-to-day life

☐ To feel comfort or familiarity (This can be a particularly strong factor when connecting with an ex.)

☐ _____

What stood out most for you as you went through this list? How did your affair impact and challenge your sense of self?

At the end of the day, the most challenging aspect of infidelity is that it shakes our sense of safety. No one likes to be deceived, especially by someone who is supposed to keep them safe. Infidelity shakes the safety of everyone involved as it is a betrayal of trust at the deepest level. Recovery requires strong motivation, commitment, determination, and desire to heal, make amends, forgive, and rebuild connection.

The next section has two parts. The first is a description of the motivation factors that drive human behavior. This is followed by a personal motivation assessment designed to help you explore the internal and external factors that helped set the stage for your affair.

I strongly suggest you work through the Motivation Assessment as it will help you assess where you are as you begin the work. This is something you will revisit later as well.

# 2

## *The* Mechanics *of* Motivation:
### *Understanding the Driving Forces Behind Human Behavior*

---

*"If we are clear and committed, we will feel high levels of motivation. If we are unclear or uncommitted, motivation will be low... The mother of motivation is choice... a choice toward something, a deeply held reason to act. It is an energy that results from thought... if we want more motivation in our lives, we must make clearer choices and more deeply commit to them."*
—Brendon Burchard, *The Motivation Manifesto,*
*9 Declarations to Claim Your Personal Power*

Human behavior is driven by a complex interplay of factors, including genetics, experiences, relationships, desires, and what you were and were not exposed to growing up. It is also impacted by cultural and societal norms, religious traditions, and the desire to be loved, accepted, and belong.

**There are two competing needs that come into play within human relationships: the desire for connection versus the desire for freedom; attachment versus autonomy.** Often those needs come into direct conflict with one another. Learning to effectively balance those needs continues throughout the human lifespan.

As children we develop behavioral strategies that help us adapt to our environment and navigate our need for both autonomy and attachment. We do this by observing what brings contentment or distress to our caregivers and adapt our behavioral responses to those that tend to generate approval. When parents turn away from these bids for attention, a child either acts out in an effort to get their attachment needs met or withdraws.

A child can be the source of a parent's need for approval as well, which can result in a parent's overinvolvement in their child's life. Parental overinvolvement can result in an unhealthy enmeshment which can stifle a child's need for autonomy, frequently resulting in the child turning away or withdrawing from the parent. This is particularly true during teen years when a child's healthy development includes the need to establish themselves more firmly as an autonomous being. The need for autonomy becomes a more prominent motivating factor during adolescence.

Motivation is the driving force that propels people into action even when the odds seem stacked against them. In his book, the *Motivation Manifesto*, author and motivational speaker, Brendon Burchard, teaches that motivation is a choice driven by a *"deeply held reason to act.* Applying this concept to your current situation, the strength of your desire to make your relationship work has a direct bearing on your motivation to act, which in turn helps direct the effort you put into the recovery process.

Motivation is impacted by both internal and external factors that influence our thoughts, emotions, and actions. Individual beliefs, values, relationships, and personal goals contribute to the motivation behind behavior as well as the desire for rewards or the avoidance of potentially negative consequences. Let's take a deeper look at these motivational drivers.

**Internal (intrinsic) motivation arises from within.** It is fueled by personal desire and driven by a sense of purpose, passion, and the pursuit of personal growth. It's rooted in the desire to move toward personal fulfillment or a goal like increasing your skill level in a sport you enjoy, or learning a new language because you will be traveling and find it satisfying to converse with people in their native language. This drive to move forward is driven by something you *want*.

**External (extrinsic) motivation is rooted in an outside situation**—another's needs, wants, or desires, and/or environmental factors, cultural or societal norms, or the desire to meet external obligations. Let's say you have an important meeting with a potential client, and you are responsible for making a presentation to demonstrate that your company is the best choice to help her grow her business. Your actions are motivated by the company's need to prosper and grow and perhaps a potential promotion. External motivation is driven by what you *will get or avoid*.

**Sometimes motivation is driven by both intrinsic and extrinsic factors.** In considering the last example, while external motivation is the drive to meet a deadline and complete an assignment based upon your agreed-upon role and reward you may receive with completion, such as acknowledgement, a raise, or possible upward movement, doing so can satisfy an intrinsic need to feel successful, valued, and needed.

**Affair recovery is driven by both internal and external motivating factors.** Internally, you could be driven by fear of loss, not wanting to feel like a failure, the desire to feel loved, and the potential relief you anticipate being forgiven would bring. External drivers could be the avoidance of divorce, or the financial repercussions it could bring.

The stronger your willingness, desire, and sense of urgency, the greater the likelihood that you will take the actions necessary to make things work, even in those moments when you may feel exhausted or defeated. If your motivation is high, you are off to a great start.

**Motivation alone, however, doesn't create staying power.** Motivation is your starting point. Your staying power will require the tenacity, determination, and discipline to stay the course, even in the face of disappointments and setbacks. (We will talk about what you can expect and how to move through challenges as our work continues.) For now, what's important for you to know is this:

---

## Your relational connection is built and rebuilt by the actions you take and the decisions you make on a moment-by-moment basis.

---

Let's take a look at your motivation as you begin the affair recovery process.

# The Motivation Assessment

The following set of questions have been designed to help you clearly assess your beginning motivation, mindset, and confidence in the rebuilding process.

You can take as much or as little time as you need to work through your responses. The important thing is for you to be honest with yourself about your goals, intentions, and expectations as you embark upon the path to relational repair. Answering these questions helps you assess the strength of your current desire for making your primary relationship work, and can give you an idea of how likely you are to succeed in doing so.

**Directions:** Where there is a rating scale, please rate the items listed on a scale of 0 to 5. (Note: Your rating is based on your *willingness* and *belief* about what is being addressed. Even if you don't know what to do, if your willingness/belief is strong your rating can be a 5.)

My desire to engage in the work necessary to make my primary partnership work right now is:

☐ Low

☐ Fair

☐ Average

☐ Strong

☐ Very Strong

**INTERNAL AND EXTERNAL MOTIVATION**

What are your primary motivations for wanting to make your relationship work? (Check all that apply.) Circle your top 5. Put an asterisk* next to your top 2.

Intrinsic:

☐ I feel guilty

☐ I feel ashamed

☐ I don't want to feel like a failure

☐ I realize how much I love my partner

☐ This isn't the person I want to be

☐ I want to align my actions with my values

☐ I realize what I stand to lose if we don't try to make our relationship work

Extrinsic:

☐ Divorce will be costly

☐ Divorce will break up my family

☐ I don't want to be perceived as a bad person

☐ My spouse really wants us to work on this

☐ Divorce is not permitted or approved of by my religion

☐ I want to preserve my reputation, at work and socially

☐ I will be seen as a failure

☐ I don't want my kids to grow up in a broken home

**RESPONSIBILITY, ACCOUNTABILITY, AND BLAME**

There are various factors that contribute to affair engagement. Let's take a look at how you view yours.

My primary partner bears responsibility for my affair due to her actions or inactions.

0  1  2  3  4  5

If so, how? _____

My affair partner (AP) bears responsibility for what happened (ex: because she is the one who initiated it or wouldn't let it go.)

0   1   2   3   4   5

If so, how? _____

Alcohol consumption is at fault for my initial affair engagement, and/or the continuation of it.

0   1   2   3   4   5

If so, how or to what degree? _____

Engaging in the affair was my choice and I am willing to own what happened, regardless of the circumstances that led me there.

0   1   2   3   4   5

## THE STATE OF MY RELATIONAL CONNECTION: THEN AND NOW

Rate the level of connection between you and your partner, on a scale of 0 to 5, *before, during, immediately after affair discovery*, and where it stands *now*.

| | BEFORE THE AFFAIR | DURING THE AFFAIR | AFTER DISCOVERY | NOW |
|---|---|---|---|---|
| I would rate our emotional connection as: | ____ | ____ | ____ | ____ |
| I would rate our level of intimacy as: | ____ | ____ | ____ | ____ |
| I would rate our sexual connection as: | ____ | ____ | ____ | ____ |
| I would rate our communication level as: | ____ | ____ | ____ | ____ |
| I would rate our spiritual connection as: | ____ | ____ | ____ | ____ |
| I would rate our intellectual connection as: | ____ | ____ | ____ | ____ |

## MUTUALITY AND HOPE FOR THE FUTURE

The next segment takes a look at your hopes and beliefs about the rebuilding process as you move into the future.

I have a strong belief that the two of us will be able to work through the aftermath of my affair and create/recreate a solid connection and rebuild trust?

0  1  2  3  4  5

My partner believes we have a solid chance of rebuilding the trust in our relationship and creating/recreating a strong connection. (If you haven't explored this yet with your partner, what do you believe her rating would be?)

0  1  2  3  4  5

It is my intention to make my relationship a top priority and do *everything in my power* to make it work.

0  1  2  3  4  5

I believe that my partner will find it in her hear to forgive my indiscretions.

0  1  2  3  4  5

I believe it is possible to make our relationship *even stronger* as we work through the affair and any underlying relational challenges.

0  1  2  3  4  5

I have a strong hope/belief that together my partner and I can create a life that is more joy-filled and increase our levels of happiness as we move into the future.

0  1  2  3  4  5

I have a strong desire to use this time to discover more about myself and explore ways that I can live in greater alignment with my values and beliefs.

0  1  2  3  4  5

What I hope to learn from this program is:

_____

_____

# Reviewing Your Results

### INTRINSIC VS. EXTRINSIC MOTIVATION

Take a look at the balance of your internal and external motivation. While it is natural to be both internally and externally motivated, if your top choices are primarily external, it can indicate that your heart may not be fully into rebuilding your relationship.

When your motivation centers around your desire to *be better* it creates a greater likelihood that you will *do better.* If you have too many external factors without many internal factors, you may want to take a deeper look at what you truly desire.

### RESPONSIBILITY, ACCOUNTABILITY AND BLAME

There is a direct link between your willingness to take responsibility for your actions and your ability to rebuild trust with your partner. I cannot emphasize enough the importance of owning what happened without being defensive or making excuses. Taking responsibility is a key aspect of healing.

### THE STATE OF MY RELATIONAL CONNECTION: THEN AND NOW

What stands out for you as you review specific periods of your primary connection? Often, we think that the connection within a primary relationship deteriorates during the course of an affair. This is not always the case. As you will learn in Part Four, *The Anatomy of an Affair*, sometimes, especially during the beginning of an affair, you may note that aspects of your primary connection have improved.

## MUTUALITY AND HOPE FOR THE FUTURE

Your intention, willingness, and belief in the possibility that you will be able to recover and strengthen your relationship internally and with your partner contributes to your success in doing so. This increases exponentially when both people's willingness and intention is high. Save your results so you can reassess as you work through this program.

A crisis is a wake-up call. It shakes you out of complacency and comfort. When you attend to it rather than sweeping it under the rug, it offers a tremendous opportunity for interpersonal and relational growth and healing. Each choice that you make either brings you closer or further away from what you want to build within your relationship and yourself.

## Reflection

Just to be clear, you aren't being asked to be flawless in your execution. You will make mistakes along the way. There will be moments when you feel connected and hopeful, and moments when you may question whether things will ever get better. You will experience periods of disappointment and doubt, such as when you put a lot of effort into your connection and your partner doesn't respond the way you anticipated. While you can't control how your partner responds to your efforts, you can learn how to better work your way through your own disappointments and learn how to communicate through them more effectively.

When challenges hit, refocus on your motivation for rebuilding your relationship. Doing so can help offset the feelings of frustration and potential hopelessness you may experience along the way. Don't let minor setbacks derail the process. You've got this!

# 3

# Affair Vulnerability Factors (AVFs)

—■—

*"So many frayed strands of disappointment, some barely noticeable, dangle from our hearts in the complex tapestry of a lifetime."*[7]
—*How to Be an Adult in Relationships:*
*The Five Keys to Mindful Loving,* David Richo

In this chapter, we examine various internal and external factors that play a role in infidelity. Although each situation is unique, there are shared vulnerabilities that create greater opportunities for affair engagement.

We are going to dive more deeply into the two main domains previously identified that shape choices: 1) your internal world, which encompasses self-perception and how you interpret and integrate the perception of others, and 2) your outer world, which is comprised of external situations, opportunities, and the environments to which you are exposed.

As we progress through this section, I encourage you to identify the factors that most closely align with your personal circumstances. This chapter offers both a detailed view and a summary table at the end.

# Internal Affair Vulnerability Factors:
## *Feeding the Need for Connection*

Next, we delve into five primary experiences of loss and explore the range of emotions, fears, and behavioral consequences that arise from each. We also examine the Affair Vulnerability Factors (AVFs) associated with these losses and ways in which engaging in an affair can temporarily provide a sense of connection or relief. It is important to note that acknowledging these vulnerabilities doesn't justify affair engagement, but rather serves to highlight how various losses can heighten susceptibility to becoming involved with someone who demonstrates interest.

### LOSS OF CONNECTION

One of the biggest catalysts for relational discontent is feeling disconnected from a loved one. These feelings can evolve over time or result from recurring disagreements or momentary arguments.

Loss of connection stems from a weakening of the emotional bond between two people. This can result from unresolved conflicts, lack of quality time together, shifting priorities or career challenges.

**Associated Feelings:** Discontentedness. Loneliness.
**Fear:** Relational loss. Increased disconnection.
**By-product:** Pursue-withdraw behavior. (You can refer to Chapter 21 for a more
   comprehensive look at this pattern.)

**AVF:** Feeling disconnected, rejected, or unwanted by loved ones can intensify feelings of loneliness and emotional isolation. The more often and more deeply you feel this way, the greater the hunger for fulfillment. This loss can trigger decreased intimacy, desire, and communication breakdowns.

**The Affair:** *Helped you feel connected and lessened feelings of loneliness.*

When someone shows up who needs, likes, or wants what you bring to the table, it can help fill a void you may not have even known you had. Social interactions, collaborative projects, and flirtatious exchanges can temporarily alleviate feelings of disconnection and loneliness. Feeling connected can enhance your self-worth and motivate you to actively engage in life.

## LOSS OF VITALITY

Loss of vitality is characterized by a general feeling of being drained or depleted where your energy, enthusiasm and zest for life is lowered.

Life is busy. Day-to-day requirements can take over, leaving little room for spontaneity and adventure. It can feel like life is directing you, instead of you directing it, and result in feelings of depression and a decline in motivation.

**Associated Feelings:** Depressed/Numb/Unmotivated.
**Fear:** Life has passed me by.
**By- product:** Life on Autopilot.

**AVFs:** Maybe things have become too predictable and maybe even a little boring. Perhaps things that used to interest you no longer hold the same interest, excitement, or adventure. You may find yourself de-motivated, lacking the drive to break free from your routine and maybe even a little depressed. Alternatively, you may find yourself resorting to risky behaviors such as excessive drinking, drug use, or thrill-seeking as a means to fill the void.

**The Affair:** *Helped you feel alive.*

The initial rush of connecting with someone unfamiliar can light up your *feel-good circuitry*. If you have been on autopilot for a while, feeling the rush of these excitatory chemicals can intensify the desire for more. This newness and unpredictability can help you feel alive.

The danger lies in seeing another person as *the source* of newfound vitality rather than as *a catalyst* reigniting your inner spark. Viewing an affair partner as the primary solution to fill this need—contributes to the addictive properties of an affair making it more difficult to leave.

## LOSS OF PURPOSE

**Associated Feelings:** Lack of fulfillment, purpose, or meaning.
**Fear:** I don't matter.
**By-product:** Personal loss of value.

Loss of purpose refers to a state or feeling of not having a clear sense of direction or meaning. This can occur when you feel disconnected from your values, passions, or sense of fulfillment, which can lead to a lack of motivation, dissatisfaction, and a sense of emptiness.

**AVF:** You have been feeling unfulfilled at home or at work. You no longer feel like your efforts truly make a difference; you no longer feel like you matter.

Perhaps you've found yourself feeling like something was missing or are haunted by the thought that maybe you've missed the mark. Maybe you're wondering what life would have been like had you made different choices. Perhaps your career isn't in the place you feel it should be at this age/stage, or maybe you've achieved great things and found yourself wondering, *Is this all there is?*

I often see a questioning of purpose or meaning arise in men who have become disillusioned with their careers. Sometimes this occurs when the company changes direction, or the person has reached their desired level of status and/or financial stability and doesn't find it quite as fulfilling as they thought it would be.

**The Affair:** *Helped you feel important, needed, or like a hero.*

The need to be seen as a hero is rooted in a longing to feel needed and useful. While the need to be needed and purposeful can show up in anyone, I find that it tends to be a particularly strong masculine characteristic. Men tend to be driven to solve problems and protect the ones they love and care about. They want to know that what they have to offer is wanted, needed, and appreciated.

When a man's hunger for being purposeful and/or useful is not fulfilled—when he does not feel necessary at home or work—it increases his need to feel needed. This can contribute to an increased vulnerability for appreciation and approval given by other people or situations.

## LOSS OF CONTROL OR FEAR OF LOSS OF CONTROL

**Associated Feelings:** Panic. Anxiety. Helplessness.
**Fear:** Future possibilities.
**By-product:** Uncertainty.

Loss of control is a sense of not having power or influence over a situation or your own actions. It can manifest as a sense of helplessness, uncertainty, or anxiety when you perceive that you are unable to manage or direct your circumstances.

Fear of loss of control refers to the anxiety or apprehension associated with the possibility of losing control over yourself, your environment, or certain aspects of life. This fear can stem from various factors, such as changes in personal circumstances, unexpected events, or a lack of confidence in your ability to influence a situation, or your partner's choices.

Each of us needs to feel like we have some measure of control over our environment in order to feel safe. Many disagreements among couples are rooted in the need for control, or the desire for sovereignty—that is, to feel in charge of your own life decisions.

**AVF:** Maybe you have experienced or are experiencing midlife distress, concern about growing older, or changes in stamina, physical appearance, or abilities. Perhaps your spouse is engaging in something new and this triggers a concern that maybe she will outgrow your relationship.

Unexpected life situations can trigger deep uncertainty about the future. Sometimes this occurs when you find yourself in a different financial or career position than you anticipated at a given age. These situations can throw you off balance and result in feelings of helplessness, anxiety, or fear about what could potentially happen next.

A strong need to *win* an argument can be a symptom of a heightened need for control. For example, this could play out during a small conflict when one partner chronically interrupts and insists that the other is 100 percent in the wrong—leaving no room for engaged listening, compromise, or reconciliation. While we all like to win, when the need becomes obsessive or you find yourself relentlessly pursuing *winning* at the cost of your relationship or values, you may be dealing with a control issue.

**The Affair:** *Helped you feel in charge, important, youthful, and desired.*

A new relationship can provide momentary distractions from feelings of unrest, and concerns about aging and potency. Connecting with someone who mirrors back feelings of youthfulness and admiration can provide an immediate experience of vitality, which helps you more easily compartmentalize concerns about the future.

## LOSS OF SOMEONE IMPORTANT

**Associated Feelings:** Sadness. Depression. Regret.
**Fear:** Your own mortality.
**By-product:** Loss and regret.

Losing a parent or other close relative is a significant loss that can trigger a variety of emotions, even if you had an estranged relationship with that person. If you had a challenging connection, their loss can trigger painful reminders of the past, including what was missing, and regret for things that did or did not happen. If you were close, you may experience regret and a deep sense of heartbreak over the loss. The loss of a friend can activate thoughts about your own mortality.

You are also impacted by the losses your partner experiences, whether the loss of a family member or a sense of self-loss. Your perceived inability to help a partner through their loss can trigger a sense of helplessness, which can in turn trigger your own sense of loss.

**AVF:** You experienced the death of someone important; or your partner has experienced an important death and has withdrawn, and you feel ill-equipped to help her through.

**The Affair:** *Provided a respite and comfort from a tragic situation and/or helped you feel understood.*

Losing someone is an external loss that triggers internal unrest. This loss can be a destabilizing force, drawing us closer to a partner. Sometimes it can prompt a return to a religious tradition and deeper spiritual engagement. But it can also create susceptibility to comfort offered by another. When someone shows up who has also had a recent loss or similar experience and offers a compassionate ear, it can foster an emotionally intimate connection. This can lead to a reliance upon that person, perhaps more than a spouse or other family members, which can become an emotional and potentially physical affair.

### SUMMARY

As you can see, there are a variety of factors, situations, and ruminations that can help set the stage for affair engagement. The feeling that someone or something else can provide a piece of life that is missing can be a strong catalyst for infidelity.

# External Affair Vulnerability Factors:
## *Situational Influences*

What happens in the outer world—that is the situations and conditions to which we are exposed and the opportunities we are presented with—influence how we react, respond, and interact with others. These interactions both influence and are influenced by our thoughts and feelings. Our external environment can create a strong pull in a specific direction that may or may not support optimal health and wellbeing. Following is a dramatic story that demonstrates the unexpected ways that environment can impact choices.

### THE ASSUMPTIONS WE MAKE

**"When it comes to interpreting other people's behavior, human beings invariably make the mistake of overestimating the importance of fundamental character traits and underestimating the importance of the situation and context."**

—Malcolm Gladwell

We tend to judge what we don't understand. Perhaps we judge because we feel we have a strong internal moral code, or think we are less susceptible to environmental conditions. Or maybe we judge because we consider certain behaviors offensive.

## THE STANFORD PRISON EXPERIMENT

We'd like to believe that we would be stronger than someone who *cheats,* or who is put in a position where their actions could cause pain to another. Of course, *we* would choose to do the *right thing in* the face of temptation. There have been social experiments that offer a deeper look at the complexity of how people respond under situational stressors that indicate otherwise. In his book *The Tipping Point,* Malcolm Gladwell relays the story of the controversial Stanford Prison Experiment,[6] which highlights the impact of situational factors on behavior.

Gladwell describes an experiment set up by a group of social scientists at Stanford University, led by Philip Zimbardo, who set out to answer the question "What happens when you put good people in an evil place? Does humanity win over evil, or does evil triumph?"

Zimbardo ran an ad in the paper looking for people to participate in this experiment. Seventy-five people volunteered. They ran volunteers through a battery of tests then chose twenty-one individuals that they determined to be the most psychologically healthy. The experiment was designed to observe the behavior of people in a simulated prison environment.

For the experiment they built a cell block in a 35 ft. corridor of their lab and created three 6 x 9-foot cells with steel bars and black painted doors. They also created one "solitary confinement" cell out of a closet.

The volunteers were randomly divided into two groups. One group was to take on the role of prisoners, the other guards. (An interesting observation: when they initially asked people whether they wanted to be prisoners or guards, most people said prisoners.)

To contribute to mirroring an actual situation, the *prisoners* were randomly picked up at their homes, blindfolded, and taken to their cells. They were not expecting their life as mock prisoners to begin in such a dramatic way. These *prisoners* were subsequently stripped of their clothes and dignity, sprayed with disinfectant, and issued identical khaki uniforms. Each prisoner was assigned a number, which was used by the guards instead of their names. The idea was for the prisoners to be totally stripped of not only their clothing but of their dignity and outside world identity as well.

What happened was both interesting and troubling. Each group began to fully assume their roles. Guards became controlling. Prisoners became afraid. Guards became more brutal and strategic in their interventions, attempting to make prisoners distrust each other. Prisoners banded together and fought back. Bottom line: It got ugly.

What began as a two-week experiment was halted in six days. Six days was all it took for people pitted against each other in a restricted environment—all of whom knew was not real—to become controlling, brutal, fearful, depressed, anxious, and hysterical.

## THE INTERSECTION OF CONDITIONS AND OPPORTUNITY

So, at this point you may be thinking, *Okay, I get that was tough, but what does it have to do with infidelity?* Granted this was an extreme case of environmental influence. Our homes are not prisons, even if we sometimes feel a bit trapped.

This experiment does illustrate, however, that conditions and opportunities have a far greater impact on our decision-making than we would like to think. Our environment, friendships, people we become close to at work, our discontents, frustrations, societal pressures, as well as the things that bring us excitement and joy create the context for our lives.

---

**The more consciously aware we are of the environmental factors that contribute to our lives, and the more in touch we are with what truly matters, the better the choices we tend to make.**

---

We each think that we are strong enough to choose well when presented with situations that are in direct opposition to our values and beliefs. And yet, time after time, in various experiments conducted in a laboratory or real life, it has been demonstrated that under the right conditions, any of us would be capable of behavior that we would have never dreamed possible.

# Affair Vulnerabilities and the Impact of Affair Engagement

In this chapter we have reviewed how loss, opportunity, and relational distress contribute to affair susceptibility. Here is a recap of the AVFs and how an affair can temporarily distract or soothe the associated vulnerabilities.

| AFFAIR VULNERABILITY FACTOR (AVF) | WAYS IN WHICH AN AFFAIR CAN DISTRACT, SOOTHE, OR TEMPORARILY FILL THE NEED. |
|---|---|
| **My life has felt stagnant.**<br><br>Things have become predictable, routine, and perhaps a little boring. | **The Affair helped me feel alive.**<br><br>The initial rush of connecting with someone new can spark a renewed sense of excitement. Life becomes less predictable and more engaging. The beginning of an affair can stimulate a greater sense of aliveness. |
| **I have been feeling a strong desire for a renewed sense of adventure.**<br><br>A woman you have connected with in a social or work situation, or another venue has activated strong desire and sparked renewed feelings of aliveness. | **The Affair revitalized my sense of adventure.**<br><br>An affair can temporarily fill the need for newness and adventure. A new woman offers new possibilities. She has not experienced any of your flaws. She has only had the pleasure of your best and sees you as you are now. You don't have a past with her, at least not yet. |
| **I haven't been feeling important or like a hero to my partner or family.** | **I felt needed and admired.**<br><br>Longing to be a hero is a primitive archetype in a man's psyche that longs to be fed. If a man grows hungry in this area for too long, it increases his vulnerability to affirmation received from other people or situations. |
| **I have been experiencing concerns about aging, where I am in my career, and wondering about what's next for me, or what type of legacy I will be leaving behind.** | **I felt more purpose driven.**<br><br>At midlife and beyond, individuals more frequently begin questioning the meaning and purpose of life. A new relationship can provide a momentary distraction from those feelings and increase feelings of vitality, youthfulness and usefulness. |

| | |
|---|---|
| **I have been drinking or leaning on other substances more than I used to.** | Increased levels of intoxication can be a warning signal that you may be trying to avoid addressing a challenging situation or numbing potentially negative feelings. It can also make you more susceptible to connecting with someone outside the relationship as intoxication breaks down defenses which can create misinterpretations and blur boundaries. |

| **AFFAIR VULNERABILITY FACTOR (AVF)** | **INTERNAL DRIVERS** |
|---|---|
| **My dad had an affair.** | Your father, or primary father figure, is your role model for what it means to be a man. If your dad cheated on your mom, you are more susceptible to engaging in this type of behavior. |
| **Mom had a boyfriend on the side that I knew about.** | Parental behaviors are powerful in shaping our own. Seeing mom with another man, or even just knowing about it is confusing. On some level, if her relationship with her dad was a rough one, you may be able to understand, but this can create distrust for women. This distrust can be a factor in your behavior. |
| **I have been feeling disconnected at home.** We seem to avoid talking about things that matter or that trigger conflict. I'm not sure my spouse is really all that interested in me anymore." | Relationships are complicated. When you are not feeling like you matter as much at home, having someone else smile and notice you can feed a gnawing emptiness. This can also set you up (on some level) to *want* to get caught simply to be noticed. |
| **I notice that I've been thinking more about my ex, wondering how she is doing, or thinking about how life would have been with her.** (Perhaps she has been reaching out or maybe you are tempted to contact her). | Even when a relationship has run its course, often there are remnants of attachment that remain. This can be particularly true in a "codependent" relationship. If you are someone who has reached out to an ex, or an ex keeps reaching out to you, it is important to take a closer look at your motivation and examine what you are getting from this connection. You need to be clear that you are putting your current relationship at risk. |

| AFFAIR VULNERABILITY FACTOR (AVF) | SITUATIONAL DRIVERS |
|---|---|
| **I work in an environment that is in the public eye and/or encourages socialization.** I work in the entertainment industry, politics, sales, or an influencer-type arena where socializing, alcohol, and/or drug use is more acceptable, and perhaps even an expectation of how you "land clients." | Temptation is everywhere. Certain careers provide more opportunities than others. Opportunity is a high-level AVF. (If you are continually in a place with available people who turn your head, and substance abuse is more socially acceptable, your resolve needs to be even stronger to not break your vows to your partner. This is particularly true when you are experiencing some of life's curve balls being thrown your way.) |

| AFFAIR VULNERABILITY FACTOR (AVF) | INTERNAL AND SITUATIONAL DRIVER |
|---|---|
| **My job has changed and/or I have been feeling unfulfilled at home or work.** I have been feeling like something is missing, or wondering what life would have been like had I made different choices. | Leaning on someone else can provide a temporary respite from life's musings or regrets for a time. What ifs aren't permanently soothed by an affair, but they can move to the back burner in the wake of an affair. |

## Reflection

Take some time to consider your AVFs.

Writing your answers is more effective as it prompts you to dig a little deeper. If you are working with a coach, counselor, or therapist, these are great reflections to share with them.

- Which AVFs apply to your situation? Is there something else that isn't on the list?
- Are there areas in your life where you have become complacent?
- What have you been hesitant to talk about or face within yourself? With your partner? Within your career?
- What do you realize now that you may not have been paying attention to then?

Now that we have examined how disconnection, loss, and situational factors can increase vulnerability to affair engagement, we will delve into essential initial steps in your recovery journey. This will involve understanding key information, actions to take, words to express, and things to avoid saying, all of which can greatly influence the effectiveness of the healing process as you embark on this path towards recovery.

Life provides many opportunities for learning, healing, and personal development. It's important to recognize that **internal cravings are not fully satisfied through the pursuit of external solutions**. Our desires serve as potent motivators and indicators that there are deeper aspects of ourselves waiting to be explored. Each of us is a unique work in progress, and the decisions we make play a crucial role in shaping the course of our lives.

# PART TWO

---

# Meeting *your* Challenges Head On:
## *Critical Steps in Recovery*

*"As human beings we have the unique ability to choose how we will interpret and digest each event that takes place in our lives. We've all been blessed with the very precious gift of free will. ... Free will enables us to use the events of our lives to grow and evolve or beat ourselves up."*
—Debbie Ford, *The Right Questions, Ten Essential Questions to Guide You to an Extraordinary Life*

Whenever you are considering making a change, the only place to begin is right where you are. So often, each of us spends time in the land of *if-onlys* and *what-ifs*.

*If only* I had talked to her sooner before things got out of control, maybe I would have spared us all so much heartache.

*What if* I never went out for that first drink with Sophie? Maybe none of this would have ever happened.

This type of thinking only serves to keep you stuck in the muck of regret. While it is natural to have these questions cross your mind, spending too much time in unsupportive thinking constricts your ability to heal, forgive yourself, and move forward.

Life offers each of us many opportunities to learn, grow, forgive, discover, and reclaim who we are and who we want to be. Affair recovery is a quest for self and relational discovery. It offers you an opportunity to dig more deeply into who you are, who you want to be, and helps you determine how you want to show up for those you love. It offers a path forward to help you shore up those areas of your life that have been out of alignment with your core values, beliefs, and commitments within your relationship and other areas of your life.

This section walks you through critical steps in the beginning stages of discovery and recovery.

**Emergency Dos and Don'ts:** This part can help guide you to more effectively begin the recovery process. The way you approach communicating with your spouse from the start either assists your recovery or makes it more challenging.

**Recovery Process Timeline:** A guideline to the recovery process.

**You've Been Caught, Now What?** We will examine the shock of being caught, or that pivotal moment when you decide to come clean.

**Coming Clean Assessment:** A tool to help you consider your options.

# 4

# Emergency Dos *and* Don'ts

---■---

*"You have been given the capacity to take dominion*
*within your own consciousness and choose the nature*
*and direction of your own thinking [and behavior.]"*
—Mary R. Hlunick, Ph.D., H. Ronald Hulnick, Ph.D.,
*Remembering the Light Within, A Course in Soul-Centered Living*

Let's begin with the four most critical dos and don'ts. Even if you don't reap immediate results, know that these behaviors go a long way to help with your relational recovery.

**1. Don't lie. Do set appropriate boundaries.** Getting caught in additional lies, even about unrelated things, re-ruptures your connection. While it may be challenging for you to answer questions about the affair, lying or telling half-truths only makes it worse. If she asks about something you don't feel is in the best interest of your relationship to discuss, kindly and directly let her know. It's okay to have boundaries, but not to hide things. There is a fine line between the two. Hiding keeps secrets in play. Setting boundaries helps the two of you maintain a sense of relational safety.

**Example:** If your spouse asks for specifics regarding your sexual interactions with an affair partner, **I STRONGLY caution you NOT to share explicit details.** While it is understandable that she may want to know if you had intercourse, or something similar, sharing detailed descriptions of how you engaged sexually can result in mental images that are difficult to erase, adding to her trauma. If your woman presses you on this, let her know that you don't think that hearing these details will help her heal. This is a great time for an additional heartfelt "I'm sorry" and reassurance that the affair is truly over.

This is a sensitive area that can go sideways very quickly. If you meet with resistance and are working through this material with a counselor or coach, you can defer these tougher conversations to one of your sessions.

**2. Don't overpromise. Do consider your commitments before making them.** You are giving your relationship your best shot at recovery, right? That doesn't mean you need to say yes to everything. Be careful not to get caught in the trap of making promises you simply may not be able to keep just to appease the situation.

Rebuilding trust involves following through on your commitments. Remember, your spouse is actively trying to determine whether or not she can trust you. Take care to consider what you can and can't realistically commit to. Make sure you can follow through *before* saying yes. (Chapter 13 explores this topic in greater depth.)

**3. Do discontinue communication with the affair partner. Don't lie to your spouse if the AP reaches out.** Continuing communication with the AP can significantly delay the reconnection process with your partner. If you promised your partner you will let her know if the AP reaches out to you, you must keep your word. You are building credibility every time you follow through on what you say you are going to do. Even though you may not want to stir her emotions, you need to let your partner know about any reach-outs and quickly shut them down. If she finds out on her own, it undermines the trust you are working to rebuild. (We will discuss how to end your affair with clarity, respect, and kindness in Chapter 11.)

**4. Don't defend your Affair Partner. Do convey to your spouse that she is your priority.** Even if there has been discord at home, your partner will struggle with you forging a connection with someone else. While she will be hurt and angry with you, much of her anger can be displaced onto the AP. She may say some horrible things about the person with whom you connected. Your SO needs to know that you value her more than the AP. Put her feelings first. Resist any temptation to defend the AP.

Once again, this is an opportunity for extending compassion and an apology—saying something like, "I can see how (upset, angry, etc.) you are. I'm so sorry I hurt you." (Chapter 25 helps guide you through the apology and amends-making process.)

**5. Don't Expect to see immediate results. Do Keep Your Expectations in Check. Be patient with the process.** Thorough healing after an affair takes time. Patience can be tough. Maybe you are the kind of man who prides himself on your problem-solving prowess, especially in the business arena. This is not the type of challenge that is quickly resolved. Think of your relational healing as a longer-term project that requires focus, ongoing commitment, and the cultivation of new ways of thinking and responding. More like chess than checkers, slow down. This is an opportunity to build your patience muscles.

These five seemingly simple (but not necessarily easy) behaviors will help keep you from inadvertently making things worse by operating from a state of panic. When you take a few moments to breathe and recenter yourself in the face of your partner's emotional upset, you will be better equipped to make choices for the relationship.

Your spouse needs to see your humility. She needs to feel the sincerity of your apologies. She needs to know that you realize and own the behavior that hurt her. She will probably need to hear you apologize and express remorse many times. Remember, she wants reassurance that she can trust you again. Her world has been turned upside down, and she wants to feel safe.

## Roadblocks to Repair

I have seen men do things immediately after ending their affair that significantly interfere with the recovery process. Here are some of the roadblocks that will make your recovery more difficult:

**Acting like the affair never happened and trying to resume *business as usual* within your primary relationship.** A looming sense of shame makes talking about an affair difficult. Most men would like their partners to just forgive and forget. Unfortunately, the heaviness of an affair can linger for quite some time after it ends. As you have heard me say before: *Slow down. Be patient.*

**Feeling so consumed by missing the AP that you just can't seem to reconnect with your spouse.** Your desire may have taken a big hit. The adrenaline rush of feeling wanted is a strong one. Now you are working to prove to the woman you love that you are trustworthy and want her. Reconnecting physically may be difficult. You may not be up for the task, especially if you are feeling rejected.

Remember, this is a vulnerable time for you as well as your partner. You may need to enlist some outside help to process your grief and regroup. Don't get caught in the inner rumination trap of wishing things were different. If you are not fully ready to reconnect with your partner, for whatever reason, it is important to acknowledge it first within yourself and then to your partner. (See the Reflections portion of Chapter 10, *Affairs Phase Two: Stuck in the Middle with You,* for a more detailed walkthrough of what to do if you are stuck and not fully ready to work on your marriage.)

**Sharing with your partner too many details about the AP, what a good person she was, and how sorry you are that you hurt her.** While all of this may be true, remember, you are trying to rebuild your primary relationship. Things you share during these vulnerable times leave a lasting footprint. You need to share enough to have your partner feel you are being honest but not so much that it re-traumatizes her. If you need help working through the grief or confusion of letting go of your AP please reach out to a professional.

One client of mine told his wife, *"You know, I think you would really like her. Under different circumstances, you would probably be friends."* Nooooo! While you may believe this to be true, don't **ever** say it. Your partner has been incredibly wounded by what happened. Saying positive things about the AP can cause your wife to feel like you are taking the AP's side over hers. This is like pouring salt into a wound. Bottom line: It hurts and lengthens recovery.

**Moving back into physical connection before your partner is ready.** Often when an affair is discovered (and possibly while it is occurring), sex at home becomes either absent or scarce. You cannot expect to jump back into a healthy sex life with your partner simply because you have given up the other person. As frustrating as it may be, rebuilding trust and connection takes time.

Waiting for your spouse to be ready for sex can be challenging. Quite often sex can be viewed as an indicator that things are okay, or at least heading in the right direction.

**Don't assume that because you are having great sex with your partner that things are okay.** Sometimes the opposite happens and the two of you engage in passionate, mind-blowing sex. Keep in mind intensity in the bedroom doesn't mean things are okay. Your partner may jump back in sooner than she is ready because she is afraid of losing the relationship. This intensity can also result in extreme emotions and a strong emotional rebound as she wrestles with the fear of losing you vs. losing herself and compromising her values.

**This isn't a race.** Work on rebuilding your relational connection before, or even along with your sexual one. One time sex doesn't mean sexual engagement is totally back on the table. She may say *yes* one moment and *no* the next. Sex is a form of intimate connection that is often difficult for couples to talk about. Let her know that you are following her lead. That doesn't mean she needs to initiate or be available when you are. It does mean you need to respect her choices.

**Take care not to become impatient with your partner's progress.** While some women tend to forgive very quickly, others take quite a while to process. If you can see this process as an opportunity to improve your relationship, it can be a vehicle to help you shore up any leaks that were in place before this outside liaison ever happened. Affairs that are quickly swept under the rug run a greater risk of being repeated.

## Reflection

- As you reflect upon these points, which ones feel most difficult for you?
- Are there areas that you need to revisit or reclarify with your spouse? If so, you can reaffirm your commitment. Let her know that you will make mistakes along the way, and that you are diligently working on better understanding yourself, your motivations, and ways to communicate, listen, understand, and be there for her.

Remember, rebuilding your relationship takes time, attention, and commitment to the process. This could be some of the most challenging and rewarding work you have ever done.

# 5

## Recovery Process Timeline

———————————————— ■ ————————————————

*"Martin Luther King, Jr., understood that underneath all of the struggle and sorrow there is a force of life that is unstoppable."*
—Jack Kornfield, *A Path with Heart*

This work offers you too the opportunity to activate within you that *"force of life that is unstoppable."* Doing so requires grit and guts. If you are a solution-driven man who thinks on his feet, you may find the ability to both act and have patience difficult. In any type of recovery work, especially the work involving yourself and another person, both are required.

Many people ask how long infidelity recovery takes. While this differs among couples, solid recovery typically takes at least a year. That doesn't mean that after a year the topic is never brought up again. It does mean that the frequency and intensity of triggers and discussions is significantly lower. The couples who do the best are the ones who set aside time each week to actively work on recovering and rebuilding their relationship. Recovery is both an individual and a relational process.

It is important for you to find the balance between offering comfort and giving her space. Be patient with her emotional highs and lows as best you can without taking it personally, as her needs and moods will fluctuate. If you are unsure what she needs, ask. Here are some suggested questions: *What do you need from me right now? Do you need time to yourself, or would you like to connect? How can I support you? Would you like a hug? Would you like to go for a walk or a drive?*

As a couple, it is important for each of you to carve out time to explore your own wants, needs, and desires, and learn how to best communicate and actively listen to each other.

The following timetable offers an approximate window into diligent recovery and an overall theme for each period. This process is not linear, which means you may feel like things are progressing, then you hit a snag, which feels like a setback. Try not to get discouraged. Movement will fluctuate. **It is important to work through feelings as they occur AND set up reconnection/fun time that excludes talking about the affair.**

### Phase I – Months 1 to 4. The predominant question during this time is: Can I ever trust again?

During the first few months, you are both recovering from the shock of what happened. Each person is discerning whether they believe the relationship is salvageable and deciding if they are willing to fully engage in the recovery process. The work involves learning how to best answer questions, set boundaries, and balance the need for connection and space.

- **For the betrayer:** How can I trust myself to ensure that I remain faithful to my commitments?

- **For the betrayed:** How can I ever trust my partner again or feel safe in this relationship?

### Phase II – Months 4 to 8. The overriding question during this time is two-fold: Can I truly forgive? What does true forgiveness look like for yourself and from your partner?

You begin diving more fully into the work of self-discovery, cultivating a greater understanding of your partner's emotional state, and learning how to engage in productive conversations. Cultivating behaviors that rebuild trust and reinforce the safety of the relationship are big components of this time frame.

- **For the betrayer:** Can I extend forgiveness to myself for the pain my actions have caused?

- **For the betrayed:** Can I extend forgiveness to my partner for his behavior? Can I forgive myself for not speaking up, perhaps ignoring signals or a gut feeling?

**Phase III – Months 8 to 12. The dominant questions during this phase revolve around the partnership: How can we strengthen our connection? How can we create a supportive, loving, trustworthy partnership?**

While relational work is an important part of the infidelity recovery process from the beginning, during this phase the affair itself becomes a less frequent focal point. The work involves a more in-depth exploration of what each person wants to create as individuals and as a couple—in the present and into the future. In this phase, you will continue fine-tuning the skills of authentic communication—both listening and speaking your truth. While the topic of the affair can still unexpectedly rear its head, it is occupying less headspace.

- **For both parties:** What am I willing to do to strengthen our connection? What do I need, want, and desire in this partnership? How can I continue to choose engaging in loving actions over my need to be right?

**Phase IV – Months 12 and beyond. The dominant question here is: How can we maintain a thriving connection that fills our needs as individuals, as a couple, and if applicable, as a family?**

This is a time of continued building and maintenance. It is important to pay attention to the tendency toward complacency and take care not to slide back into old patterns. Your relationship needs time and attention. Learn how to nurture each other and engage in behaviors that light up each other's world. It is important to prioritize connection and set aside quality time to work through day-to-day needs as well as engage in planful interactions that feed your connection.

- **For both of you:**
  - o Make a commitment to deeply listen to your partner and pursue curiosity about their interests.
  - o Work through whatever blocks you from more consistently asking for what you need and desire, in a clear manner—without complaint or blame.

Hint: Instead of complaining about what you don't have/like, kindly and directly ask for what you would like, and then give your partner room to let you know if they are willing/able to provide it.

  - o Speak your truth with kindness, compassion, and clarity.

Working through Phase IV can set you up for a solid, satisfying relationship.

## Reflection

- Where do you see yourselves on the relational timeline? These timeframes are impacted by the work you are doing as well. If you are just beginning to dive into the work, you may be chronologically in stage three or four, but from a recovery perspective you may be in stage one or two.

- What would you like your relationship to look like? While the exploration of this question will be ongoing throughout your review of the material/recovery, it doesn't hurt to start thinking about that early in the process. Creating a vision for your relationship gives you something to work toward.

- What are your most challenging aspects of the recovery process thus far?


In the next segment, we are going to dive into affair discovery, its associated dilemmas, and the feelings stirred.

# 6

# You've Been Caught. Now What?

∎

*"The first time I dared look within myself, I was terrified.
I had made a life practice of avoiding myself, by any and all
means. I craved and clung to any addiction, relationship, or
outside distraction. I did this because I was afraid— … Maybe
I was afraid I would find nothing inside or simply darkness."*
—Melody Beattie, *Codependents' Guide to the Twelve Steps.*

You may feel caught in your affair well before being confronted by your spouse. The longer an affair continues, the more difficult it is to maintain its secrecy, and the more you may feel caught between both relationships.

*Actually getting caught* in an affair—whether through suspicion, discovery, or admission—however, is a whole new ballgame. Like setting the first domino into motion, the impact triggers a long trail of reactions. The top three emotional reactions men experience are terror, shame, and relief.

**Terror:** During an affair, one of the biggest fears is exposure. Once you acknowledge the affair or are discovered, that fear comes to fruition and terror builds, forcing you to confront what's next. *Is she going to leave me? Can she ever forgive me? Is my relationship over?* Time and time again I hear from guys that they never intended their affair to end their primary relationship. And yet once the affair is discovered, they realize that is a straight-up possibility.

**Shame:** Upon discovery, most men tap into a deep sense of shame. Facing the anger, hurt, and questioning of an aggrieved partner is no fun. In most cases, guys will say almost anything to make it stop. Unaddressed shame can lead to depression and self-loathing, which can be difficult to shake.

**Note:** This is a vulnerable time for you both. It is easy to overpromise to soothe her emotions. Be careful. Remember, you are working to rebuild trust. Your SO will be paying attention to how well you honor your agreements. So don't make them lightly. We will discuss this more in-depth later.

**Relief:** Many men describe breathing a sigh of relief when their spouse finds out, because it means they can finally quit worrying about discovery. Getting caught provides an extra impetus to back away from a connection you may have been struggling to end.

But, what if you haven't been caught, *yet?*

## The Power of Stories

Every relationship has its story, and there is a healing power contained within each. When facing a challenge, we can find solace in knowing others have found their way through. In the stories throughout this book—including the one that follows—you may see yourself. Some stories may surprise you. At the very least, hopefully these stories let you know that you are not alone, and that you can utilize this time to cultivate a life more in sync with who you are and who you want to be, within and outside of your relationship.

## Facing Your Choices: The Story of Jim, Liz, and Shelly

This chapter highlights the story of Jim, Liz (Jim's wife), and Shelly (the AP).

Listen as Jim wrestles with what happened:

*"I guess I quit paying attention to Liz's needs. Problems at work just kept getting bigger and became all-consuming. When I came home, Liz complained about how much time I was spending at work. Instead of making her a priority, I found more reasons to work late. The more she complained, the more I retreated. Work became my safety net and my excuse.*

*"In the process, I found myself spending more time with Shelly at work. Shelly didn't complain. She was interested in me and what I was doing, always willing to help, and great at her job. We began working on more projects together. As lame as it sounds, I felt like Shelly liked me. And it didn't seem like my wife liked me very much anymore.*

*"I began stopping at a bar to grab a drink or two on the way home from work, just to chill. I rationalized that would help me better deal with the upset I knew I'd absorb when I walked in the door late. One night, I invited Shelly to join me. We had just finished a project together. I thought it would be nice to celebrate this corporate and personal victory with her.*

*"After that first drink, we had another. I felt all this pent-up energy welling up inside. She was so sweet and attractive, sitting there on that barstool. So, I went for it. I leaned over and kissed her. And she fully kissed me back. I knew it was wrong, but she was there for me. My wife wasn't. I don't know, maybe I didn't give her the chance to be. That was the beginning of our ten-month affair that I never should have let happen in the first place.*

*"At first, even though I felt guilty, I felt happier at home. My wife's complaints didn't bug me quite so much. But as time went on, weekends began to get tougher. It didn't feel like Liz and I were connecting. She didn't seem happy, at least not with me. Maybe I was just looking for an excuse. I don't know.*

*"I began working more Saturdays. So did Shelly. We found ways to be together. My mind got all tangled up. I managed to justify what I was doing because it minimized frustration at home. Liz and I didn't seem to be arguing quite as much. It all seemed to work well, for a while. Until one day it didn't.*

*"It was like I was living in two different worlds, and it became more and more difficult to keep them from colliding. Something inside me began to shift. I noticed my desire to be with Shelly beginning to taper off. It happened just before Christmas, which has historically been our favorite family holiday.*

*"Liz wanted to decorate, so I pulled out all the Christmas decorations, and we spent the entire weekend fixing up the house. The kids were coming home from college a little*

*early this year, and we wanted to be ready. We had a great weekend together preparing for the kids. We laughed and talked about holidays past. We even made love that weekend. It felt like old times.*

*"The kids got home late Sunday afternoon. We were both excited to see them. I grilled for dinner, and Liz made the veggies and her famous twice-baked potatoes. Our daughter, Jess, made pumpkin cheesecake muffins. We had our family back together, and it felt great. Later that evening it hit me how fucked up everything had become. And I was the one who did the fucking!"*

**Commentary—A Point of Reckoning**

That weekend, Jim came face to face with his affair. It's not like he hadn't struggled with it before, but engaging with his wife over the weekend and preparing for the holidays jolted him into a deeper reckoning with himself and his choices. He began thinking about his marriage and the family they had created together. In his own words:

*"It's like that weekend, I did a 180. It's difficult to describe, but it was a wakeup call that what I was doing wasn't going to end well. Prior to that weekend, as strange as it sounds, I didn't give much thought to how this would end. Granted, I thought about what would happen if I got caught in the past, but this was different. Being with Liz that weekend, it's like I experienced the woman I chose to marry and raise a family with. I thought about her, and what she had sacrificed to be a great mom and create a great home for us. Yes, I helped, but she did most of the work to make our family work. Damn. I knew what I was doing, even if she didn't know about it, was hurting her – hurting our relationship – making things worse. I was living a lie. This isn't something I ever thought I would do. That's the man I want to be. It's not who I am."*

Many men reach a point of reckoning when they know they need to firmly end things with their AP. This moment can arise like it did with Jim, when something at home jars you into *seeing* your partner, feeling appreciation for her – even through whatever conflicts you may have been experiencing—reflecting on the life you have built together, and the reasons you connected in the first place.

This point of reckoning can also occur when the reality of getting caught hits too close to home. In the case of work affairs, coworkers can sense what is going on. The energy between two people in the throes of an affair is difficult to keep under wraps. People can see it, feel it, and detect it in the actions and looks of consenting parties. Those involved believe they are doing a great job hiding it, but more often than not, others sense it and are talking about what they believe to be true.

These reckoning moments hit hard, shocking your system with thoughts about the people you never intended to hurt, coupled with the realization that that your actions may have caused you to lose everything: Your partner. Your family. The respect of your community. And even respect for yourself.

These moments are decision points that frequently result in a man questioning himself and pulling back from his AP. He often realizes that whatever drew him into his affair—whatever he has been receiving from this connection—isn't worth the pain he is potentially causing his wife. He knows his affair needs to end.

## THE COVER-UP

Trying to end an affair, particularly the first time around, can be challenging, especially when your AP isn't ready to call it quits. Sometimes affair partners go back and forth several times before breaking it off for good. Let's look at what happened when Jim reached his own point of reckoning and realized he needed to end the affair.

Jim continued: *"Shelly kept texting me over the weekend. When I didn't respond, she started calling. It scared me. I didn't want Liz to see her name pop up on my cell phone, so I changed her name to George. Liz asked why I wasn't answering 'George's' calls. I think she suspected something, but she kept her cool. I told her I didn't want to focus on work over the weekend, and that I had been spending way too much time there. She smiled and agreed.*

*"I didn't sleep well Sunday night. I dreaded what was to come but vowed to keep my resolve. My wife and family were what was important here, not my connection with Shelly. I was ready.*

*"On Monday morning, Shelly came in dressed to the nines. She was very sweet and affectionate. Although I knew she must have been upset I ignored her calls and texts over the weekend, she treaded lightly. She smiled and said she wanted to figure out a time to be together over the holidays. I felt trapped. I didn't want to hurt her, but I knew it was over. It simply had to be. I knew I had to tell her, but I didn't exactly know how."*

### Commentary—Breaking Things Off

Ending things with an AP can be particularly challenging, especially when she doesn't see it coming. Even when your AP knows you are married, letting go isn't an easy thing to do—particularly for women.

Your message must be clean, clear, and definitive. Leaving wiggle room helps no one. Even if you are trying not to hurt the AP, she will be hurt. Not being clear or trying to keep her hanging on in the hopes that things change at home only hurts her more. Knowing a woman is holding on, "just in case," can seem like a great ego boost, but trust me, keeping a window cracked open, even just a little, hurts everyone much more in the long run.

## THE BREAKUP ATTEMPT: TAKE ONE

Jim said, *"Needless to say, things didn't turn out as planned. I tried to tell Shelly we were through, but I just couldn't. She questioned my weekend disappearance, and I made up an excuse. Shelly started to get angry, stating that I could have found some place to call or text what was going on. I told her I was sorry, and her demeanor quickly changed. She shifted the topic and tried again to pin me down to a date for 'our Christmas.' Our Christmas! The sound of it made me cringe. Christmas is a time for family and is our family's favorite holiday. I turned away. She must have seen it in my face. I certainly could read the upset on hers. Once again, her anger flared.*

*"'What is happening?' she asked. 'You promised to carve out some holiday time for me. For us. You told me you were looking forward to time together. And now you can't even look at me! What the fuck, Jim!'*

*"I stammered, trying to come up with an excuse—anything to calm things down. I told her it was becoming more difficult for me to get away. Then she said something shocking. 'Well, maybe I should just call your wife!'*

*"I couldn't believe she even went there! That was the last thing I wanted her to do. My weekend with Liz really shifted things. It caused me to realize I wanted my wife and my life back. And I was determined to do everything in my power to make that happen.*

*"It seemed that the tables were turned, and now Shelly, who was always affirming, understanding, and there for me, was the one unhappy with me. I just wanted to get the hell out of there. What kind of a mess have I gotten myself into?"*

### Commentary—The AP's Emotional Response

One thing that men engaging in affairs often forget is that at some point, they will have to deal with their lover's *unpleasant* emotions, not just the happy ones. You can't stay bathed in the enchantment of "new love" forever. Disappointment is inevitable.

A woman scorned reveals other sides of her personality that may have been neatly tucked away under the blanket of an affair. Ultimately, the stressors of real life are uncovered, breaking the spell of enchantment. I have had men tell me that they found that the stress of keeping a lover from cracking had become even more challenging than any stress they had been experiencing within their primary relationship!

### IS CONFESSION *REALLY* GOOD FOR THE SOUL?

Should Jim tell Liz? What would you do in Jim's situation? If you haven't told your partner yet or are beginning to discuss the nuances of your particular affair, know this:

---

## A woman can be forgiving if she feels you are truly sorry, and if you acknowledge the gravity of what you did and the impact your actions had on her.

---

This, however, will take time.

# To Tell or Not to Tell? That Is the Question.

So, you have decided to call it quits with your Affair Partner (AP). Perhaps you haven't been caught *yet* and aren't quite sure how to handle things, especially at home. Should you confess?

There is a high likelihood that your spouse suspects something is off and that you could be engaging with someone else. Affairs are quite difficult to hide indefinitely; even if she doesn't find out now, she could learn about it later, especially if others suspect or know about it, or if you have any electronic "paper trail." Even if she doesn't know, many experts say whether you have been caught or not, you must confess. Carrying such a big secret can weigh heavily on your soul.

Relational honesty and authenticity are important values to honor, but what else must be taken into consideration? Is moving forward authentically impossible without telling your spouse about the affair? Can you hold yourself accountable and re-sculpt your relationship without revealing your indiscretions? What is the healthiest decision for your relationship?

It is difficult to be authentic when you are hiding something this big.

———————————————— Coming Clean Assessment ————————————————

Is honesty *always* the best policy? As you consider your options, it is important to examine your situation, your partner, and your motivation for coming clean. Here are some questions to consider as you decide the best course of action for you and your partner. **Please circle each one that applies and put an asterisk next to your strongest three:**

1) You want your partner to understand that there are things she has been doing or not doing that have caused you to look elsewhere.

2) You want to alleviate your guilt or clear your conscience.

3) You are tired of carrying this burden alone.

4) You believe she probably already knows anyway.

5) You are having trouble focusing on work or home tasks, and feel telling her would help you get back on track.

6) You need help letting the other person go. You believe that telling your primary partner will hold you accountable.

7) You don't feel like you can totally be yourself in your primary relationship if you don't tell her about the affair.

8) You want to lay it all out on the table so that she can make an informed choice about your relationship. While you are hopeful you can start fresh, you feel you cannot do so unless she knows.

9) You value trust and honesty and don't believe you can truly move forward without sharing information about your transgressions.

So, what do these results tell you? Consider your top three asterisked answers and which quadrant below they fall into:

- **Questions 1-3:** These three are more about you than about your primary relational partner. If these are your strongest reasons, you may want to do a little more introspective work before talking to her. With these as your primary reasons, the likelihood of this talk going well is probably slim.

- **Questions 4-6:** If these three are your primary motivators, then you are moving up a bit on the scale. While they are still more about your state of mind, they point to a greater desire to share with your partner to put the affair behind you.

- **Questions 7-9:** These are the most potent reasons for sharing your indiscretions with your SO, as they are more focused on her and your relationship.

What stood out for you as you considered your motivation? If you are still unsure whether you want to discuss the affair with your partner, talk to a trusted friend, coach, or therapist who specializes in infidelity recovery. You may also find greater insight as you work through this material and identify the drivers that led to your affair.

**Talking to your partner helps hold you accountable and create a clean slate. If you decide to** handle it on your own without coming clean, it may be wise to engage in some counseling to strengthen your relationship and work through relational challenges in general, and specifically related to your affair.

We will continue with Jim, Liz, and Shelly's story in an upcoming chapter. First, we are going to explore the ways in which your upbringing and how your needs were and were not met contribute to the formation of your interpersonal relationships.

# PART THREE

—■—

# Unpacking *the* Past:
## *How Our Needs, Desires, and Family Shape*
## *Our Self-Perception and Relationships*

The way we internalize childhood and teen experiences plays a significant role in shaping our perspectives on the world and influencing the formation of adult relationships. Our early experiences, such as interactions with family members, friends, and societal influences, can leave lasting impressions on our beliefs, values, and emotional responses.

Positive experiences during each developmental period can foster a sense of security, self-worth, and trust, which can contribute to healthy adult relationships. Conversely, negative experiences, such as trauma, neglect, or dysfunctional relationships, can lead to the internalization of negative beliefs, insecurities, and attachment issues that may hinder the formation of healthy adult relationships. Understanding and addressing these internalized experiences is crucial for personal growth and the development of fulfilling and meaningful connections in adulthood.

During this segment we will explore the following questions:

**The Quest for Completion:** What happens when you hit periods of doubts or wondering whether there was something in life you missed out on or could have handled differently?

- **Three Core Needs:** What are they? What types of experiences fulfill them? And, how does it impact you when they are not being met?

- **Pain and Pleasure:** How do they drive decisions and behavior?

**The Influence of Family on Who and How You Love:** What is the impact of upbringing and childhood exposure on adult relationships and affair engagement?

# 7

# The Quest *for* Completion

■

*"You complete me."*

—From the movie *Jerry Maguire*, directed by Cameron Crowe

Fairy tales and movies both shape and reflect our views on love. They accentuate the human quest to discover and connect with that ever-elusive soulmate, the one perfect person without whom we will never quite feel whole. Many of these tales end with *and they lived happily ever after*. Unfortunately, we typically do not get a window into what the *happy* in the *ever after* looks like.

Encounters with new people, situations, and adventures can activate an inner chemistry in ways that can create some doubt about your primary connection activating thoughts like: *Are we still meant to be together? Maybe she isn't 'the one' after all. Have we outgrown each other?* You may wonder whether there is someone else out there who is a better fit for who and where you are now. While this doesn't occur in all cases of infidelity, it is normal for a strong connection with a new person to awaken the inner doubt monsters and activate ruminations over what may be missing.

# The Missing Piece

There is a beautiful children's story by the prolific writer, poet, and philosopher Shel Silverstein, titled *The Missing Piece*, which powerfully illustrates this concept.

The story begins with a young boy who suddenly realizes he is missing a piece of himself. This realization sparks him to set off on a quest, determined to find the perfect *piece* to complete him.

He begins with an external, exhaustive quest, only to discover that nothing is really missing after all. In the end, he makes peace with himself exactly how he is. Like Dorothy in *The Wizard of Oz,* he discovers "there's no place like home" and that he *is* home.

Many of us will, at some point, bump up against the notion that something is missing. This is frequently referred to as a *midlife crisis*, although it can occur at any age. For some, this feeling bursts into awareness like a freight train traveling at full speed. For others, it shows up as a gnawing in our gut that we just can't seem to quench.

Sometimes a man experiences a haunting feeling that he might have *missed the boat* in life. Have you ever had the feeling that you are not where you should be at a particular life stage? Feelings of this nature can trigger a host ruminating thoughts, sometimes activate a heightened career focus, and spark a plethora of questions.

- Is this all there is?
- Did I make the right career choice?
- Did I choose the right person?
- Does she still want me?
- If I had to do it all over again, would I make the same choices?

And the age-old existential questions:

- Do I matter? Does my life matter? Who do I matter to the most?
- What's it (life) all for? What is my bigger purpose? In what ways am I stepping more fully into my purpose or living a purpose-driven life? Is there anything I need to change?
- What type of mark am I leaving on the world?
- What if ...?

Existential stirrings and musings can be catalysts activating a desire for deeper exploration one hand, and just wanting things to return to that ever-elusive *normal* on the other. What do these questions stir up or reveal to you?

## The Impact of New Relationships

When two people first meet, they each create an idealized image of one another. This is based on their interactions, views on love, what they witnessed as a child, and prior relational encounters. Since new relationships inspire us to act like our best selves and keep less desirable traits tucked away, interested parties are not initially connecting with the whole person, only their projection of who they believe that person to be.

Additionally, new romantic relationships often trigger an influx of hormones like oxytocin and dopamine, which are the natural chemicals that make us feel good. Sometimes these feel-good chemicals can act like a drug, blocking out much of our rational thinking—along with our ability to see our partner's flaws. These hormones are critical in our biology, as they create the bonding necessary to (one day) procreate. But they can also "trick" us into thinking our new partner is "perfect for us." (More on this later.)

As blossoming connections are explored, you may encounter longings that you didn't even know you had. New experiences can serve as a temporary reprieve from obligations such as parenting, building a financial portfolio, and honoring social obligations—all of which can diminish quality time to engage with your partner, resulting in feelings of disconnection and an *ever after* that isn't quite as happy as you assumed it would be.

You can become so wrapped up in life's routines that you lose sight of your critical human needs. Let's take a deeper look at three core human desires and how they play out in our lives.

## Three Core Needs

**"May this be a safe place full of understanding and acceptance, where you can be as you are, without the need of any mask of pretense or image."**

—*To Bless this Space Between Us,* John O'Donohue, author, poet

Each of us has three core emotional/psychological needs. I refer to them as the "Three No's" (not because they are negative but because calling them that makes them easier to remember). These are the desire to: **Be Known**, **Noticed**, and to **Know You Matter.**

These are primal needs that predominantly run beneath the surface of our awareness. Let's take a closer look at each.

## THE NEED TO BE KNOWN

The type of *known* I am speaking of is when someone is attuned to who you are. It is a way of being seen that honors the whole person. Dr. Daniel Siegel,[7] a neurobiologist, author, and professor of psychiatry at UCLA, refers to this phenomenon as *feeling felt* by someone, meaning that the person has a good sense of who you are. They read and respond to your signals in ways that encourage openness and increase feelings of acceptance and respect. Feeling known promotes greater relational intimacy, as it increases a partner's willingness to be vulnerable and express their needs, rather than move into patterns of anxiety, avoidance or discontent.

Within every relationship, there are certain traits that we find more appealing or relatable than others. When our partner embraces all aspects of who we are, not just the ones they prefer, it creates a foundation for deeper relational bonds that can lead to mutual growth and flourishing.

Acceptance doesn't mean agreeance, and it doesn't offer an excuse for *bad* behavior under the guise of "That's just who I am." In a solid relationship, each person strives to consider the other person's needs, as well as their own. They can show their playful side, discuss things that make them anxious, and express their excitement as well as their sorrows without *walking on eggshells* out of fear of upsetting their partner.

Feeling known and accepted by those we love is a gift that empowers us to more fully explore and discover our true nature.

## THE NEED TO BE NOTICED

A parent's perception of a child influences how the child sees themselves. As we move into adulthood and have a stronger sense of our individuality, our need to be noticed takes shape in different ways. Completing a complex project that results in acknowledgment from bosses and peers, being promoted, having a loved one offer positive feedback on what we've done or even comment on our physique or outfit can feed this need. Being noticed is a critical component in cultivating self-worth. When we are noticed, we feel like we matter. When the important people in our lives quit paying attention, we can feel isolated, unimportant, and alone.

**Important Note:** If you have experienced abandonment or neglect growing up, the need to be noticed can surface even more powerfully within your adult relationships. This can result in attention-seeking behaviors that sometimes feel overwhelming to a partner. It is important to have various people, activities, and interests that help fulfill this need.

---

## A partner cannot be the sole provider of anyone's needs.

---

Conversely, living in an unpredictable household can also have the opposite effect. If being noticed as a child or teen resulted in a possible negative reaction, punishment, or abuse, in adulthood you may tend to try to *fly under the radar* as being noticed at home was dangerous. This can result in strong conflict-avoidant behavior within intimate relationships resulting in disengagement during a potential partner's upset. This can be problematic within a relationship, as avoidance can feel like abandonment, particularly when the other person's upbringing included parental disengagement. **Avoidance can result in the creation of repetitive patterns making it difficult to bring challenges to a workable resolution.**

When the people we spend time with take an interest in our activities and interests our connection with them flourishes. Being noticed also impacts how we feel about ourselves. Self-esteem and self-confidence increase in the presence of people who notice, acknowledge, and appreciate our efforts. This is particularly true of intimate relationships, people in power positions (in work and social settings), and our peers.

The need to be noticed is one of the reasons social media has such a strong grip on our culture. It can become an electronic substitute to satisfy the desire to be noticed. The inherent danger is when becomes tied to self-worth and the number of *likes* and comments we do or do not receive.

## THE NEED TO KNOW YOU MATTER

The final leg of the trilogy is knowing that what we do and who we are positively impact those around us. Knowing we inspire others or make a difference in someone's life is motivating. It can inspire us to give more generously and open our hearts more fully. Giving to others is a gift with give ourselves as well. Giving, particularly when it is well-received, increases our sense of meaning and purpose.

Each of us wants to know that who we are matters to someone. For some, contributions made at home to family and friends feed this need. (This can be particularly true in strong familial cultures where individuals work for the good of the extended family, either financially or to take them to new and safer places to live.) For others, contributing to charity or engaging in meaningful work endeavors helps feed this need. Others are driven to engage in high-profile giving that impacts many lives.

Knowing we matter to our partners strengthens connection and helps us feel loved.

## WHAT HAPPENS?

Often in my couples work, I hear individuals expressing disappointment that they don't feel that what they do or who they are makes a difference. Sometimes I have each person list the things they do for their partner and the relationship. This gives the other person an opportunity to acknowledge contributions they may not have noticed. Acknowledgment helps a partner feel like they matter. Knowing you matter, like the other two "No's," is a critical core need for emotional and psychological well-being.

While these core needs may go dormant for a time, eventually they do resurface. At first blush, engaging in an affair can spark the embers of a need that you didn't even realize you had. It feels good to be the focus of someone's interest and attention. The challenge lies in the link you make between the person and the fulfillment of the need. When you see someone else as the source of your needs' fulfillment, it can stimulate a desire to want more—more of their time and attention, and more frequency of their presence in your life.

In relationships, more frequent arguing over the *little things* is a signal that one or more of these needs is not being met. While it isn't the responsibility of any one person to totally fill another's needs bucket, it is important to cultivate an awareness of ways in which these core needs are and are not being met. Talking about the Three No's creates a framework for each partner to assess their needs and create solutions to better address them as individuals and as a couple.

# Pain and Pleasure

Two other factors that influence human behavior are: 1) the avoidance of pain, and 2) the desire for pleasure. Affairs check both boxes.

## PAIN AVOIDANCE

One of the primary drivers of human behavior is the avoidance of pain. Individuals engage in all sorts of activities, including spending more time at work and relying upon mood-altering substances to avoid *feeling* pain. This is especially true within intimate partnerships. Over time, couples can go to great lengths to avoid discussing topics that can lead to disapproval, disappointment, disconnection, or rejection.

Difficult conversations with a partner may be avoided in the hopes that problems will simply remedy themselves if you just wait long enough.

As you will hear me say repeatedly:

## You can't heal what you don't talk about.

You may be able to set it aside for a time, but eventually those pesky little inner thoughts will intrude upon your world, no matter what you do. Avoidance can provoke passive-aggressive behavior or detonate a bomb that leaves much shrapnel in its wake. Sometimes both. Regardless of how these inner musings show up, they have the potential to wreak havoc within your relationships.

## PLEASURE SEEKING

The second driver of human behavior is the desire to experience pleasure. Receiving attention from someone new floods our neural networks with endorphins. This surging chemical overload can hit like a bolt of lightning charging every cell in your body with a jolt of electricity. Its intoxicating effects can be extremely difficult to resist. The high of connecting with someone you are attracted to can hit the dopamine circuits hard.

These feel-good feelings can spill over into your life at home. Many people find that during the early stages of an affair, the little things that bothered them at home are not quite so bothersome.

---

## Reflection
### *Exploring Core Needs*

The following has been designed as a couples exercise when your partner is ready to explore. It also offers a powerful exploration on your own or with a professional.

These questions refer to the 3 Core Needs (the need to be known, noticed, and know you matter). If you are working on this exercise as a couple, each of you can choose one core need to focus on. Take ten minutes to jot down what resonates with you about this core need and reflect on how it has been fulfilled or unmet in your life. If you are working on this exercise alone, you can go through the questions by yourself and consider inviting your partner to explore them independently or at a later time.

1. Consider your child and teen years. What stands out for you about how this core need was met and not met?
   a. Who showed up for you, and what did this "showing up" look like in your life?
   b. Who did you want to show up for you who wasn't quite there? What did you want this person to do differently?
2. Where in your life does this core need now get fulfilled the most? The least? Work? Home? With your kids? With friends? In your relationship?
3. What are two things your partner currently does to help you feel known, noticed, or know that you matter?
4. Moving forward, what are some things you can do that could contribute to greater satisfaction in this area?

**Designate one person as the explorer, the other as the listener.**

**When you are the explorer**, use your answers to these questions to further explore and share your experiences and thoughts with your partner. You are not limited to sharing what you wrote. If more ideas surface while sharing, feel free to offer them. If some of your unmet needs involve your partner, take care to share without blame. This is about sharing your feelings, and brainstorming ideas for ways to better meet these needs moving forward, not assigning blame.

**When you are the listener**, it is your job to listen without interruption. Remember, this is about your partner, not you. You don't need to defend any actions or inactions on your part. Just listen and nod your head—indicating you care, empathize with, and understand. Write down any questions or ideas you may have as your partner is talking.

**When your partner is finished**, you can ask clarifying questions to better understand what they have shared. You can invite your partner to share more about a particular topic you would like to understand better. *"Would you be willing to share a little more about _____?"*

After your partner feels complete, you can offer ideas or inquire into ways you can help enhance their experience. *I have a couple of ideas I think could be helpful. Would you like to hear them.* Or, *How can I help you feel more fully known, noticed, or know that I value you—that you matter to me?*

Make note of key ideas and ways you can help your partner better feel Known, Noticed and Know they matter. Then switch roles.

Like the little guy in the story, each of us can periodically feel like there is a piece missing, and if we can just find it, life will be better. If is important to take note when you are feeling particularly vulnerable and not *whole*. These are the times when placing a greater emphasis on self-care, and partner communication, are particularly important.

The more thoroughly you work through this process, even the most painful parts, the greater the possibility of rebuilding trust and creating a solid relational foundation to build from.

Next, we take a look at how family-of-origin experiences shape adult decisions, particularly when it comes to affair engagement. We will explore ways in which what you witnessed growing up affects your adult choices.

# 8

## Influences *of* Your Family *of* Origin *on* Who *and* How You Love

■

*"Whether we realize it or not, it is our woundedness,*
*or how we cope with it, that dictates much of our behavior,*
*shapes our social habits, and informs our ways of thinking*
*about the world. ... For many of us, it rears its head in our*
*closest partnerships, causing all kinds of relational mischief."*
—Gabor Maté, M.D. with Daniel Maté, *The Myth of Normal:*
*Trauma, Illness & Healing in a Toxic Culture.*

Your childhood experiences deeply affect how you navigate adult relationships. This is important to understand as you are recovering from an affair, since your family of origin offers your first taste of love, which is the foundation of your personal relational blueprint. How you were and were not loved and cared for influences how you express love, who you are drawn to, and shapes your expectations in relationships. Gaining a greater understanding of these early connections helps set the stage for healing and rebuilding your relationship.

Family interactions, culture, and beliefs, as well as exposure to religious institutions, coaches, teachers and interactions with friends and their family members each play a role in the formation of your values and beliefs about the world and yourself. In addition, exposure to parental depression, anxiety, addictions, and trauma influences how you interpret, react, and connect with others. In essence, your values, beliefs, interpretations, and the ways in which your nervous system responds are shaped by what you are exposed to as you grow.

During this chapter there will be three reflection exercises designed to help you more deeply explore attitudes, beliefs, and patterns formed during the course of your childhood and adolescence and the impact they have had upon your current relationship. The more insight you gain about yourself and your response patterns, the greater your ability to understand past choices, make more mindful future choices, and create a healthier connection between you and your partner (or any future relationship.) During the next chapter, we will explore affair stages and then move on to the affair recovery process.

## The Impact of the Past Upon the Present

**"Until you make the unconscious conscious, it will direct your life and you will call it fate."**

—Carl Jung, *Man and His Symbols*

As we have discussed, an important part of affair recovery is to bring more conscious awareness to underlying patterns that when not addressed, can lead to impulsive or automatic reactions rather than thoughtful responses. Uncovering the roots of these patterns can be challenging as they tend to run beneath the surface of conscious awareness. Left unchecked, however, these patterns can hamper a couple's ability to effectively address challenges and create positive change.

## Reflection I
### *Exploring Family Dynamics*

**"Our relationships with one another are not a luxury but an essential nutrient for our survival."**

—Dr. Daniel Siegel

This initial round of questions offers you the opportunity to take an in-depth look at the structure, dynamics, and influence of your family. These may be areas you have previously thought about, or they may be totally new. Take your time to explore the questions and jot down your thoughts based upon what you experienced and witnessed at home.

**Beneath each topic are discovery questions** designed to help you explore the impact what you witnessed growing up had on your childhood and the views you formed about yourself, as well as the influence your upbringing had upon your adult choices and relationship/ family.

This is a great exercise to work through with your spouse as it can give you both insight into each other's family dynamic and ways in which it has impacted your lives, response patterns, and beliefs.

**Family History and Legacy:** What were the stories you heard from your parents and grandparents? What were their struggles and triumphs? Did they immigrate? How were they educated? Did career successes and/or failures play a role in your family legacy?

> **Impact on Childhood:** How did these stories shape your childhood and your perception of your family and yourself? Did they motivate or demotivate you?

> **Influence on Adult Life:** How have your family stories impacted your choices in adulthood, such as education, career, and relationship choices?

**Family Structure:** Did you grow up in a traditional or less traditional family? How was your family viewed by your friends? Was yours the place where people congregated, or did you avoid having friends over?

> **Impact on your childhood:** What type of impact did your family structure have on you growing up? Did you enjoy being at home or did you tend to avoid

going home? Did you spend more time at other people's houses? How did you interact with parents/siblings? Were you embarrassed by your family? Proud of your family?

**Influence on your adult life:** How do you feel your upbringing impacted your views on marriage, family, and fidelity and how you parent (or will parent if appliable)?

**Parental Roles and Childcare:** How were your parents' roles defined in terms of childcare? Were both parents involved, or was one more dominant in caregiving? Were you raised by a solo caregiver, and if so, who else helped out, such as grandparents or other family members?

**Impact on Childhood:** How did your parents' relationship impact how you viewed yourself and formed relationships as a teen/young adult? Did you see them as loving, arguing, or belonging together? Was one parent more dominant than the other? Were you afraid of either parent? How did these interactions influence your self-perception?

**Influence on Adult Life:** How do you believe your parents' relationship influenced your relational choices? How has your upbringing shaped your approach to parenting now or in the future?

**Changes in Family Dynamics:** What types of changes did your family experience in your home environment? Separation? Divorce? Significant moves?

**Impact on Childhood:** How did these changes affect your childhood and views of yourself? What role did you assume as a result? (Sometimes a parent can become overly reliant upon a child for support. Sometimes children can take on a caregiver role for other siblings, act out in school, or become even more determined to succeed.)

**Influence on Adult Life:** How have your family dynamics influenced your beliefs about marriage, relationships, fidelity, and divorce? What impact has your upbringing had on your relationships and family dynamics?

**Religion/Spirituality:** What religious or spiritual beliefs did your parents have, and how did they help shape your worldview as a child?

**Impact on your childhood:** What were the positive or negative effects of the way religion/spirituality was handled in your household? Were you required to attend religious services? What type of impact did the beliefs and practices of your parents influence you? Your beliefs?

**Influence on your adult life:** Which of these views have you embraced? Rebelled against? Carried into your own marriage? Where do you and your spouse agree? Where do you differ? How has your faith, or lack thereof influenced your life, recovery, and what you believe now?

**World Views:** What were your parents' views on the world, country, and culture?

**Impact on your childhood**: How did their beliefs impact you as a child?

**Influence on your adult life:** How have their views influenced your perspectives as an adult? How well do your views align with those of your spouse? Are you able to discuss and work through differences?

Next, we discuss human psychosocial development and ways in which experiences during specific time frames optimizes or stifles emotional and psychological growth.

# Psychosocial Development

Professionals in the fields of medicine, psychology, and education have developed models designed to help us better understand the inner workings of human development and how we relate to others. One of my favorite theorists for age stage development is social psychologist Erik Erikson. His work on social and psychological development examines the ways in which relationships and social interaction contribute to human development and growth.

Erikson has outlined eight stages of human development. Positive experiences and interactions in each of these stages support growth, self-esteem, and confidence, fostering specific competencies in preparation for the next stage. Conversely, traumatic experiences and inconsistencies can hinder development. Delving into each stage in detail is beyond the scope of this work. However, there is one stage that I thought would be worth visiting as it is a crucial stage in the development of personal identity and relational growth: adolescence.

(If you would like to explore each of these developmental stages and competencies more fully, you can refer to an article written by Kendra Cherry in *Very Well Mind.*[8])

# The Impact of Adolescence

**"Adolescence is a period marked by unique brain remodeling processes known as pruning and myelinization, which create an ESSENCE that is the basis for well-being both during this important period of growth and change, as well as throughout the lifespan."**

—Dr. Daniel Siegel

**"Adolescents need freedom to choose, but not so much freedom that they cannot make a choice."**

—Erik Erikson

Adolescence is a critical period characterized by significant individual and relational growth, as well as notable neurochemical changes and brain development. This stage, second only to the first year of an infant's life, plays a crucial role in shaping personal identity and self-acceptance. It involves navigating the delicate balance between the desire to fit in and the need to stay true to oneself. Peer relationships hold considerable sway over behavior, risk-taking tendencies, and the formation of identity during this time.

To explore adolescence, we will be relying upon the work of Erikson, and another expert in the field of human development, neurobiologist and psychiatrist Dr. Daniel Siegel, as presented in his book *Brainstorm: The Power and Purpose of the Teenage Brain*. While unresolved trauma can stem from experiences in any stage of development, adolescence often emerges as a significant subject of discussion during my client sessions.

Erikson identifies the primary conflict of adolescence as "Identity vs. Role Confusion." Successful navigation of this stage leads to the development of "fidelity," which Erikson defines as "establishing an ideological commitment to one's beliefs and values."[9] While Erikson suggests that adolescence spans from twelve to eighteen years old, Siegel extends the upper age limit to twenty-four. This extension overlaps with Erikson's life stage "Intimacy vs. Isolation," which focuses on cultivating and maintaining intimate, loving connections.

According to Siegel, adolescence is a period characterized by immense growth, creativity, passion, and moodiness. It is the most intense growth a human being experiences outside of the first year of life. Adolescence is characterized by a marked shift in focus from parental influence to peer acceptance. Increased levels of dopamine and other hormones also occur during this stages which can lead to heightened courage for exploration which can contribute to greater risk-taking behaviors.

A parent's role is to balance their adolescent's need for greater independence while still demonstrating interest, nurturing, and care. Keeping the lines of communication open during a time of an increased need for independence can be trying for a parent. Teens need parental attention, love, boundaries, respect, and encouragement. Having strong, caring adults who model respect and integrity is particularly important during adolescence.

When a teen experiences or is exposed to trauma, bullying, excessive criticism, intense parental disagreements, a contentious divorce, a lack of acknowledgment/interest in their life, parental infidelity, or excessive alcohol or drug use, it can negatively impact the formation of their identity, causing them to question themselves. The ability to stay true to their values, what they believe is the right thing to do (fidelity), while exploring the world in new ways can be tricky. A teen is cultivating self-trust, self-acceptance, the ability problem-solve, and is relying upon strong, loyal friendships and caring relationships to help them navigate this adventurous and often tumultuous time.

An adolescent develops confidence and/or insecurity in navigating love interests as they balance strong chemical attraction and desires with the needs, desires, and insecurities of another. They are beginning the journey of discovering themselves through the eyes of crushes and love interests working through puberty, and curiosities about sexuality, body parts, and attraction.

If you are currently parenting adolescents / young adults, this is also a great section to review. Parenting children through their life stages often activates our own experiences during these stages. I invite you to pay attention to what you experience as you move through your children's life stages.

**Relational struggles arising from this stage** can show up as difficulty being truthful, or telling the full truth; insecurity, which may be masked as sarcasm, bravado, or excessive judgment of others; indecisiveness and/or a lack of trust in himself or others; and self-doubt or difficulty sustaining healthy relationships. Confusion regarding one's role/identity arises more frequently from difficulties arising during this life stage.

**Successful resolution of the adolescent stage** leads to a stronger ability to stay true to oneself and make self-supportive choices, even in the face of pressure to do otherwise. Strength in one's ability to empathize, care for, and be loyal to a love interest, and an openness to trust in love are attributes that are seeded during this time as well.

While the internal framework we form for how relationships and love work is influenced by all life stages, adolescence is a particularly pivotal time of individual identity formation and relational development.

---

**Adolescent experiences are strongly tied into how we form and maintain relationships as adults.**

---

## Reflection II
### *Exploring Adolescence*

There are three pivotal developmental stages during adolescence: middle school, high school, and early college (or entrance into tech school, the work world, or the military). This exercise offers you the opportunity to reflect upon your own adolescent experiences—between the ages of twelve and twenty-four—and reflect upon experiences that helped shape your development.

### MIDDLE SCHOOL • HIGH SCHOOL • EARLY ADULTHOOD
#### (life after high school)

**Parental relationships:** How would you describe your relationship with your parents? Whose attention did you have to work the hardest to get? Were each of your parents involved, too involved, distant, or absent? How did each of them participate in your upbringing?

- Who attended sports and school functions?
- Who handled discipline? Did you ever feel afraid?
- What did you long for from each parent that you never received or wanted more of?
- How did you work to get each parent's affection or attention?
- Who was more nurturing? Who could you turn to in a crisis?

**Peer relationships:** How did your closest friends influence your decisions? Did you face challenges or experience bullying?

**Influential people:** Often coaches, teachers, and others serve as powerful role models, influencing our lives in a variety of ways. Who were the key individuals/role models in your life? How did they help shape your decision-making? How did they influence your self-esteem / self-confidence?

**School experiences:** How did you perform academically? What type of involvement did your parents have in your education?

**Traumatic experiences:** What were the most challenging experiences during each age range? Did you face divorce, arguments, or emotional, physical, or sexual abuse? Were you bullied? Did you bully others?

**Freedom and management:** How much freedom did you have? How did you handle it? What did you keep hidden from your parents? What did you lie about?

**Sense of self:** How did you perceive yourself? Were you confident, shy, or somewhere in-between? When did you feel most/least confident? The most powerful/powerless? How did you manage aggression? Bonus: If you had to choose a character or movie that represents your life during this time, who/what would it be?

**Accomplishments and recognition:** What are you proud of achieving? Did you receive validation or recognition for it?

**Love interests:** Who stands out among your love interests? How did your significant relationships develop emotionally and physically? How did they end?

**Sexuality:** What type of physical interactions did you engage in during these age ranges? What was your first sexual experience like? How did these early physical experiences impact later interactions and your view of yourself and potential love interests?

**Pivotal experiences:** What is a standout memory from each age stage? What did each of these experiences signify to you? How did they shape your perception of yourself and others?

**Summary:** Take some time to summarize what you discovered about yourself and your key relational experiences. How do you see these interactions shaping the way you view yourself? Your relationships? Your career pursuits? Your views on life? Your views on male/female relationships and roles? What correlations can you draw from these experiences upon your current relationship and choices?

This too can be a great exploration project to engage in with your partner. As always, my suggestion is that you each work through the questions on your own first then set up a time to explore together. It is important not to pressure one another to share about areas they feel hesitant to discuss. Treat each other with interest, curiosity, and respect.

**Remember:** This is a time of personal and relational exploration and healing. It isn't a race. It is okay to work through things slowly, or at whatever pace works for you both.

Let's look at a story that highlights the impact of adolescent experiences in shaping adult behavior.

# The Intersection of Opportunity and Parental Infidelity: Frank's Story

Frank's dad was a successful corporate executive whose income created a nice life-style for the family and gave Frank's mom the option of being a stay-at-home mom. From the outside, they looked like a typical middle to upper middle-class family. Some even saw them as the perfect family—successful and happy.

Yet on the inside, everything was far from fine. Frank's dad had been engaging in an affair with his assistant since Frank's teen years. The entire family knew about the affair, yet pretended like things were normal. Frank's dad's behavior was disturbing to everyone in the household and helped set the stage for how Frank internalized relationships.

When Frank's mom first suspected the affair, she confronted his dad, who denied it but did not alter his behavior. He continued to spend late nights at work, and sometimes spent weekends away even after being confronted. Ultimately his mom decided that she didn't want to risk upsetting the family with a divorce, so she just quit asking about it.

On one occasion, Frank saw his dad sitting in the car outside their house talking to a "woman from work" who dropped him off at home because his car was in the shop.

When Frank's dad came in for dinner, the only thing mom said was, "I can't believe you let *her* drop you off at the house." Frank's dad ignored her and asked Frank about his day. Frank was fifteen at the time, which places him in Erikson's developmental stage of "Identity vs. Role Confusion."

This was a confusing time for Frank, who realized that Mom wasn't as okay as she pretended to be. He heard her crying in her room at night on several occasions when his dad came home late from "a work event." He tried his best to pick up the slack left by his dad's absence by becoming a dutiful son who tried his best not to rock the boat. On a personal level, Frank channeled his energy into sports and running.

Frank's mom coped with things by trying even harder to be a *good wife* and mother. She began doing everything for everyone. Frank said, *"I think she thought if she prioritized being the perfect wife and mother, ultimately my dad would end the affair. He never did. He was with this woman until the day he died of a heart attack in our driveway."*

**Frank learned there was an unwritten family rule that you don't talk about things that could cause upset. He learned the best way to deal with potential conflict is to ignore it and pretend like things are okay.**

Even though Frank knew in his heart that dad's actions were wrong, the unconscious message Frank received was that it is okay (or even acceptable) for a married man to have a relationship with another woman as long as no one talks about it.

As an adult, Frank became a successful corporate executive, just like dad. But Frank stepped into dad's shoes in more ways than just his career choice. Frank's rise to the top included forming a very close relationship with a woman at work, which ultimately turned into a full-blown affair.

## Frank's Affair Vulnerability Factors (AVFs)

Let's take a quick look at Frank's vulnerability factors and see how they played out.

Frank was attractive, charismatic, and friendly. People enjoyed working and socializing with him. Six months before the affair began, Frank was promoted into his second high-profile corporate position. One of his direct reports was a newly promoted woman who managed one of his key departments. She was organized, efficient, attractive, and excited about her recent promotion. Frank became Gracie's mentor, and she began to soar under his leadership. There was an attraction from the beginning—they both could feel it—but Frank chalked it up to work chemistry.

One evening at the conclusion of a successful regional meeting held at a prestigious hotel, Gracie made her first presentation to Frank's entire division. The meeting and her presentation were a smashing success. A group of Frank's managers went out to celebrate. The energy was high. Frank and Gracie were the event's star performers.

One by one, the rest of the team retired to their hotel rooms, leaving Frank and Gracie alone at the bar having one last drink together. When they stood up to leave, Gracie leaned in and hugged Frank, and he kissed her. That was the day they both acknowledged the spark growing between them and acted on it.

Gracie looked up to Frank as a mentor who ignited her confidence. She felt seen by him, and that helped her see herself. Frank felt a great sense of pride and importance helping Gracie and seeing her blossom. He felt like her hero; that he made a difference in her life. He felt needed. And with this new turn of events, he felt wanted and desired as well.

## FRANK'S RECKONING

Frank stared blankly at the rug beneath his feet in my office as he described his anguish.

*"I swore I would never be like my dad. Never. I remember my mom crying at night when Dad said he was going to be working late again. We all knew where he really was. And now, here I am, doing the exact same thing to my wife, Susan—making up lies to cover up what is really happening, and just pretending like things are okay. I love my wife; I do. I mean we've had our ups and downs, but I never wanted to hurt her. I'm so fucking ashamed.*

*"When Susan confronted me about the affair, at first I denied it...told her she must be imagining things...I would never cheat on her. The next day while sitting at my desk, I flashed back to that day when I saw my dad sitting in the car with his secretary. I remembered how he ignored my mom when he came inside and how we all pretended things were okay. Then I flashed to my mom crying. What an asshole I thought he was. I wished I had called him out. I tried so hard to be there for my mom, to make up for the pain my dad caused. I swore I would never end up like my dad, hurting the people he loved and living in a sea of deceit and lies until the day he died, and yet, there I was doing the same damn thing. That was the moment I knew I had to tell Susan the truth."*

**Commentary:** As Frank stopped to reflect on the circumstances that led to his affair, he admitted that he hadn't been putting much energy into Susan or the kids for a while. He had grown accustomed to Susan taking care of things at home. Life was comfortable, almost on autopilot. Family activities centered mostly around the kids, and Frank and Susan hadn't been engaging much outside of sports games and neighborhood gatherings. Frank felt a great sense of aliveness at work where he felt like he could have a powerful impact. He didn't feel as impactful at home but did not talk to Susan about his feelings. Instead, he put his home life on the backburner while he plugged into work.

Frank's dad's affair during his formative teen years also had an impact. Even though Frank swore he would never be like him, his dad's infidelity and his parents' "normalizing" it, had left an imprint. Remember, this life stage is about identity formation. One of the ways our identity is formed is through the role modeling of significant adults around us. Frank's parents' conflict resolution style was silence. He didn't learn successful skills from observing his parents. Basically, he learned Dad (men) had the power to do what he wanted. Mom (women) were charged with making things run well at home. Unconscious patterns run deep and tend to fly under the radar. Frank had unknowingly replicated what was modeled to him growing up.

Combine that modeling with the opportunity at work, and the sense of aliveness and value Frank felt in mentoring Gracie, and you have the foundation for Frank's affair.

Remember those three core needs, the need to be known, noticed, and know you matter? Frank's career and connection with Gracie hit at least two and possibly all three. He definitely felt noticed and knew that he mattered. Gracie also knew that part of him that he took such pride in—his ability to lead and mentor others. So, in that regard, he felt known as well.

## DECISION TIME

Frank continued: "*I decided to go home early and own up to what happened. I stopped at that Thai place Susan loves and brought home dinner. She seemed a little suspicious that I was home earlier than usual, yet she gave me a big hug when I walked in. She smiled and genuinely looked happy to see me. I love when Susan smiles!*

"*In that moment, I looked at the woman I had fallen in love with years ago. Truth is, I still do love her. I realized I had let my excitement and passion at work kind of take over my life and I quit paying attention to her. Well, I guess we kind of quit paying as much attention to each other. I hadn't felt as important in her life the past couple of years, but I hadn't done a damn thing to try and change that."* Frank sighed.

*"I could tell Susan knew something was up. We both did. Yet we sat down to eat and just acted like everything was okay. In some ways that felt more comfortable. I flashed to that scene at the dinner table with Mom and Dad pretending like things were just fine.*

*"Susan opened a nice bottle of wine, and we sat there for about an hour eating, talking, and laughing together. Part of me just wanted to end the evening there. I wanted to tell her, but I didn't want to spoil the moment. Then she asked, 'I haven't laughed like that in a long time. You have been spending so much time at work lately and things have been feeling distant with us. Are you sure there isn't something else going on?'*

*"For a moment I waffled. Did I really need to tell her? In that moment, part of me understood why Mom and Dad didn't really talk about his affair. Maybe it was easier to just deny what was happening outside the family and pretend like everything was okay. I mean when I was a kid, life at home wasn't bad. They made it work for the most part. And if I told her, would it break up the family? Could she ever forgive me? If I were to end things at work, would I really need to tell her?*

*"And yet there it was, staring me in the face. My opening. I could just be like Dad and continue denying things, or I could tell her the truth. Even though I was scared to tell her, I was tired of lying and pretending. So I swallowed hard and began, 'I really need to talk to you about something that's not easy to talk about, but I owe it to you to tell you the truth...'"*

Frank proceeded to tell Susan about his affair. He apologized for not being up front the first time she asked. Even though she strongly suspected Frank was having an affair, it was difficult for Susan to hear Frank confirm her suspicions. He tried his best to comfort her through her tears.

Frank apologized repeatedly for lying and betraying her. He asked Susan if she thought she could ever forgive him. She said she wasn't sure. He told her he was committed to being a better husband and asked if she would be willing to give him a second chance. She told him they needed to get some help, as she had many feelings to sort through, and she wasn't sure what she wanted. That's when they reached out to me.

## "IF ONLYS" AND RECOVERY

Frank sat in my office shaking his head. *"What the hell was I thinking?"* Frank then looked me in the eyes and asked, *"Do you think we can ever get back to what we had?"*

Even though the circumstances surrounding your affair may differ from Frank's, perhaps you too are wondering, *What the hell was I thinking?* And questioning whether you can get back to what you had.

The answer to that question is*: No. You will never go back to what you had.* Engaging in an affair permanently changes your relationship. You can't ever go back to the way things were.

Frank continued: *"I ended things with Gracie. I apologized to her too for pushing the boundary between us that should have never been crossed.*

*"I know it may be an uphill battle, but I hope Susan can forgive me. I realize that my marriage is what's really important to me. The truth is, I took my eye off the ball. We both did. I would like another chance to see if we can make things right.*

*"Now I'm questioning whether Gracie and I can even work together. It's tough, you know. We make a really good team at work. Things just got out of hand. If only..."*

Like Frank, you may be filled with *"if onlys."* And like Frank, if you too are willing to own what happened, explore the vulnerability factors that led to your affair, and act in alignment with what you want and who you want to be, you *can* recover and rebuild your relationship and your life. You can even fortify your connection in ways that will make you stronger and less susceptible to future temptation.

**So, with all those powerful factors pulling on you, how do you move forward toward strengthening the relationship with your spouse?**

The first step is to recognize that having an affair didn't fix your problems or fill the void you may have been feeling inside, even if it seemed to at the beginning. Turning toward another person created a host of additional problems that will need to be addressed. Affair recovery work offers the opportunity to more intentionally clean up areas of your relationship that you may not have been actively addressing.

As Frank discovered in our work together, what he witnessed in the past played an integral role in the decisions he made in his marriage and, luckily, in his healing process as well.

## Reflection III
### *Connecting the Dots*

In this final exercise we will compare and contrast your parental relationships with your spousal relationship to uncover adult relational response patterns rooted in childhood experiences.

You will go through the exercise three times. The first time through you will reflect upon your family of origin; the second - your behavior toward your spouse; the third – your spouse's behavior toward you.

If you and your spouse are working through this material together, these questions can help the two of you explore your relational dynamics prior to your affair. These explorations can also be useful if you are working with a coach or therapist to help you identify and work through ineffective relational patterns that have developed over time.

These questions involve taking a look at messages you received from your family of origin— (parents, stepparents, or primary caregivers) either directly or through observation of their actions.

### YOUR FAMILY OF ORIGIN

1) How did your parents demonstrate affection toward each other? Toward you?

    a. Did you witness your parents saying, *I love you*? To each other? To you?

2) How did your parents comfort you when you were sad, anxious, or angry?

    a. How did they respond to your struggles at school, at home, or with friends?

    b. What conclusions did you draw from these experiences about life, friends, yourself?

3) What messages did you receive from each of your parents regarding your achievements in school, sports, and other endeavors?

    a. Were their responses predominantly positive? *I'm proud of you. Great job. You worked really hard on that, and it shows.*

b. Or mostly negative? *You're too sensitive. Can't you do anything right? You got a C on a test? You are so lazy. You're just like your dad/ mom.*

4) How did your parents manage money?

a. Were there differences in financial management?

b. Did they ever argue over finances or spending habits?

5) Were your parents' emotional responses predictable or unpredictable?

a. Did either of them suffer from anxiety or depression or have mood swings, meaning they were sometimes extremely sad and other times excited, agitated, or angry?

b. Were either of your parents quick to anger? What happened when they were angry? How did they manage their anger?

c. How did each parent treat you *when they* were sad, anxious, or angry? How did they treat each other?

d. How did you respond/protect yourself from the intensity of their moods (if applicable)?

6) Did either or both have challenges with alcohol or use other substances? Did personalities change when they were under the influence?

a. How did their behavior impact you?

7) How did your parents manage stress, deal with challenges, and resolve conflicts?

a. Did they distance themselves or avoid each other during stressful moments? Become angry? Sweep things under the rug?

b. Did they collaborate to create workable solutions?

For the next two rounds you will reflect upon your relational dynamic with your partner/spouse.

## YOUR BEHAVIOR TOWARD YOUR SPOUSE

Go back through the questions and replace "your parents" with yourself.

Example: **Question 1:** How do you demonstrate affection toward your spouse? **Question 5:** Are your moods predictable or unpredictable? **Question 6:** Do you or struggle with substance use issues?

### YOUR SPOUSE'S BEHAVIOR TOWARD YOU

Go through the questions again and answer based upon your spouse's behavior toward you.

Example: **Question 1:** How does your spouse demonstrate affection toward you? **Question 5:** Are your spouse's moods predictable or unpredictable? **Question 6:** Does your spouse struggle with substance use issues?

### SIMILARITIES AND DIFFERENCES

What are the similarities and differences between your parents' way of responding and the way you and your spouse interact? Are your spouse's reactions similar to either or both of your parents? What about your reactions? Are they similar to either parent?

In what ways has your family dynamic had a positive influence on your life and life choices? In what ways has your exposure growing up made life more challenging? What would you like to do differently in the future?

# Defining and Working Through Trauma

I want to take a moment to address a word that is frequently bantered about these days and that you will see referred to periodically in this text, and that is the word *trauma*. The word originates from a Greek word meaning "to wound or pierce." Its original meaning referred to an external wound, but its later definition was expanded to a "wound inflicted not upon the body but upon the mind."[10]

We typically associate trauma with some type of catastrophic occurrence like receiving or witnessing physical abuse, the impact of parental death upon a child, incest, the ravages of war, and other devastating experiences. These are often referred to as *big-T traumas*. This type of trauma can either occur as one big event, or an accumulation of multiple incidents over time. Dr. Gabor Maté is an M.D. and author who works with and has written multiple books on addiction and trauma. He tells us that *"...capital-T trauma occurs when things happen to vulnerable people that should not have happened."* These types of occurrences underlie many mental and physical illnesses and impair healthy development.

There are also *small-t traumas* that each of us experience to varying degrees throughout our lives. Maté writes, *"Children, especially highly sensitive children, can be wounded in multiple ways; by bad things happening, yes, but also by good things not happening, such as their emotional needs for attunement not being met, or the experience of not being seen and accepted, even by loving parents."* He goes on to state, *"Trauma isn't what happens to us. It is the internal wound suffered as a result of what happened."*

Traumas of any kind, large or small, inflict wounds and result in the development of coping mechanisms designed to help a person adapt and protect themselves from future occurrences. *Small-t* trauma coping mechanisms are typically aimed at maintaining connection with caregivers and other important people. Experiences of *Big-T* and recurring trauma results in the development of more robust defense-mechanisms designed to keep individuals, and sometimes other family members, safe. These traumas tend to have more devastating effects on an individual's ability to trust, form a positive self-concept, and create and sustain healthy relationships.

Trauma wounds are activated in response to any stimulus that even remotely resembles the original woundings. These activations frequently occur without any recollection of the original infliction. We often refer to this as being "triggered." Triggering experiences tap into prior woundings. This is important to know as you are working on healing, helping your partner heal, and establishing a stronger connection. Exploring childhood experiences and woundings can help you identify where your own traumas, big or small, occurred which can offer greater insight into relational response patterns which have carried over into your adult relationships.

Betrayal is a traumatizing experience which stacks on top of earlier traumatic occurrences within the current and prior relationships, as well as childhood and adolescent interactions. We discuss ways to help your partner work through the trauma of betrayal in Part Six.

The people we are closest to have the greatest power to both fill our needs for love and affection and trigger deep seated trauma. Over time a couple too develops its own defense mechanisms and coping strategies which can include becoming overly attached to filling a partner's needs in order to maintain connection, and/or turning away from a partner when their need for attention feels overwhelming or controlling. These patterns can become automatic defensive reactions which hampers a couple's ability to effectively navigate and discuss challenges, particularly those they believe may upset their connection. Affair recovery creates an opening to explore and shift old patterns that may have been contributing to more frequent misunderstandings and the inability to work through differences. We explore the process of implementing change in Part Eight.

**Summary:** The formation of human relationships is intricate and complex. We are each shaped by the cumulative experiences of our lives. Our expectations, aspirations, vulnerabilities, and dreams are deeply rooted in the ways we've been treated and the manner in which we've assimilated our past encounters – whether disheartening or enlivening. These experiences influence the assumptions and judgments we hold about the world, our partners, and ourselves.

In the next section we will be taking a look at how affairs begin, develop, and the most effective ways to end them.

**"I realized that my perspective of life was being determined by beliefs that I had been taught as a child even though they were not what I believed as an adult. ... I felt like I was a victim of life ... that I was blaming others for not making me happy."**

—Robert Burney, *Codependence, The Dance of Wounded Souls*

---

## An unexamined past is destined to repeat itself.

---

# PART FOUR

---------------------------■---------------------------

# The Anatomy *of an* Affair:
## *How Affairs Begin, Evolve,*
## *and the Best Way to End Them*

Understanding how affairs work can help demystify them. In this section we explore how affairs begin, take shape, and the most effective way to end them.

The material walks you through the three distinct phases of an affair. It offers insight into various forms of infidelity and some pre-affair warning signs you may have ignored, which can help ensure you don't slide back into future affair behavior.

We will dive into:

**Phase I – In the Beginning:** Details of the powerful pull of a new affair and the various forms an affair can take.

**Phase II – Stuck in the Middle with You:** Exploring what is typically the longest stage of an affair and the one with the most ambivalence, including the addictive properties of an affair.

**Phase III – Closing the Door:** How to end your affair clearly and decisively.
In the sections that follow, we will more fully explore relational recovery.

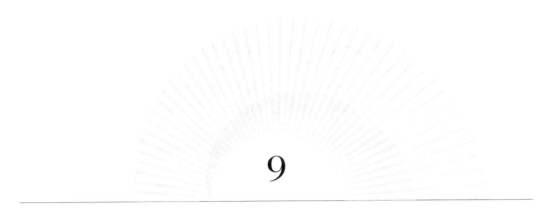

# 9

# Affairs Phase One:
## *In the Beginning*

---■---

*"You are enough to drive a saint to madness or a king to his knees."*
—Grace Willows, *To Kiss a King*

*"I feel the need to endanger myself every so often."*
—Tim Daly, actor

Like the beginning of any new endeavor, affair beginnings are filled with anticipation, uncertainty, and excitement, all of which can bleed over into your primary relationship. It is the shortest and most enlivening phase.

The excitement and anticipation of connecting with someone new can spark a renewed sense of aliveness, resulting in an increased release of those feel-good chemicals like dopamine, oxytocin, and serotonin. This chemical surge can promote greater life satisfaction and the appearance of greater contentment at home. You may find that things that were *troubling you* take on less significance. An affair's beginning sometimes fuels more passionate interactions at home.

Engaging with an affair partner doesn't just impact the AP. It impacts your primary partner as well, even if she isn't consciously aware it is happening. An energy flows within and between relational partners. The activities, thoughts, and feelings of one partner impact the dynamic of the relationship within each person and between them. We will discuss this in more depth in *The Neurobiology of Change* chapter.

So, what constitutes affair behavior? Even if you have already engaged in an affair, it can be helpful to assess when and how it started. Let's take a look.

# Defining Infidelity

In the past, sexual intercourse was frequently thought of as the sole defining criterion for labeling an extramarital connection as infidelity. With the proliferation of technology, there are many more entry points into affair behavior than in years past. So, what exactly is infidelity? Let's break it down by looking at the root of the word *infidelity*: **fidelity.**

**Fidelity** is defined in *Merriam Webster's Collegiate Dictionary* as: "Faithfulness to a person, cause or belief, demonstrated by continued **loyalty** and **support**."
**Loyalty:** "Giving or showing firm and continued **support** or allegiance to a person or institution."

**Support:** "To bear all or part of the weight of."

The prefix *in-* means "not." So, distilling this down, **relational infidelity means not being loyal to the commitment made to a partner or helping to *bear the weight of* things that can disrupt the connection**.

Each of us wants to be able to trust that our partner has our best interests at heart. We want to know that they will help *bear the weight* of the relationship when things get heavy. One of the most important aspects of the Affair Recovery Process is rebuilding trust, which is about being loyal to your commitments and mindful of to whom you give your word.

## A BRIEF NOTE ON ETHICAL NONMONOGAMY

"Ethical nonmonogamy (often abbreviated to ENM) is an umbrella term used to describe relationships that aren't 100 percent exclusive."[18] There are a wide range of connections that can fall into this category, from an occasional connection with someone outside the relationship to a couple's active engagement in polyamory. While it is outside the scope of this work to include an in-depth discussion on nonmonogamy, I would be remiss not to include mentioning it in the context of infidelity recovery, as it has become a more frequent discussion topic in recent years.

While the makeup of a nonmonogamous relationship differs from a monogamous one, the essential parameters of fidelity still apply.

The key for each couple is engaging in clear, honest, authentic discussions to gain consensus on what types of interactions work and don't work for each person. It is critical to keep the lines of communication open. Whenever something new arises, like the need for exploring something that lies outside your original agreement, it is important to discuss it with your partner and create new agreements as needed.

**Engaging in behavior that you are hiding from your partner, which goes against what you have committed to as a couple, violates your commitment to fidelity. Deception is the hallmark of infidelity and the area that poses the biggest challenge to recovery.**

## Reflection
### *Fidelity*

- What constitutes fidelity in your primary partnership?
- What actions or types of engagement violate fidelity?
- Do you and your partner agree on what fidelity looks like and the behaviors that constitute infidelity?
- Where do you think you first began *crossing the line*? (What did you choose to ignore or not pay attention to that may have set the stage for your indiscretions?) What are three things you can do to help fortify you against a reoccurrence?

## Can Men and Women Be *Just Friends*?

Friendships between men and women can be tricky, particularly when there is an attraction felt by one or both parties.

Just because someone is married or in a committed relationship doesn't mean they will never be attracted to someone else. We can fool ourselves into believing that the attention being given to, or received from, someone outside of a primary relationship isn't in danger of sliding into an affair. However, spending a great deal of quality time with someone you feel attracted to builds connection. This is how human beings are wired. The challenge lies in how the connection is managed.

It's important to pay attention to the thoughts you have about this relationship and how this person makes you feel to help ward off sending signals that help set the stage for more.

We can conjure up all sorts of reasons to internally minimize a connection we feel with someone:

*She is just interested in what I have to say.*

*She just really needs my help with* _____ (insert problem here).

*She laughs at my jokes.* Or simply, *I feel good around her.*

Initial sparks can be intoxicating. Sometimes we can misinterpret those sparks to mean there is something wrong in our primary partnership. That is not necessarily the case. It's important—particularly if you are feeling a strong chemistry with an individual, especially one with whom you frequently interact—to keep in mind your commitments, the state of your primary relationship, and your AVFs.

Without the pressures of day-to-day life, other connections may, at first, seem much easier to maintain. This is because when we first meet someone, we typically step forward as our best or most dynamic self (as they most likely are too!).

I am not suggesting that male/female friendships are impossible to maintain. Establishing friendships across gender lines can offer different perspectives on relationships, problem-solving, and life in general. Good friends contribute to our emotional and psychological health and well-being. It is simply important to be aware of the type of signals you may be sending and receiving from another human being you connect with.

Your inner commitment to fidelity and to the agreements made with your primary partner must be strong enough to override any temptation to engage in behavior that compromises your connection. This is why self-awareness is so important. Being in touch with your life conditions, needs, and feelings are critical elements to making mindful choices. When you feel more vulnerable, and your agreements are not as solid, you are more at risk of engaging in behavior that opens the door to the affection and acknowledgment offered by another.

# Types of Infidelity

Let's look at some of the conditions, feelings, and behaviors that can lead to infidelity, as well as the various types of affairs.

The segment has been designed to: 1) offer you a window into the conditions that contributed to your specific affair; 2) provide anyone reading this with a greater understanding of types of affairs and their properties; 3) increase your awareness of affair warning signs to help prevent a future occurrence.

**As you review this material, consider the beginnings of your own affair. Which of these apply to your situation?** Are there any points which may have led to your affair that you find surprising or unexpected? You may also refer to this material whenever you begin to feel a spark of attraction to help fortify yourself against possible future engagements.

# Physical Affairs

Touch is a basic human need. It stimulates a neurochemical release of oxytocin, which is often known as the *cuddle hormone*. Neurochemical reactions increase the desire for bonding. Hormones released during sexual connection can contribute to growing what may have started as *just sex* into a stronger emotional bond.

Touching, kissing, cuddling, giving shoulder or back rubs, slowly rubbing the arm of a person of interest standing next to you, spending the night in the same hotel room at a convention, being in the same bed, being naked or partially naked together, or engaging in *any* type of sexual interaction or sexually suggestive behavior that violates your agreement with your primary partner constitutes physical affair behavior.

**RED FLAG: If you find yourself frequently touching, being touched by, or desiring touch from someone you feel attracted to, you may be heading into a physical affair.**

## Reflection

- Do you find yourself touching or being touched by a particular person, more than others you encounter in similar situations (like in a work setting, at the gym, etc.)?

- Have you engaged in any physical connection, like touching her back as she walks out the door? Or perhaps a quick kiss goodnight after a happy hour event?

- Are you finding yourself hugging her goodbye a bit too long and feeling the connection lasting well past the hugging?

- Are you finding yourself replaying the interactions with her in your head?

- Are you fantasizing about physical connection?

- Do you notice a difference in your level of attraction or ability to hold firm to your boundaries while drinking?

## Emotional Affairs

An emotional affair is at play when you cultivate a deep connection with someone, sharing intimate parts of your life in ways that distance you from your primary partner. When another person becomes your *go-to* for emotional support, it can build a bond of intimacy that can interfere with the connection you have built with your primary partner.

Working through a difficult challenge or intense project at work can provide opportunities for deepening conversations and cultivating a friendship outside of work. There is increased vulnerability to the attention of another when unaddressed issues at home have created distance in your primary relationship.

If you find yourself more frequently turning to this other person when something exciting or challenging occurs and/or sharing more intimate details about your life, even perhaps challenges in your marriage, instead of your spouse, these are signs that the friendship may be drifting past the friend zone.

**RED FLAG: If you find yourself hiding your interactions, or the frequency of your interactions, with another person from your partner, or if you find yourself lighting up at the possibility of seeing this person—setting up scenarios to meet**

with them, or designing projects to work on together—consider taking a deeper look at the state of your primary relationship and what this relationship, or your fantasy of it, may be fulfilling for you.

## Reflection

Following are some questions that may be helpful to review if/when you feel a spark of attraction to someone outside your primary partnership. Is your attraction to her, or the chemistry between you, growing?

- Do you think about this person when you are not with her?
- When something important or challenging happens in your world, is she the first person you think about sharing it with?
- Are you finding the banter between the two of you beginning to contain sexual innuendos?
- Are you going out of your way to spend more time with her?
- Are you finding yourself more inclined to keep your rendezvous secret from your partner? From coworkers?
- Do you text her from home?
- Do you feel a deep sense of caring for her?

If you find yourself answering in the affirmative to many of the questions above, take a step back and consider what you are/have been receiving from this relationship, or what you may be avoiding discussing or addressing at home.

**Emotional stirrings triggered through new relational connections can offer a window into desires we put on the back burner to deal with the day-to-day life.**

## Online Affairs

The digital world offers many ways to connect. There are even websites for married people to connect and pursue *extracurricular activities* with willing participants. It can feel safe to engage with someone online, but I caution you these connections can become another way to distract yourself from facing whatever may be brewing internally or at home.

It can be quite embarrassing to get caught engaging in suggestive dialogue with someone online. I have seen men fall victim to online scams that end up threatening their primary relationship. What can begin as a titillating conversation can end up in extortion. The online partner may be using a false identity to obtain credit card information and other identifying factors. I have seen people get fooled into connecting with someone only to have them ultimately turn the tables and threaten exposure (to a spouse and others) if the person doesn't comply with their financial demands. I know it sounds far-fetched, but I have seen it happen more than once.

**RED FLAG: If you find yourself engaging in behavior that is difficult for you to stop, or stop thinking about, there is a good chance you are in the grip of an addiction.** Connecting with women online can serve as an ego boost; however, getting caught can shatter the image your partner holds of you. Just think about what would happen if your partner read or heard an exchange between you and this other woman. (I have seen this happen as well. Not a pretty picture, I can assure you.)

## Reflection

- Are you finding yourself making excuses to lock yourself away to connect with your online buddy?
- Are you fantasizing about the possibility of meeting her in person?
- Is she asking you for money to connect or making promises for more in-depth interactions or photos if you send her money?
- Are you finding her compliments flattering and enticing?
- Is your partner beginning to question the amount of time you are spending "working" on your computer or phone?

## Pornographic Affairs

**"Sexual fantasies and pornography reflect a man wanting a woman to want him completely with no strings attached."**

—Robert Augustus Masters, *To Be a Man*

Each couple has their own preferences and guidelines regarding what is okay or not okay when it comes to viewing sexually stimulating material. Some couples enjoy watching pornography together. Others view it as taboo behavior. In either case, pornography becomes problematic when it turns into an addictive behavior you can't seem to stop, or your biggest go-to for stress relief, or a way to escape addressing internal and relational challenges.

When pornography becomes an obsession—that is, something you struggle to *not* do and/or something you have agreed *not* to do—it can interfere with your ability to connect with your spouse and undermine her trust in you. Viewing pornographic materials, particularly the type that includes aggressive or abusive sexual behavior, can represent unresolved childhood woundings.

If you find yourself becoming overly focused on pornographic stimulation—stuck in a cycle of obsession until you get relief upon viewing it, often followed by shame—it's important to identify your drivers and look at what you may not be attending to within yourself or your primary relationship.

Sometimes a man can get so wrapped up in visual stimulation that it interferes with his ability to make love. Gentlemen, I have seen this happen. A visual fantasy can become so overpowering that it begins to take precedence over the real thing. Guilt, shame, and excessive pornographic stimulation can even impact a man's ability to maintain an erection when being sexual with his partner.

One woman told me, *"When we had sex, it was as if my partner wasn't really there. I believe he stopped seeing the real me and instead got lost in a fantasy. The problem was I couldn't fulfill that fantasy in the same way an on-demand video could. For years I didn't interfere with his pornography use since he reassured me he only wanted to be with me, but when I gave birth and temporarily couldn't have sex, he started an affair with a real person. I could never satisfy him with the frequency or type of sexual activity he wanted, because I was competing with something that wasn't real."*

**RED FLAG: If you find yourself reaching for pornography more and more often, or if it has become your go-to for stress relief, it may be time to reach out for some additional help**—perhaps including an addiction recovery program. Here are some questions that can help you discern if your behavior has become problematic.

---

## Reflection

---

- Does it feel more stimulating to watch sex than to engage with your partner?

- Are you finding an increased craving for this type of visual stimulation?

- Are you hiding your viewing from your spouse?

- Are you finding it more difficult to get or stay aroused with your partner?

- Does the frequency of your pornographic viewing correlate to an increased frustration that your partner is not meeting your sexual expectations?

- Are you avoiding initiating sex with your partner out of fear of rejection?

- Has the intimacy between the two of you diminished?

- Are there topics, particularly around sex, intimacy, and connection, that you may be avoiding discussing with your partner?

Each couple has their own *rules* on what is okay. If you find yourself violating those rules frequently or becoming obsessed with engaging in visually erotic stimulation as a substitute for connection, it is important to take a deeper look at the underlying causes, either with your partner or a professional.

**Does fantasizing constitute a breach of trust?**
Fantasies in and of themselves are not an indication that something is wrong in your primary partnership. If, however, fantasizing interferes with your ability to connect with your partner, there may be some deeper issues at play that could be useful to explore.

**RED FLAG: Frequently fantasizing about someone you know and are connected with can blur boundaries when you encounter that individual in real life**. What you fantasize about can offer hints about some of your affair drivers and an attraction that could move into the danger zone.

We discuss more about this topic, including how to address differences in desire, in Chapter 19.

# Contributing Factors

## WORKPLACE AFFAIRS

Many affairs are rooted in workplace connections. The first stereotype that comes to mind is that of a powerful man forming a deep connection with his assistant. Some people have even referred to this person as a *work wife*. As you know by now, I believe language is powerful. References to this dynamic harken back to a woman serving a man. The danger lies when her *care* extends past workplace duties. While people may chuckle at this label, it speaks to the close dynamic between two people and a power imbalance that can serve as a setup for forging intimate connections.

Workplace affairs can occur between colleagues working closely together in a variety of ways. They may engage together on projects, through running a company, pursuing sales, or working for companies who do business together. Humans are attracted to other humans. Business connections can easily bleed into more when boundaries are not firmly set.

According to a survey conducted by the job site Vault.com and published in *Forbes*, 58 percent of all employees surveyed admitted to engaging in a workplace romance. These statistics increased with time on the job. In fact, 72 percent of those over fifty said yes to engaging in a romantic interlude with a coworker at some point in time during their career. And 19 percent of respondents were either married or in a committed relationship at the time.[11]

## ALCOHOL CONSUMPTION – ADDING FUEL TO THE FIRE

When it comes to affairs, alcohol and attraction can be a deadly combination. Alcohol consumption frequently sets the stage for physical connections. Work events—including colleagues getting together for happy hours, conventions, and sales dinners with drinks—can open the door to letting your guard down. It is easier to be friendly and flirty after a couple of cocktails. A hug goodbye can lead to a kiss. A kiss can lead to a make-out session after walking someone to their car or hotel room. Once lines are blurred, it is easier to blur them further during the next encounter.

**RED FLAG: Excessive or frequent alcohol consumption with someone you are attracted to.** Be especially mindful of your alcohol intake when you are attracted to someone. Alcohol and drug use makes it much easier to cross a line that you may not cross when sober.

# 10

## Affairs Phase Two:
### *Stuck in the Middle with You*

———————————■———————————

*"Growth is painful. Change is painful. But nothing is as painful as staying stuck somewhere you don't belong."*
—Amanda Hale, *The Single Woman Life, Love and a Dash of Sass*

The middle phase of an affair is typically the longest and most confusing. The hallmark of this stage is uncertainty and indecision. A man can feel caught between that part of himself that wants to do the right thing, and the difficulty inherent in telling someone it's over and losing what the AP has been providing. (And as we have discussed, it's not just sex!)

In this phase, the high of engaging in something new begins to fade. As the excitement wears off, so too does the magic. Fantasy comes face-to-face with reality as you try to balance the needs of two women vying for your time and attention—not an easy undertaking. As life and the affair begin to *normalize,* practical life challenges begin disrupting the connection, making things increasingly more difficult.

It is easier to keep lives separate during the beginning phase, when it can feel like the affair is something that more or less *happened*. Continuing the interaction past this phase requires more deliberate deceit to keep it in play.

The three stressors that tend to occur more frequently during the middle stage are: 1) guilt, 2) the fear of getting caught, and 3) increasing demands for connection from the AP.

It is during this phase when the primary partner more frequently begins questioning her man's behavior. Questions from a suspecting spouse are often met with vehement denial: a) either that this is really occurring, or b) in the case of a repeat offender, that it could be happening again.

It is not uncommon for me to hear the man who has betrayed say something like: *"How the heck did this happen? How did things get this far off track? I don't know what the hell I was thinking."* While the beginning of an affair can bring euphoric relief, the push and pull of the middle stage often has the opposite effect, as the affair more frequently bleeds into life at home and becomes more difficult to maintain.

Sometimes you know you *should* leave, yet you can't quite end it. Or maybe you have tried to end to end it several times only to find yourself getting pulled back in. Too good to leave, too challenging to stay. It's like being stuck in quicksand. Sometimes the more you try to pull out, the deeper you sink.

This is also the time that the addictive properties of an affair become more prevalent: rationalization, increasing levels of tolerance, engagement in risky behaviors, denial, and behaving in ways that increasingly compromise the primary relationship. As with all addictions, the craving for another *dose* can overwhelm the senses and trigger withdrawal symptoms when you try to walk away (like moodiness, depression, and anxiety). The hallmark of any addiction is secrecy and the inability to stop. Let's take a look.

## The Addictive Properties of an Affair

**"Addiction is a complex psychological, emotional, physical, neurobiological, social, and spiritual process. It manifests through any behavior in which a person finds temporary relief or pleasure and therefore craves, but that in the long**

term causes them or others negative consequences, and yet the person refuses or is unable to give it up."

—Gabor Maté, M.D. with Daniel Maté, *The Myth of Normal: Trauma, Illness & Healing in a Toxic Culture.*

In his book *The Myth of Normal*, Gabor Maté, M.D. in partnership with his son, Daniel, offers a more holistic view of addiction than the current disease model. Addiction is reframed as a *complex process* which impacts and is impacted by key elements of a person's psychological and physiological makeup as well as the influences of the social structure to which the person is exposed. He goes on to describe the **three main hallmarks of addiction** as: *"short-term relief or pleasure and therefore, craving; long-term suffering for oneself or others; and the inability to stop."*

We typically associate addictions with substances like alcohol or drugs. However, when examining an affair through Maté's lens, we can see how an affair can meet all three of Maté's addiction hallmarks. As with all addictions, it is what the substance provides, or creates freedom from, that a person becomes addicted to. In the case of an affair, we can view the connection with an affair partner as the substance, and the sensations, feelings, and distractions it provides as the superglue that creates a bonding that is difficult to release.

When we can better understand the psychological, emotional, physical, neurobiological (chemical), social, and spiritual impact of affair engagement, we can more effectively root out those elements within the *system* that needs to be healed moving forward. The *affair system* includes the person who engaged in the affair, the relational dynamic with their primary partner, and what was soothed, avoided, or gained through the connection with the affair partner.

What is sometimes difficult to for people outside of an affair to understand is that the strong attractor factor is not as much the affair partner themselves, as it is what that person evokes or touches inside their betrayal partner. This is described by Maté as follows:

## The issue is never the external target but one's internal relationship to it.

In attempting to help his audience better understand the broader scope of addiction, in his talks Maté frequently poses this question to his audience: *"Who, by the definition just given, is now or ever has been addicted?"* Typically, everyone's hand goes up.

He continues his discussion stating that all addictions are not created equal. Some clearly have far more detrimental effects than others. Such is the case with affairs which can have a much broader devastating impact than anticipated.

For those of you who want to take a deeper look at the ways in which an affair mirrors the characteristics of addition, listed below are addiction characteristics (AC's) adapted from *Symptoms of Addiction, Medical News Today*,[12] followed by their affair corollaries.

# Comparison Between Signs of Addiction and Infidelity

**Addiction Characteristic (AC): The person cannot stop behavior.** In many cases, at least one serious attempt is made to stop the behavior of misusing a substance, only to relapse, often multiple times.

**The Affair:** Quite often, several attempts are made to stop the affair before firmly calling it quits. Initial attempts tend to leave the door open for future re-engagement. Once begun, an affair tends to take on a life of its own.

**AC: Withdrawal symptoms begin.** When bodily levels of the substance of choice dip below a certain level, the person using develops physical and mood-related symptoms. This may include cravings, bouts of moodiness, bad temper, poor focus, a feeling of being depressed and empty, frustration, anger, bitterness, and resentment. Withdrawal can trigger violent outbursts, trembling, seizures, hallucinations, and sweats.

**The Affair:** During periods when an individual is unable to connect with an AP he has become attached to, he can become edgy, moody, and more easily upset. In the beginning, an affair can be a source of relief from various life stressors. As it continues, however, an affair tends to become its own stressor, as the individuals involved attempt to figure out ways to connect while keeping their secret intact.

**AC: Behavior continues despite awareness.** The individual continues regular use of the substance, even though they are aware of its hazards.

**The Affair:** Awareness of the impact on others and potential pitfalls is frequently not a strong enough factor to halt affair engagement.

**AC: Risk-taking increases.** An addict may engage in risky behaviors either to obtain, or while under the influence of, the substance. While using, people tend to be less thoughtful about how they are acting and interacting with others. This is due to the ways in which the substance directly impairs their ability to make wise choices.

**The Affair:** An affair puts the lives of many people at risk, and by the time this is realized, much of the damage has already been done. Risk taking can include lying even when directly asked if something is "going on." As an affair continues, the two can engage in flirtatious behavior at the office, attend lunches or happy hours together, or exhibit more public displays of affection.

**AC: Substance use replaces problem-solving.** An addicted person commonly feels they need their drug to deal with, aka avoid, their problems. They can develop a psychological (as well as a physical) dependence on their substance of choice, which means they can become more anxious without it and the frequency of the need for it increases.

**The Affair:** This can ring true with affairs, particularly in the workplace. The liaison becomes someone to lean on when work difficulties arise. A rationalized dependency can easily develop, particularly if this is a boss-subordinate relationship.

**AC: Obsession snowballs.** An addicted person may spend more and more time and energy focusing on ways of getting hold of their substance, and in some cases, how to use it.

**The Affair:** It takes more time, effort, and energy to find ways and places to connect with the AP and to keep the affair hidden from a partner as time goes on.

**AC: Secrecy and solitude prevails.** In many cases, the addict may take their substance alone, and even in secret—which increases the attraction factor.

**The Affair:** Secrecy heightens the adrenaline rush of an affair. Where and how to connect can become an all-consuming problem to solve, which serves to strengthen the high. Also, shared secrets can deepen attachment.

**AC: Denial takes root.** A significant number of people who are addicted to a substance are in denial. They are not aware (or refuse to acknowledge) that they have a problem.

**The Affair:** Denial is particularly true during an affair's beginning stages. The parties involved do not typically see the bigger impact of affair behavior until it is too late and has already compromised their life and their marriage.

**AC: Social impact/disengaging in hobbies or activities:** As the addiction progresses, the individual may refuse social invitations and stop doing things they used to enjoy.

**The Affair:** As an affair progresses, it begins to encroach increasingly on time previously devoted to family, social activities, or hobbies. Things that used to matter at home may not take on as much importance as they did in the past. Since stimulation is found elsewhere, there is more of a tendency to "check out" at home; the thrill of an affair can fulfill the need for adventure and excitement.

**AC: Financial difficulties ensue.** If the substance is expensive, the addicted individual may sacrifice a lot to make sure their supply is secured.

**The Affair:** Engaging in an affair can involve expenses such as dining out, booking hotel rooms, and purchasing gifts, which can be financially burdensome. However, the true cost goes beyond money. The revelation of these expenditures can indicate a deeper emotional connection, causing even more pain for the betrayed partner when exposed.

**AC: Relationship problems worsen.** Addictions interfere with the quality of relationships.

**The Affair:** On this one...well, enough said.

Addictions can overpower reason until they are faced. Once you become clear on what you want and know the risk factors for continuing substance use, you are better equipped to choose options that are congruent with what matters most.

## The Power of Secret-Keeping

### One of the primary adrenaline rushes of an affair is its secrecy.

The excitement inherent in this secrecy can be difficult to walk away from. There is something about entering into a connection with the forbidden that fires up those neural pathways—making pursuit more exhilarating. Think of adolescence when a parent forbids their teen from dating a particular person, or hanging out with a friend group they don't approve of.[13] Adrenaline is heightened during these risk-taking activities—compelling a repetition of the behavior.

Ultimately, though, an affair's secrecy can become more of a burden. As the affair begins to normalize, fantasy is replaced by the concrete reality of two people attempting to navigate the complexity of their lives. Vigilance tends to wane. Receipts get left in coat pockets. Text messages come in during inconvenient times. The AP can vie for more time and attention. It is during this phase that the affair is in more danger of discovery.

As the weight of guilt becomes heavier, there can also be more back-and-forth movement within the affair itself—a waffling between excitement and guilt. When things are difficult at home, it is easier to rationalize your decision. When things are going well, an affair serve as an interfering reminder that you are compromising your integrity and marriage. Perhaps you made this choice when things at home were not going quite so well, and now that they are better, you are more haunted by guilt.

All relationships, including affairs, ebb and flow—resulting in fluctuating feelings of connection and disconnection. The challenge arises when disconnection becomes the norm, making it difficult for a couple to find their way back to each other. As we have discussed, affairs aren't necessarily an indicator that things at home are *bad*. A momentary slip or attraction may simply fire up a connection that you didn't see coming.

At specific times, the desire for newness, adventure, or immersion into something all-consuming is stronger than others. Some men (and women) tackle extreme sports, run a marathon, go mountain biking, climb a mountain, go white-water rafting, etc., to feed the part of their soul that craves adventure. Others find their wildness in deep intellectual banter, passionate kisses, stolen moments, secrecy, sex, sex with a new partner, or sex in a new place. As discussed, the adrenaline rush sparked by a flirty connection, a couple of drinks, or a kiss goodbye at a bar can easily turn a spark into a flame. Once ignited, the fire of desire can be difficult to squelch.

There are other ways to stimulate the parts of the brain that craves newness, which we will explore later. For now, let's take a peek into Joe's middle-stage uncertainty.

## Navigating Uncertainty:
### *The Story of Joe, Carol, and Jessica*

Joe and Carol have been married for nine years. Joe has been engaging in a physical affair with Jessica for almost two years. Let's hear Joe describe his story.

*"Jessica is a gal I met at the gym. We worked out at the same time every day and started talking after workouts. Jess was going through a rough patch in her marriage, trying to decide whether or not to end it. She said she wanted to get a man's perspective and told me that it had been six months since they had sex. I let her know it*

*had been a while for me too. A couple of visits later, she asked me if I would be interested in a 'no strings attached' arrangement. She said she wasn't interested in diving into another relationship, but she missed being physically intimate with someone and wasn't connecting with her husband.*

*"That conversation marked the beginning of what has been a two yearlong on-and-off affair. Jess recently ended up filing for divorce and moving out on her own. The other day she reminded me that we had been connecting for about two years and wondered about 'our future.' She asked if I would consider leaving my wife. I must admit I was surprised by her question. She said she felt really close to me and now that she'd left her marriage, she was ready for more.*

*"A couple of times over the course of the past year, I pulled back from Jess, as it felt like I was thinking about her a little too much. Then she would text, or I would get in a fight with Carol and reach back out to her.*

*"For at least a year before connecting with Jess, my wife Carol just didn't seem to have a lot of interest in me. She'd frequently complain that she didn't feel like a priority. She was upset that she was always the one initiating plans and complained that my main focus was work. Sex used to be really good with us and helped me feel connected, but it became less frequent. She said she just wasn't feeling emotionally connected to me and that impacted her desire.*

*"I began to wonder if she even liked me anymore. I grew tired of getting turned down, so when Jess approached me with the no-strings-attached arrangement, it sounded intriguing. It felt like it was a way to stay in my marriage and relieve some of my tension. It seemed that Carol was always complaining. I know that's no excuse, but the idea that somebody wanted me was very appealing.*

*"After the affair began, things seemed a little better at home. I was less edgy, and I think I started trying more with Carol. While we still weren't connecting very often physically, it felt like maybe she was beginning to like me again. It seemed like this arrangement was working for everybody, until it wasn't.*

*"I definitely wasn't prepared for that question from Jessica. I admit there have been times when I wondered if Carol would be happier without me. But leaving her? That's much more complicated. We've had nine years together. I guess maybe there's no such thing as a 'no strings' arrangement!"*

Joe slumped back on the couch and sighed. *"I still love Carol. I do. I'm just not sure I'm still 'in love' with her, as cliché as it sounds! What kind of a mess have I gotten myself into?"*

**Commentary:**
Joe isn't alone. The *"I love but am not sure I'm in love with...."* phrase weaves its way into the fabric of many relationships at one point or another. Have you ever felt that way? Has your spouse ever said those words to you?

In my practice, this idea of loving but not being *in love* is one of the catalysts for couples reaching out. What happens to raise doubt about whether we are *in love* or *out of love* with a partner?

While it is natural for a relational connection to ebb and flow over time, sometimes the *ebbs* can cause us to question the connection. *Are we/Am I really still in love?* A mature love can look vastly different from the emotional high of a new connection.

So, what do you do when you feel less connected? Talk about it. Authentically engage. This can be as simple as: *"It doesn't feel like we've been as connected lately. I've been missing that. Do you feel the same way?"* Or, *"I'd love to brainstorm ideas for ways we can better connect."*

In his book *How to Be an Adult in Relationships*,[22] author David Richo discusses what he calls *the five keys to mindful loving.* His work supports the idea that love isn't just a feeling, it's a choice. The actions you take either move you closer or further away from each other. You can increase your feelings of love by taking actions to be more loving.

Examine your own efforts. Have you, like Joe, been putting your relationship on the back burner? If so, try initiating an evening out. Often making the effort to create a plan goes a long way toward reengagement. And engaging in something new or different can help forge a path toward reconnection. *"Saturday night, I have something special planned. The attire is (dressy, nice casual, hot jeans, etc.) We leave at seven."*

Unlike fairytales that end at the altar with "and they lived happily ever after," real coupling involves learning how to sustain the *ever after,* which never quite looks like we imagine it will!

# Questioning It All

You heard Joe's description of his life-questioning, which he was not bringing to the table at home. Leaning upon someone outside your primary relationship can provide *just enough* comfort that it becomes easier to talk yourself out of engaging in difficult conversations that you need to have with your spouse. Talking about the tough stuff is hard. It is easier to avoid challenging conversations when someone else is satisfying some of those relational needs.

As we have been discussing, the middle phase of an affair is a time of confusion and doubt. You can begin questioning everything relational. Love. Lust. Loss. What's really *real*?

**If you are in the middle phase and unsure which way to turn, rather than pretending with either of these women, it's time to face your ambivalence.** You must first be honest with yourself. Before making a solid commitment to anyone, get in touch with your own truths. Engage in self-exploration. Don't commit to anyone if you aren't ready. If you need some space to sort things out, let your spouse know. The last thing you want to do is feign commitment to either of these women if you aren't sure where you want to land.

---

## Reflection

### *Exploration at the Crossroads*

If you find yourself at a crossroads—unsure or not fully committed to your next steps—following are some questions to help you navigate this middle stage and discern what you want.

I encourage you to jot down your initial uncensored thoughts, and then revisit these questions within the next week or two and see if you've gained more clarity. Some answers may come right away. Others evolve over time.

**Consider your future. What your life would be like if ...**

- You left your primary partner? What would things be like for the kids (if applicable)?
- You chose to create a life with your affair partner full-time?
- You were on your own—partner-free?
- You treated your relationship like a critical work project and gave it 100 percent effort?

- You both learned how to communicate more effectively and made your relationship a high priority?

## Consider your primary relationship.

- What first drew you to your spouse? What did you love about her?
- What caused you to choose to marry her?
- What is something that you have worked through in the past that was difficult for you both?
- What are you proud of about this relationship?
- What is something you have done in the past that demonstrates how much you love your partner?

## Consider your own goals and aspirations.

- Which choices are in alignment with your deeper purpose?
- What is your intellect telling you?
- What is your heart telling you?
  - Where do my intellect and heart intersect? Where do they collide?
- Who will be affected by your decisions?
  - Are you willing to sit down and talk about your ambivalence, thoughts, and ideas?
- What does your ideal life look like moving forward?
- What are you inspired to accomplish?
- Which choice best supports you in realizing your vision and dreams? (How about your partner's?)
- Who can you bounce ideas off of?
- What is the wisest choice you can make in this situation?
- What have you been avoiding talking about?

## Consider your hopes and beliefs.

- Do you *really* want to make your relationship work? (If it's helpful, you can rate it on a scale of 0 to 10, with zero being not at all and 10 being 100 percent.)
- To what degree do you believe it's possible to repair your relationship and make it work?

Our relationships are part of us. They exist internally and externally. The picture you paint of your spouse, the way you interpret her actions, and your intent, impact how you see and show up for her, and the quality of your relationship.

It is important to consider the whole picture of your relationship, not just your most recent state of mind or the state of your relationship just prior to the affair.

If you are still wildly uncertain, save these questions. Revisit them in the next week or so to see if anything has changed as you sit with the importance of consciously choosing what you want instead of allowing yourself to be pulled by your situation or the chemical rush of what momentarily feels good.

As always, if you continue to feel really stuck, reaching out for help can be the best decision. Sometimes just talking it out with a professional can help you gain the clarity to make the best choices for all concerned.

# 11

## Affairs Phase Three:
### *Closing the Door—How to Clearly and Respectfully End Your Affair*

---

*"There comes a day when you realize turning the page is the best feeling in the world, because you realize there is so much more to the book than the page you were stuck on."*
—Zayn Malik, singer

### Unwinding Your Affair

When you are ready to end it with your affair partner—and I mean *really* end it, not just think maybe you need to end it, but truly let her go—this chapter offers you a way forward.

If you are ending an affair your primary partner knows about, it is important for her to know that you are putting her first. Your words and actions, even the little ones, help demonstrate that she is your priority. It is also important for you to understand her needs moving forward. You are beginning the trust-rebuilding process as you recommit to your partner, which requires clear and conscientious choices on your part.

## AND THEN SOME ...

Here is a quick little tip that can help your primary partner feel like a priority as you are ending things with your AP. I call it *and then some.* It entails looking for special things you can do for her or adding something extra to your routine. It doesn't have to be a grandiose gesture. In fact, it's the little things that really indicate you are paying attention. Does she have a favorite coffee or tea? Wake up a little early and either make it for her or go to your local coffee shop and order it. Perhaps there is a cute coffee mug at the store with a hummingbird on it (and you know she loves hummingbirds!). Have the barista make her favorite drink and give it to her in this new mug. Don't underestimate the power of the little extras.

To set the stage for healthy recovery, you must clearly end things with your AP. Your final conversation is critical in ending your connection: It's over. No wiggle room.

---

## The best way to unwind things is clearly, kindly, respectfully, and directly.

---

Perhaps you have tried to end things in the past and it didn't stick. Or maybe you have recently said things to passively indicate it's over in hopes that she takes the hint. Until you have this final conversation, you are keeping the connection in play.

Here are three ways engaging in this final dreaded conversation helps with recovery:

1. **For you:** This final conversation helps solidify inside of you that the affair is over, and that you are choosing to end it. You are not keeping the door cracked open just in case, as this isn't fair to anyone. While keeping someone waiting in the wings can feel less scary, doing so increases the likelihood of a repeat offense, and it keeps the AP from moving on.

2. **For your Primary Partner:** This final conversation is a testament to your SO that you have put a period on this relationship, not a comma, not a question mark. No maybes. You are committed to doing what it takes to make your primary relationship work. Period.

3. **For the Affair Partner:** This final conversation helps her let go and move on. For her to heal and begin her own recovery, she needs to release the hope that you two will one day reconnect. The more clearly you end things, the more quickly and completely she can heal and move on. And this conversation helps unwind the energetic entanglement the two of you have created.

## COMMUNICATING WITH THE AFFAIR PARTNER

While you may have told the AP all along that you have no intention of leaving your spouse or family, your behavior may have indicated otherwise. In case you don't already know this, words are no match for the fantasies a person can create in their mind. You can defend your position all you want, but when you are engaging in an affair—particularly an intensely emotional or steamy sexual connection—there is a darn good chance a woman will fall for you. (It is quite likely that you may be experiencing loving feelings for her as well.)

Many women engage in affairs because they, too, feel like something's missing in their lives. Perhaps she has a primary partner who hasn't been quite as attentive, or maybe she's single and has been in a series of unfulfilling relationships, or perhaps she hasn't engaged with a man sexually in a while. For a time, you become her *missing piece*, the outlet or fantasy for fulfilling her relational desires.

Remember, she too is taking a risk in being with you. If she's married, she risks the fallout of her husband's discovery and the shame of being exposed to her children, family, and neighborhood. She risks being labeled as a woman who can't be trusted around other women's husbands. She risks losing her friendships. Being found out can be catastrophic for her as well.

If she's single, she's probably more available than you and possibly frustrated that you are not. In many cases, having an affair with an unmarried woman puts you in the center of her relational desire, and there's likely a strong part of her that is staying because she believes, whether implied or assumed, that you will leave your SO for her. Or maybe she likes having her freedom and doesn't want to engage with a fully available man.

I have seen many single women become very attached to the married object of their affection. This attachment can be so strong that she believes she must inform her lover's wife about their affair. There are two primary reasons for this: 1) If she tells your wife, maybe your wife will leave you; 2) If she feels angry that you have pulled away from her, the revenge monster may rear its ugly head. In this case, you may see a side of the AP that you haven't experienced before. Trust me, this is *not* the way you want your wife to hear about your indiscretions.

## When you engage with someone outside your marriage, you are playing with fire. No one comes out unscathed. No one.

That doesn't minimize the growth that may occur, or what this may have sparked inside of you.

### SAYING YOUR GOODBYES

Even though you have decided that you want to make your marriage work, saying goodbye isn't easy. As painful as it may be, you must make it clear to your ex-lover that you are breaking things off. You need to be direct, firm, and kind in your delivery and request that she honor your decision. You both knew the risks going into the affair. But now, you are choosing to work on your marriage.

Let's take a quick look at how George ended his affair with Katie.

## Ending Things with Clarity and Compassion: *George, Kelly, and Katie*

George was a corporate executive who had been engaging in an affair with Katie, a woman he had grown close to after working on several high-level projects together. His wife, Kelly suspected he was having an affair. When she confronted him, George confessed. He let Kelly know that he was sincere about wanting to make his marriage work. He told her that he would clearly and directly let his AP know that the affair was definitively over when he went back to work on Monday.

Kelly agreed to give him the space to end things with his AP in person, if he agreed to let her know any time the AP reached out afterwards. That was one of several agreements they made during the course of their recovery. While George and Kelly hit a few bumps along the way their unwavering commitment to their relationship, themselves, and each other helped them successfully rebuild a strong foundation of trust and create a thriving connection.

Here's how George told his AP Katie that it was over.

*"Katie, you have been very important to me. You showed up at a time when I was confused about a lot of things, and I leaned on you way more than I ever should have. Last night Kelly confronted me with some things she'd found out about us, and I confessed. It was a rough night. We talked about a lot of things. I don't want to lose Kelly. We're going to give it our best shot to see if we can fix what has broken between us. Kelly is looking for a counselor to help."*

As George spoke, tears rolled down Katie's cheeks. She knew this day was coming, yet she just wasn't ready for everything to end so abruptly. George gently continued.

*"I think it will be too tough for both of us to work so closely together anymore, so I'm going to request a transfer to a new region. I know it sounds cliché, but I really do wish you the best. I hope—no, I know—you will find a great guy who can give you what I can't. You deserve to be with someone who can really be there for you."*

*"I'm sorry too,"* Katie said. *"I never should have let things go this far. Do you have to change regions? We work so well together. I don't want to lose our work connection too."*

*"Yeah, I know. I just think it would be too tough and tempting for us to continue working together. And I promised Kelly. I'm sorry."*

*"This is so tough, but I get it. I knew the risks, but you've meant so much to me. You've been such an important person in my life. I'm really sad about this—about all of it. I hope we can still touch base from time to time."*

*"I know it is abrupt,"* George said, *"but I have promised Kelly that I would end things and that we will no longer be in communication. So, we won't be able to call or text each other at all. I really need to stay true to my promise and give my marriage 100 percent of my focus. I am counting on us both to respect my decision to focus on my marriage. And again, I'm so sorry for hurting you."*

Katie knew not seeing or communicating with George would be tough, but she heard the sincerity in his request. She responded, *"I get it. I hate losing you, but in truth I never really had you anyway. Of course, I will honor your decision. And I will genuinely miss our connection. At the end of the day, it is your friendship I will miss most. And we worked so well together. I wish we could just rewind and do things differently. Can I give you one last hug?"*

They embraced. Then George left.

While that may sound like an episode from a soap opera, affairs often involve deep emotional connections. We have this notion that if a person is married or in a serious relationship, their love and commitment alone should keep them from developing a connection with someone else. That simply isn't the case. Human beings are complex, and there are so many factors that impact how and why we connect with other humans.

George's ability to speak with Katie with compassion and clarity helped her move on. Katie heard his sincerity and was able to express her feelings one last time. Their final conversation provided closure and set the framework for both to part ways with dignity and respect. It helped Katie begin the grieving process cleanly, engage in her own healing work, and create what was next in her life without keeping her sights set on a future possibility with George. It helped George strengthen his inner integrity by honoring his commitment to his wife, Kelly, and creating a clean ending.

George took things one step further to tie up all loose ends by talking to his boss about the affair. The two of them were able to carve out a plan that would create more distance between him and Katie, helping fortify him against future temptation.

Some men believe they can continue to maintain communication with their AP. This rarely works. If this is a woman you work with, ideally one of you should change positions, or even companies, if possible. At a minimum, you need to no longer be working directly together. If that isn't feasible, do something to create distance and minimize non-work-related interactions.

## Reflection
### *Staying the Course - What to Expect*

Leaving someone you formed a relationship with is never easy. Once you have let the AP know that you are breaking things off, allow yourself some time to grieve. Set boundaries, and do not continue engaging in discussions with her about your decision. That is why that final conversation is so critical. It helps you close the door with her and within yourself. Once you have it, you need to be finished.

**There are two patches of vulnerability you will likely hit after breaking things off with the AP.** The first tends to occur in the days and weeks immediately following the breakup. No matter how confident you feel that working on your primary relationship is the right thing to do, you may find yourself waffling a bit with your decision. This is completely natural. Don't let missing your connection confuse you. It will get easier.

The second can occur as things settle down at home. When the heat is off and life becomes more routine, you may find yourself thinking about reaching out to the AP—maybe just to check in and see how she is doing. Don't. The impulse will pass. This can be a great time to seek support from your coach, counselor, or a trusted friend. It's also essential to prioritize self-care by engaging in activities that bring you joy. Allocate time for your personal interests and plan quality moments to bond and explore new experiences with your significant other.

The person you have been connecting with occupied a space in your life that is now vacant. While throwing yourself into work overload or other distractions can provide a temporary respite from the pain, the sooner you face your sadness over this loss, the more solidly you will build the foundation for your recovery.

Don't keep someone *waiting in the wings* just in case your attempts at marital reconciliation fail. This isn't fair to your spouse or your ex. Women naturally tend to build fantasies about men they love, and if you leave any room for doubt, she'll undoubtedly climb into it. While it may feed your ego to know that she's willing to wait and see how things turn out at home, you're hurting her and your own integrity in the long run. Keeping the window even slightly open keeps her from bandaging her wounds and moving on with her life. If you truly care for this person, the best thing you can do for her is to let her go completely.

## If You Think YOU are Bulletproof, Think Again

Often men pride themselves on being strong in the self-discipline department. *"Once I set my mind to something, it's made up. There is no going back. I am strong that way."* I've heard comments of this nature more than once. Don't let your ego get in the way of maintaining your boundaries. If you say to your spouse that you aren't going to communicate with your AP, don't.

It takes an extremely high level of self-discipline, commitment, and introspective awareness to maintain a connection with an AP that doesn't ultimately lead you back into the bedroom (or wherever your liaisons occurred). Don't be fooled into thinking you are the exception and that you can stay connected and stay away. Like a newly sober alcoholic walking into a bar that specializes in his favorite cocktail, the temptation to *have just one* is simply too great. Don't risk it.

# PART FIVE

---■---

# Expanding Recovery:
## *The Power of Commitment, Establishing Boundaries, and Honoring Promises*

This section is designed to help you continue navigating through affair recovery. We dive into the next phase of the recovery process using Jim, Liz, and Shelly's story as the backdrop.

We also explore what marriage means to you and dive into an example of delivering a heartfelt apology.

In this section, you will read about:

**Paths to Recovery: Putting the Pieces Back Together**

- The conclusion of Jim, Liz, and Shelly's story
- The five A's of recovery

**The Impact of Making, Breaking and Keeping Promises**

- How to deliver a heartfelt yes and an authentic no
- Exploring your views on marriage and being a husband
- The nuances of recovering from a repeat offense
- Ways to navigate powerful connections without crossing the line
- How to prepare for a fresh start

# 12

## Paths *to* Recovery:
### *Putting the Pieces Back Together*

———————————————— ∎ ————————————————

*"Let us not forget that our actions form, piece by piece, a structure that is either upright or crooked. And so let us aim to be our highest selves, keeping our character and values intact, meeting every situation with solid integrity and generous humanity."*
—Brendon Burchard, *The Motivation Manifesto,*
*9 Declarations to Claim Your Personal Power*

Remember Jim, Liz, and Shelly from Chapter 6? As a quick recap, Jim was struggling trying to decide whether or not to come clean with his wife about his affair. As you may recall, his affair partner Shelly had just threatened to tell his wife, Liz, about their connection. Let's listen to his words and see how things played out.

*"When Shelly threatened to tell Liz I panicked. She didn't even know Liz. They met once at a work function, but that was their only interaction. How could she threaten me like that? Never in a million years did I think she would go there! I had trouble keeping my cool, but I didn't want to make her any madder than she already was.*

*"I told Shelly to slow down and take a step back for a moment, that her threat to tell Liz was a real turnoff.*

*"Shelly responded, 'But it's not fair, Jim. I sat around all weekend waiting for you to call, and you just ignored me. Don't tell me you couldn't find five minutes to call or text me back. Did you even think about how that would make me feel?'"*

## JIM'S REFLECTIONS

*"The truth is, that weekend I didn't think about how Shelly was feeling. I was enjoying my time at home with Liz. We were really connecting. I guess I should have texted her something, but I knew if I did, she would have tried to talk me into meeting her somewhere. I didn't want to deal with the hassle. It started to feel like I had a noose around my neck and that Shelly was pulling on the end of the rope."* Jim let out a deep sigh.

*"Sounds like it was starting to get pretty intense,"* I responded. *"What was going on inside of you as you came face to face with Shelly's disappointment and the possibility of her talking to Liz?"*

*"Truthfully, I felt like crap. I just wanted to disappear. I certainly didn't want her talking to Liz. If anyone was going to tell her, it was going to be me. I just stood there for a moment, thinking I'm fucking up two women's lives! I knew I needed to calm Shelly down, but I also knew I needed to figure out how to unwind it all. In an instant everything seemed to be unraveling."*

## UNWINDING THINGS WITH SHELLY

Jim continued: *"I told Shelly that I cared about her, but that I was really thinking I needed to try and make things work at home with Liz. I told her that I thought we needed to take a break, that this was all becoming too intense and confusing.*

*"Shelly started crying. Then she got angry again. 'So, you're breaking up with me? Right before Christmas? Maybe I really will tell your wife, Jim. Who knows how you will spin this? You'll probably pretend that nothing happened or paint me out to be the bad guy. She needs to know the truth about the guy she's married to.'"*

## JIM'S REFLECTIONS

Then Jim said to me, *"That was so unexpected. Suddenly, she's acting like she's protecting Liz. What the hell was I dealing with? I felt trapped. I paused for a moment, took a breath, and somehow, I found the courage to tell Shelly straight up that we were through. I knew I had to do it, right then and there. Putting it off would just make things worse. I told her we needed to be done; that I needed us to be done."*

## COMING CLEAN

Jim later decided to come clean with Liz about Shelly. Shelly, it seemed, *had "gone off the deep end,"* and if anyone was going to tell Liz what happened, he wanted it to be him, not her.

Jim set up an uninterrupted time to talk with his wife. He explained that while working closely on projects together, he began to feel a pull toward a woman at work. He acknowledged that he should have seen it as a warning signal, rather than allowing things to cross the line. Jim took 100 percent responsibility for what happened.

When Jim told Liz, she was devastated. She let him know she had felt something was going on but didn't know how to talk about it. She kept ignoring it, hoping it would all settle down and go away. *"I wish I'd had the courage to talk to you,"* Liz told Jim. *"I guess maybe I was afraid of what I'd find out. It felt easier to ignore it than risk asking and finding out it was true. I never thought you'd cheat on me. On us. What the hell, Jim? What happened to us?"* Liz let out a big sigh, put her face in her hands, and began to cry.

Each woman has her own way of expressing and dealing with emotions. She may cry. She may explode in anger. She may withdraw or be silent. Her self-respect has been shattered, and she's not sure how to get it back. While you may be able to help her as time goes on, there are some things she must figure out on her own.

This is a tricky time for any guy. After an affair comes to light, things will be bumpy. Focus on *her*. Be responsive in the moment to her reactions and provide her with what she needs as best you can. Does she need to vent? Does she need comfort? A little space? Time to process? There's not one right answer that fits all. You aren't aiming for perfection here. You're working toward reparation, which will have its hits and misses.

# Five A's of Recovery:
## *Acknowledge. Admit. Apologize. Ask. Adapt.*

Here's a formula you can use as a recovery guide. I call it the five A's:

- **Acknowledge** her emotions
- **Admit** your shortcomings
- **Apologize** and express remorse
- **Ask** her what she wants and ask for what you would like
- **Adapt** and reassure her. Adapt to her needs and allow her the space and freedom to choose what she wants.

### THE FIVE A'S IN ACTION

Liz and Jim's emotions were running high. Jim began to wonder whether he did the right thing by telling Liz. He felt bad that his actions caused her so much pain. Liz was sobbing. He wasn't sure what to do next. Here's how Jim applied the five A's:

"I can't even imagine what you must be feeling right now, Liz. I know I effed up big-time. This is not the kind of husband I want to be. I'm so incredibly sorry for all the pain I caused you…for all of it. I took my eye off the ball and compromised our relationship. You didn't deserve any of this. I am so incredibly sorry. Is there anything I can do for you right now? I'd love to hold you and comfort you, but I'm not sure if you want that from me. Just tell me what you need. A hug? Time to think? I'll do whatever it takes to win you back. I love you. I hope one day you can find it in your heart to forgive me. I want to grow old with you if you'll let me. I want to make this right, Liz."

Let's look at how Jim applied the five A's.

Jim began by **acknowledging** his wife's emotions.

> *"I can't even imagine what you must be feeling right now, Liz."*

Then he **admitted** his shortcomings.

> *"I know I effed up big-time. This is not the kind of husband I want to be. I took my eye of the ball and compromised our relationship."*

Jim offered a brief descriptive **apology**.

> *"I'm so incredibly sorry for all the pain I caused you...for all of it."* Then again, *"I'm so incredibly sorry."*

He **asked** Liz what she wanted and then offered a suggestion of something that might comfort her.

> *"Is there anything I can do for you right now? I'd love to hold you and comfort you, but I'm not sure if you'd want that from me."*

Jim concluded by offering some choices and reassurance while being open to **adapting** to Liz's needs.

> *"Would you like some space? Time to think? Can I give you a hug? I'll do whatever it takes to win you back. I love you. I hope one day you can find it in your heart to forgive me. I want to grow old with you. I want to make this right, Liz."*

Jim wanted to reassure Liz that his connection with Shelly did not mean he didn't love Liz. At that moment, Liz let him know she wanted a hug and then some space to think things through.

Hopefully you can see that the five A's formula isn't too difficult to implement. What's most is your sincerity and openness, and letting her take the lead. In so doing, you offer her the space to consider what she wants and express it, hopefully in a calm manner. You reassure her that she's valued and reinforce your willingness to meet her where she is by "doing whatever it takes" to show up in new ways and recreate a thriving relationship.

This set the stage for this couple to engage in a deeper discussion about the state of their relationship prior to the affair.

## TAKING STOCK OF WHERE THEY WERE

Liz decided to take a walk and asked Jim if he wanted to join her. He agreed. After about five minutes of silently walking together, Liz shook her head and said, *"I just don't understand how this happened."* Jim told her that he had been thinking about that too. He told Liz that in looking back, he realized he'd felt disconnected for some time, and instead of talking to her, he'd pulled away. Once again, Jim told Liz how sorry he was that he hadn't come to her to talk about things. *"I think we just weren't spending as much time together. I didn't think you were interested in some of the things going on with me. I was busy at work and threw even more of my attention into my projects. At work, I felt successful. At home, well, I guess I just quit trying. I know that's not an excuse and I really am sorry I didn't have the smarts to talk about it with you. It all seemed to happen so quickly. I'm so sorry, Liz."*

Even though it was challenging to hear about the affair, Liz told Jim that she was relieved he told her. At times she'd felt like she was going crazy. She'd even started checking his phone. That's not the kind of wife she wanted to be. She realized she, too, had been pulling back. She'd interpreted his working so much as him not caring about her needs. She'd quit asking for what she wanted.

They realized they were living together and living apart at the same time. They both had been feeling lonely and weren't sure how to reconnect or bridge the gap.

## LIZ AND SHELLY

Two weeks after Jim's confession, Shelly reached out to Liz. She asked her to connect over coffee to *"talk it out, woman to woman."* She let Liz know she had important things to share that she thought Liz should know about.

Shelly's reaching out caused Liz to question everything all over again. Was there something Shelly could share that would give Liz additional insight? Maybe there were more things Jim was hiding or lying about. Liz was tempted to meet with Shelly. She was curious and wanted to make sure she wasn't being fooled again. Were they still secretly seeing each other?

While the possibility of hearing an AP's version of "the truth" can be enticing, unless the two women had a prior friendship they were trying to salvage, meeting with an AP would most likely do more harm than good and lengthen the recovery process.

Liz declined Shelly's request to talk. She let her know that she wasn't interested in hearing what she had to say. Shelly tried several more times to convince Liz that it would be in her best interest for them to meet. Ultimately, Liz blocked Shelly's number.

Shelly also reached out to Jim several times over the next two months. The final text was letting him know she received an interesting job offer and was moving to Chicago. Per their agreement, Jim let Liz know each time Shelly texted. Even though it momentarily stirred things up with Liz, telling her about the texts reinforced his commitment to his marriage and helped the trust rebuilding process.

# The Recovery Process

### SHELLY'S RECOVERY

While Shelly's actions may seem a bit over-the-top, it's not uncommon for a woman who feels wronged or misled to react in unexpected ways. Shelly believed she had found true love with Jim. While she hoped he would one day leave his wife, she had reconciled herself to sharing him. She enjoyed his company, attention, and affection and panicked in the face of Jim's abrupt withdrawal. Her provocation for wanting to connect with Liz was a mixture of a desire for retribution for Jim's sudden departure, and the need for redemption, which she believed could be gained through telling Liz her side of the story.

After her move, Shelly began engaging in her own healing work—examining the ways she had compromised her values and settled for less than she wanted or deserved by connecting with a married man.

### LIZ'S RECOVERY

*"When I reflect back on what happened, the truth is I knew something was off. I just knew it. Yet I kept ignoring it, hoping things would get better. We were going through a rough patch, but don't all marriages go through tough times? I guess I just didn't want to accuse him of anything if it wasn't true. Maybe I was afraid it just might be true, and then I didn't know what I would do. Would I leave him? Would the marriage be over? What if he fell in love with someone else? I guess I just wasn't ready to face whatever was going on, so I just tried my best to carry on, hoping that underneath it all we'd be okay."*

Liz began looking at other ways she didn't speak up in her relationship or with friends. Through her recovery process she was able to let go of any self-blame she harbored for ignoring her intuition, and for contributing to the growing distance by not talking to Jim about her concerns. She ultimately faced her pain and talked to Jim about all of it. Liz was determined not to sweep anything under the rug.

## JIM'S RECOVERY

Instead of running from the discomfort of hearing Liz talk about her heartbreak, Jim sat by her side and listened, without defending, as she shared her heart and mind. He took responsibility for his choices and let Liz know repeatedly how truly sorry he was for hurting her. He also told her that none of what happened was her fault.

The way Jim listened without becoming defensive helped Liz see how much she really did matter to him. As Liz was able to experience Jim's listening and deep remorse for hurting her and not talking about things before the affair, she began to soften. Over time, their trust in one another grew. Jim explored his AVFs, which resulted in identifying some internal and external experiences that helped set the stage for his affair. Eventually, Liz forgave him, and he began to forgive himself.

## JIM AND LIZ DISCUSS THEIR RECOVERY PROCESS AS A COUPLE

*"We both used this as an opportunity to sit down and discuss what we wanted our marriage to look like,"* Jim shared. *"We made a vow to each other not to just say yes without thinking things through. I became much more conscious of my commitment to Liz. And she worked on giving me time to consider things instead of pushing me for a quick answer. We've learned how to better navigate disagreements and resolve things instead of sweeping them under the rug. I'm giving my marriage much more thought now than the first time around. I'm so grateful to Liz for letting me back in and letting me prove to her how much I really do love her."*

Liz agreed. *"I trust and love this man more than ever. He really turned things around. I feel like he's truly committed to our marriage. I feel that I can trust that he means what he says. He doesn't just say it; he does it! And I'm trusting myself more too. I'm not allowing myself to slip back into old patterns of impatience and avoidance.*

*"We talk about things now and don't let the little things become big."* Liz paused. *"Yes, thoughts of the affair still surface from time to time, but I'm able to more quickly work through them. And Jim listens. He genuinely seems interested in what I have to say. And I'm more conscious of not pushing him into an important conversation when I'm frustrated about other things. While this wouldn't be the way I would have chosen to get here, our marriage is more solid than ever. I really do love this man."*

**MY REFLECTIONS ON JIM AND LIZ**

So, what happened and what changed with Liz and Jim? Their pre-affair marriage wasn't that *bad* in the sense that they weren't prone to arguing. They just weren't feeling much aliveness. Over time, life had pulled them in different directions, and they quit prioritizing their connection. They had created two separate lives and were living more like roommates than as husband and wife.

During recovery, they each gained greater clarity on who they were, what they wanted, and what they were each committed to doing to create a thriving marriage. They worked on spotting discontentment early and learned how to engage in *courageous conversations* to set the stage for healthy dialogue. They quit taking things so personally and cultivated a greater trust that each of them had the other's best interests at heart. They focused on themselves too by engaging in activities with other people that brought them joy. Together they created a vision of what they wanted their lives to look like and engaged in ways that helped them move in that direction.

Jim and Liz weren't perfect, but they learned to reprioritize what was important to them and continued to work on strengthening their connection, relational understanding, and setting aside time to discuss matters of importance so that little things didn't become big things.

## Reflection
### *On Jim Liz and Shelly's Story*

- What stands out for you about Jim, Liz, and Shelly's story?
- Do you agree with Jim's choice to come clean? What would you have (or have you) done?
- How fortified do you now feel to resist the temptation of outside influences?
- Have you discovered the aspects that are toughest for your spouse to work through in order to begin healing from your affair?

# How to Deal with Powerful Connections to Ensure You Don't Cross the Line

Collaborating with someone you feel chemistry with can be exhilarating. To capitalize on a great working relationship without crossing the line, the biggest key is to clarify your position before the lines begin to blur. Clear communication may be a little uncomfortable at first, but it's the best way to set the stage for strong working relationships that don't compromise your integrity, career or relationships.

One of the core connecting factors in workplace liaisons is how projects and deadlines stimulate adrenaline rushes and dopamine surges, which in turn light up specific neural pathways. It requires more brain juice to think in new, un-patterned ways. Neurobiologist Dr. Dan Siegel describes this as, "Brains that fire together, wire together." What this essentially means is that there is a neurobiological connection formed when engaging in something stimulating or meaningful with someone else.

There can be intense exhilaration when meeting a tough deadline, creating a successful solution, or even failing at an important assignment together. Emotional arousal stimulates connection. The more intense and frequent the arousal, the greater the desire for more. Throw in a powerful physical or intellectual attraction, and sparks begin to ignite. The danger occurs as we begin to view the person, not the exhilaration from the experience, as the source of powerfully charged feelings. This can be particularly challenging if connections at home have been running a bit cold.

## SETTING AND HONORING BOUNDARIES

When chemistry is sparked between you and someone outside your primary relationship, it is important to acknowledge what you are feeling, first to yourself, then to the other person in ways that are appropriate for the nature of the project and your connection. Weigh things out internally before deciding what must be said to the party sparking interest, and then determine if and how to address this with your SO.

Below is a dialogue illustrating a respectful way to talk about a strong connection before lines become blurred. This conversation takes place between two people experiencing an attraction to one another who have just completed a difficult and successful project together at work. This instructional dialogue is intended to be a template that can be modified as needed based on your particular situation.

**Begin by acknowledging the project**, the excitement of its success, and the appreciation for how amazing it was to work together. *"We did it! I can't believe we finished in record time. We kicked ass! It was awesome to collaborate with you."*

**Follow the acknowledgment with a boundary-setting statement**, such as, *"I want to be sure that in all the excitement of this project, it's clear that I'm a married guy. I would never want the thrill of working together to blur boundaries. I enjoy working with you and want to make sure we're both committed to maintaining a solid professional relationship."*

She may respond, *"Of course. Me too."* Or perhaps, *"I would never question that."* Even if she seems a bit surprised that you brought it up, it is clarifying for you both to state out loud where you stand. Setting boundaries helps avoid misinterpretation and gives you more freedom to enjoy a solid working connection.

**Follow up with an affirming statement about the future,** *"Great! I'm looking forward to diving in on the upcoming project. We work well together."*

That's it. Short and sweet. Acknowledge the project and set the boundary. Then close with another acknowledgment of the project. No room for ambiguity or assumptions.

## Reflection
### *Assessing Dynamics at Home*

It is important to periodically assess the state of your connection at home. The following questions are designed as thought starters. Reviewing them on a monthly basis helps ensure that you prioritize proactively addressing any challenges that you may have ignored in the past.

- Does it feel like things at home are more frequently drifting into autopilot mode?
- Where have you allowed competing interests to take precedence over your relationship?
- Is there anything you have been ignoring or avoiding?
- Is there anything you believe your spouse has been ignoring or avoiding?
- In what ways has your relationship grown?
- Where do you feel stuck?
- What do can you do better?

- Where would you like more support from your partner?

This is a great exercise to engage in with your partner. You can each review the questions first on your own and then set up a time to discuss.

As an example: If you feel like you have been spending more time at work, you can acknowledge this and let her know you would like to find ways to reconnect and spend more time together. You can let her know that you have been feeling a bit disconnected, distant, or are missing her, and that you would like to spend some time exploring new ways to connect.

Together, create or review your vision for the rest of the year (travel, life goals, etc.) and make some plans. What would you both like more of? Less of? Plan some fun things to do together.

---

### Recovery is about gaining self-awareness and rediscovering who you are as individuals and who you want to be as a couple.

---

Hopefully hearing about Jim and Liz's recovery process helps you see what is possible. You and your partner can also grow stronger through the recovery process. Creating a calm space to listen as she works through her emotions is an important aspect of recovery. Couples with a high degree of determination are more thoroughly able to process and create an even deeper connection and commitment to themselves and each other.

In the next chapter, we will focus on marriage, commitment, and the importance of staying true to your word.

# 13

## The Impact *of* Making, Breaking, *and* Keeping Promises

---

■

---

*"Be impeccable with your word."*
—Don Miguel Ruiz, *The Four Agreements*

Can you imagine a world of impeccable promise-keeping? Just think about it for a moment: What would your life be like if you knew unquestionably that when someone gave you their word, you didn't have to wonder if they meant it, but could unequivocally count on it?

During infidelity recovery promise-keeping is crucial. It can be challenging when you're conflicted about a request and don't want to hurt or disappoint someone else. So, what gets in the way of impeccable word-keeping?

Cultivating impeccability with your word is a form of truth-telling. Keeping your word requires: 1) diligence, 2) an inner commitment to truth-telling, and 3) the ability to decline a request when it doesn't work for you. When someone gives their word, they typically mean it at the time it is given. Or do they? Let's take a deeper look.

Have you ever made a half-hearted promise? Said yes to something you didn't want to do just to appease your partner or avoid an argument? If there was one thing I could convince you to change, it would be not making half-hearted promises or saying yes under pressure. Because they are given reluctantly, promises made under duress are more likely to trigger inner resistance when it comes time to deliver.

Impeccable word-keeping requires self-awareness and self-trust and helps build relational trust. It requires you to cultivate the art of giving a full-hearted yes or a kind, direct no.

## If you are unable to say no, then your yeses aren't true yeses.

Your promises are rendered meaningless when you haven't built up your "no" muscles.

Hesitance to say no, particularly to his partner, most often stems from one or more of the following five things:

1. The desire to please and not disappoint a partner
2. The fear of reprisal that a no may bring
3. Not taking time to consider the request in the context of prior obligations
4. Wanting to shut down a conversation that you are either tired of having or fear will start or continue an argument
5. Growing up in an environment where you took on a people-pleasing role, which essentially meant that you received positive attention from your primary caregiver(s) when you were "good" and disapproval or withdrawal of parental attention when you were "bad" (meaning that you behaved in a way that a caregiver deemed disappointing or unacceptable).

Figuring out what will be considered "good" (pleasing) behavior, to either avoid pain or receive positive affirmation or affection, can be a constantly moving target. Growing up in a dysregulated household, or with an unpredictable parent, can create children who become hyper-focused on pleasing others. This behavior frequently carries over into adulthood.

When you say yes because you don't want to upset, disappoint, get into an argument or hurt someone's feelings, you're doing more of a disservice to the relationship than helping it. Making an inner commitment to being faithful to the word you give is a great muscle to begin strengthening as it helps build greater trust in all areas of your life.

Relationships built on trust are better able to weather life's storms. Granted, it isn't easy to tell someone something that might disappoint them or potentially disrupt your connection. But when you choose to engage in a kind, honest conversation, you open new possibilities for growth, healing, and connection.

**Here's the tricky part:**

---

## While your partner needs to know that you're genuinely sorry for the pain your choices have caused her, regaining her respect requires you to demonstrate both humility and vulnerability without giving up who you are as a man.

---

**There is a danger that in your quest for redemption, you lose your ability to say no.** Let's take a deeper look.

No takes many different forms:

- *Not right now or Not yet.*
- *I'm not sure I can get it done in that time frame.*
- *That is not something I can (am willing to) commit to.*

Being in the recovery stage of a relationship doesn't mean you have to become a *yes man.* While you may be tempted to say yes to everything she asks for out of fear that she will get angry or leave you,

---

## Saying yes out of desperation sets you up for the most challenging F word in a man's vocabulary—failure.

---

You most assuredly will fail to keep your commitments if you don't take the time to consider your yeses in the context of the bigger picture. Most people have some type of electronic scheduling system. Check yours to make sure the requested dates work. If need be, tell her you will check your work schedule to verify and then follow-up.

During the early parts of recovery, you'll probably be called on to say or do a bit more than you're used to. Prioritizing her requests is part of how you make amends and help restore her faith in you. Just make sure your actions align with your commitments.

**A respectful no helps to make your yeses more meaningful and believable.**

**Try This:** The next time you're faced with a request, especially one that has been challenging to fulfill in the past, pause before answering, and consider the probability that you'll be able to honor the request. If you're someone used to saying yes, you can let your partner know in advance that you intend to be more mindful of the commitments you make. You want her to know that she can count on you, which may mean that you take a little more time answering. You also want her to trust your yeses, which means she will sometimes get a "no," a "not yet," or an "I need more time to make an informed decision."

This may be a little tough to implement at first if it isn't something you are used to, but trust me, it will help strengthen your relational trust in the long run.

Next, let's take a look at one of the biggest promises of all: the marriage promise.

### "I PROMISE TO LOVE, HONOR, AND CHERISH..."

No one enters into a marriage thinking they might have an affair. And yet temptation is everywhere—an attractive gal who strikes up a conversation during an evening out with the guys, the attentive woman in the office who seems more into you than your wife, someone you have a few drinks with during an out-of-town convention, an ex that has reached out for a favor that "only you" can take care of.

The woman in each of these situations is more likely to turn your head, when things aren't running quite so smoothly at home, or when you are struggling with other more personal challenges. You are more susceptible to outside influences when things are rocky in another part of your life, or when you are out of alignment with yourself.

States of inner unrest can be difficult to identify at first, as they typically lie slightly beneath the surface of awareness. As we have discussed, there are a variety of personal and relational vulnerabilities that contribute to discontent.

Sometimes discontent shows up early in a marriage. This can particularly be true for couples who have known each other for a long time before tying the knot.

## For Better or for Worse

Traditional marriage vows include a pledge to be there for one another not just during the good times, but through life's difficulties and challenges—"for better or for worse, through sickness and in health, till death..." They don't say, "I'll stay with you until I get bored, or until I find someone who pays more attention to me!"

---

**The more work a couple does to prepare for marriage, including ways to resolve conflict and work through challenges, the stronger their foundation will be for weathering life's storms—which *will* arise.**

---

Whether you're newly married, planning on getting married, or contemplating a re-commitment ceremony, the rest of this chapter offers you an opportunity to dive more deeply into your thoughts on marriage. As you move into relational recovery, you'll be afforded new opportunities to reconsider your promises and how you intend to live them into the future.

Let's peek under the covers of a newer marriage—exploring what led to the man's affair—to examine how a couple can begin to fortify itself upon entering into marriage recovery. To set the stage, a key component for this story is that the husband is a repeat offender. This wasn't his first affair.

## Working Through a Repeat Offense: Justin, Sophia, and Jen

Justin and Sophia had been together for a total of six years—married for almost one. A couple of months before they got married, Justin formed a relationship with a woman at work.

When Justin started with the company, it was Jen who spent time *showing him the ropes.* Jen found Justin funny and went out of her way to make sure he was adapting well. Justin appreciated the extra time Jen spent helping him acclimate. What began as friendly banter and seemingly innocent flirtations between two coworkers ultimately led to their affair, which continued on and off through Justin and Sophia's short marriage.

My work with this couple began as they were about to celebrate their one-year wedding anniversary, when Sophia discovered that Justin had once again connected with Jen. (Her initial discovery occurred shortly before their wedding.) The couple came to see me to sort through what happened and determine whether their relationship had enough traction to withstand the latest round of Justin's indiscretions, or if it was time to call it quits.

During our session, Sophia began by talking about how hurt and devastated she was upon learning Justin had broken not only his promise to stay away from his AP but his marriage promise as well.

*"You know what the saddest thing is?"* Sophia said. *"I gave him the benefit of the doubt. I moved on after the first time. I trusted him, and now I feel like a fool and don't know how I can trust him ever again."* Tears began to roll down Sophia's cheeks as she continued. *"We had a great relationship. I mean, we argued occasionally over trivial things, but we were solid. When people asked me if I could ever picture Justin cheating, I said, 'Never. He's not that kind of guy.' Our friends and family had no idea that he cheated just before we were married. I never told a soul. I didn't want them to look at him differently. I just swallowed it up and kept going. That's what I do. Suck it up and move forward.*

*"He swore up and down the first time that it didn't mean anything and that it was over. I don't understand how this is happening to me again. He promised. We took vows! If he wants to be with her, I told him, just go. He said he was confused. I told him to just leave the house until he can become unconfused. I will not compete with this woman for his attention. He is my husband! He needs to make up his frickin' mind. Her or me. Or maybe we just need to be done. Never in a million years would I have thought we would be here. Again!"*

Justin sat there shaking his head and quietly said, *"I got confused. Maybe I was scared. I slipped. I didn't think it would ever happen again. But it did. I was confused, but I'm not anymore. Being away from you for the last two weeks gave me a chance to really think about things."* (Justin had moved in with his sister after Sophia found out about his most recent indiscretion.) *"I don't want her. I want you. I want us. I want our marriage to work."*

Sophia responded, *"I let my guard down. You begged me to give you another chance. And I did. You swore it would never happen again. We got married, for Christ's sake. You promised me. You promised, Justin! I never would have married you if I thought you weren't over her. You said it was a one-time thing. You said she didn't mean anything, and I believed you. Boy, was I stupid. So stupid to trust you. Again. I have no idea what to do or even what to believe anymore. I don't know if I can stay married to a liar!"*

## THE VULNERABILITY FACTORS FOR A REPEAT OFFENSE

Repeat offenses do exponentially more damage and greatly lengthen the trust-rebuilding process. The three strongest vulnerabilities for a repeat offense are:

1. Frequent exposure to someone you're trying to break it off with (This is particularly common in workplace affairs.)
2. Connections with the AP that aren't completely severed
3. The initial affair being inadequately worked through

Justin's situation included all three. He saw his AP, Jen, at work every day. They didn't cleanly cut the cord after his initial affair. And Justin and Sophia didn't engage in any type of recovery work after the first incident.

## JUSTIN PLEADS HIS CASE

*"I wanted to break it off with her, and I did. I told her we needed to stop, that I couldn't do this anymore. She started crying. I hated to see her cry, but I held my ground and told her it was all too much, that we needed to be done. I thought it was over..."*

Sophia interrupted. *"You thought it was over? You thought? Really? Doesn't sound like there was too much thinking going on. I need you to do more than 'think' it's over. What the hell happened? I need to know more than 'I tried,' Justin. I want details."*

**Commentary:**
Affair discovery is a very fragile time for all involved. It is the practitioner's role to make sure each person feels heard and to protect the couple from further injury as much as possible. The one who has been betrayed needs to be able to talk about things and ask enough questions to better understand what happened, even though full understanding is virtually impossible. While sharing the affair story is hurtful, in order to heal, it does need to be discussed in ways that helps bring a couple closure. When they shortcut the process, a recurrence is far more likely. That was a contributing factor to Justin and Sophia's situation.

When Justin's initial indiscretion was discovered, wedding invitations had already been mailed. The venue had been secured with a non-refundable deposit. Sophia was so excited that they were finally making it official. All of this weighed heavily upon her decision to quickly try to put Justin's initial betrayal behind them. He was sorry. He promised: *never again.* Sophia chalked it all up to wedding jitters. They had been together a long time. She could forgive one mistake. Right?

Well, not exactly.

---

## Yes, forgiveness is key to moving past betrayal. But forgiveness that occurs too quickly, without doing the deeper work, can be a smoke screen for avoidance.

---

Shoving an affair under the rug doesn't help it heal.

### THE NEED TO KNOW: SOPHIA QUESTIONS WHAT HAPPENED

Sophia repeated a little more softly, *"Just tell me what happened, Justin. Please. I need to know."*

Justin continued: *"Okay. Like I said, I told her that we needed to be done—that I couldn't see her anymore. She said she understood, but I could tell she was really hurt. We didn't talk to each other for at least a couple months. Then one day we both ended up in line at Starbucks before work. She asked how we were doing. I told her we were doing fine. And that was that.*

*"A week later she sent me a text. Something funny she saw on TikTok. I responded with LOL. Then we began texting a little more. About a week later, she said a bunch of people from work were going out for happy hour. She wanted to know if I'd be open to joining. She didn't see why we couldn't be 'just friends.' At that moment I thought, We're both adults. Why can't we just be friends? I thought back to when I first joined the company. She was good to me. We were friends for a while before anything more happened. I thought we could get back to that. And I felt bad about how much I'd hurt her. So, I agreed to join the group for a quick drink after work.*

*"We were going out with others from work. I figured we could keep things casual, but after a few drinks, when everyone else had left, Jen and I continued talking. I walked her to her car. She gave me a hug and then kissed me. I didn't mean for anything to happen. I really thought we could just be friends."* Justin hung his head and sighed. *"Guess I was wrong."*

*"Just friends? Really, Justin? You told me you wouldn't talk to her anymore. Broke that promise too, didn't you? And now you're sitting here telling me you began talking to her because you thought you could be just friends and didn't want to hurt her feelings? What about my feelings?"* Sophia's voice began to quiver. *"Did you even think about me?"*

## CAN FORMER AFFAIR PARTNERS BE "JUST FRIENDS"?

When Jen reached back out, Justin responded. He did feel bad about hurting her and didn't see any harm in texting. He figured being friendly would be better than being a jerk and completely ignoring her. They began texting more frequently. Funny memes. Inside jokes. Stories about other people in the office. Justin found himself looking forward to Jen's texts. She made him laugh.

They were entering into dangerous territory for former affair partners. As we have discussed, the likelihood of maintaining a friendship with someone you're trying to cut ties with is slim, especially when a breakup is still fresh. Reconnection is much more common if you don't set up strong boundaries, especially at the beginning.

As our sessions continued, it became abundantly clear to Justin that if he wanted to make his marriage work, he and Jen couldn't maintain any type of friendship. And Jen wouldn't be satisfied with being *just friends* anyway. Just before Sophia found out about their second time around, Jen had told Justin that she had fallen in love with him. That revelation shocked and confused Justin. He never intended to go down *that* road.

Having a woman say *"I love you"* can evoke different types of feelings inside a man. In the case of an affair, it can be shocking when it comes unexpectedly or when he doesn't see the relationship in the same light.

Jen's confession made him realize he was in trouble, and that he needed to end things for good. He told Jen he couldn't see her anymore, that it was all becoming too complicated. He wanted to make things right with his wife. He asked her to please not text or call him. As you heard, Jen said she would *try*.

## THE DISCOVERY

An *"I'll try"* is different than a solid commitment. It leaves wiggle room. As discussed in chapter 11, successfully closing the door on an affair involves clear, kind, direct communication. That door needs to be firmly shut. Not doing so can result in one or both parties reaching out during an emotional moment, which was exactly what happened in Justin's case.

Let's rewind a bit to see what happened after Justin's first attempt to end things with Jen.

About a week after Jen's "I'll try" in response to Justin's request to end their affair, before Sophia knew about his second indiscretion, she heard his phone beep. Justin was in the kitchen, so she picked it up and headed toward the kitchen to hand it to him. On an impulse, she clicked on the text and began reading. In it, Jen once again professed her love for Justin and asked him to reconsider. Jen said she knew that he loved her too. She ended with, "You don't have to leave your wife. Just don't leave me!"

An enraged Sophia walked into the kitchen, shoved the phone in Justin's face, and exclaimed, *"Explain this!"*

Justin panicked. He had told Jen he was done. Why was she still texting him? His immediate thought was, *Why the hell did I leave my phone sitting on the bed?*

Sophia's discovery sparked a heated exchange between the two of them. She was irate. Justin was scrambling. He said he was confused but that the affair was over. He wanted to put it all behind him and move on. *Why now? Why did she have to find out now?* he thought to himself. Justin knew getting over this one wasn't going to be easy. Could Sophia ever forgive him?

He said, *"I am so, so sorry. Nothing is going on right now. I swear. It is over. I don't know why she sent me that text. I don't love her. And I don't believe she really loves me. I love you."* At that moment there were no words that could offer Sophia comfort. She wasn't about to believe anything he said.

It turned out Justin hadn't ended things as cleanly as he thought. He needed to have one final conversation with Jen to end things clearly and directly.

## CLOSING THE DOOR ONCE AND FOR ALL

Justin told Sophia he would fix things and make sure Jen knew it was over. He texted Jen and let her know they needed to talk. They set up a time for a phone call. He told Jen that it was impossible for them to maintain any type of friendship, that he was determined to make it work with his wife, and that she needed to respect his decision. Once again, she said she would *try*. Justin let Jen know she needed to do more than try. He told her that if she reached out in the future, he would not be taking her calls. He said he would be cordial at work if they happened to pass each other in the hallway, but that he would be adjusting things to minimize any type of contact. Since they no longer worked in the same department, there would be no work reason for them to connect at work.

This time Justin's communication was intentional and direct. He got clear regarding what he wanted, and clearly communicated that to Jen, which helped her realize she needed to let go of her hope they might one day be together. Justin's strength helped Jen be strong. It was clear that she needed to let him go. No wiggle room. Jen's recovery work entailed her taking a deeper look at what she wanted and creating healthier ways to engage with projects and choose available men.

## WHAT WENT WRONG?
## THE INTERSECTION OF SILENCE AND OPPORTUNITY

Through the process of our work together, Justin examined his AVFs. We explored the conditions that helped set the stage for his affair.

Seven months before they were to marry, Justin had moved in with Sophia and her sister. Justin and Sophia were newly engaged and wanted to focus on saving money for a house. Justin moving in seemed like the sensible thing to do.

It turned out that living with Sophia and her sister wasn't as easy as he thought. The couple had little to no privacy as her sister had a boyfriend who was frequently there as well. Justin had stepped into a strong household dynamic that Sophia was much more comfortable with. While Justin had briefly mentioned to Sophia early on that he wished they had more privacy, he didn't talk about his growing struggles with their living situation.

Justin began feeling more disconnected from Sophia, who seemed fine with the way things were. She was focused on the wedding and excited about the idea that the first home they would both live in together, they would potentially own. *Just suck it up*, he told himself. *It's not forever. It will all be worth it when we can buy a house.*

Instead of talking to Sophia, Justin began talking to Jen about his struggles with his living situation. She listened and offered him tips on how to make the best of things. In addition, Jen continually let Justin know how good of a job he was doing at work. "I know it won't be long until you're promoted. You're catching on so fast!" Jen was right about that one. Justin was promoted rather quickly into a senior accounting position in another division of the company.

The challenge was that Justin was talking to a woman he found himself growing more attracted to about things he should have been discussing with his fiancé. One day, things went too far, and instead of just talking, they ended up having sex in his car. That was the first of several passionate encounters.

## JUSTIN'S AWAKENING

Here's a window into a later session when Justin was expressing his deep remorse and desire to put his marriage back together. He desperately wanted to rebuild trust with Sophia, come back home, and restart their married life together unencumbered by his past choices.

*"How do I convince her it's over?"* he asked me. *"I know I told her that before, but this time I really mean it. I want my wife back. I will do whatever it takes to make this work."*

I invited him to dig a little deeper. *"You've been down this road before. What's different this time?"*

Justin paused for a moment as he reflected on something a friend recently said to him.

*"One day I saw an old friend Johann at Costco. I hadn't seen him since shortly after our wedding. He waved me over and said to me, 'Hey man, how's your wife doing?'*

*"I gotta' tell you, there was something about hearing him call Sophia my 'wife' that struck me. Earlier that week, Sophia had said to me that she was sad that we didn't get much of a chance to be married before the affair threw a wrench into things. I finally got it. She wasn't my girlfriend anymore. She was my wife. My wife!*

*"I realize now that I was never really a husband to Sophia...never really considered what it meant to be her husband."* Justin attempted to rub away the tears beginning to form. *"Even though we had spent most of the previous five years together, I was now a husband, not a boyfriend. It hit me hard, ya know. I felt so ashamed of what I had done to her and our marriage, and even to the woman at work. My actions hurt a lot of people. And the most important one of all is my wife."*

*"I hear you,"* I said. *"I hear that the idea of being a husband stirred something inside of you. And it's as if you began to consider what that really means for the very first time."*

*"Yeah."* Justin sighed. *"And I feel so bad about that. I don't know what I was thinking, getting involved with this other person. We started out as friends. I liked her. She was a good listener, but I let it go too far. And I hurt them both."*

## REPARATION: DELIVERING A HEARTFELT APOLOGY

Listen as Justin describes his remorse and delivers a heartfelt apology to Sophia during a subsequent session when the two of them were sitting together on my couch.

*"I put everything at risk. Everything. And I hurt my wife so deeply. She didn't deserve that. I'm so sorry about all of it."*

*"Can you look at her and tell her that?"* I prompted softly.

Justin took both of Sophia's hands into his. He looked into his wife's eyes with great authenticity and humility and said, *"I'm so sorry for betraying your trust, sorry for all the pain my actions caused you, sorry for hurting your heart. I know I fucked things up, again! I truly hope that somewhere in your heart, you can find the strength to forgive me. Even if you can't right now, I hope you can forgive me one day. I'm sorry for not being the husband you deserve. I so want the opportunity to be that man. I really do. I promise I will do whatever it takes to make things right with you if you can find it in your heart to give me the chance. I love you so much, Sophia, and I'm so very, very sorry."*

Tears rolled down their cheeks as they both felt the pain, vulnerability, and significance of Justin speaking from his heart. This was a deeply moving and healing moment for them both. Justin's sincerity and his deep love and care for Sophia filled the room.

Engaging in heartfelt apologies (yes, you will need to apologize more than once!) is a critical component of the healing and reconnection journey. These types of apologies deepen intimacy and set the stage for rebuilding trust. They have the power to strengthen relationships in unforeseen ways.

Justin's apology was just that: sincere and heartfelt. While it wasn't his first *"I'm sorry"* and wouldn't be his last, it was certainly his deepest and most authentic thus far. (Chapter 25 offers a roadmap for crafting a heartfelt apology.)

Vulnerability and humility go hand-in-hand in the rebuilding process. A person who has an affair must be willing to get real, own their mistakes, and truly want to make amends; otherwise, the likelihood of repetition looms large. And little by little, a spouse must be willing to let her partner back into her heart.

Thorough recovery from infidelity requires time, patience, and a steadfast commitment to yourself, your spouse, and your relational health.

## RECONCILIATION

Sophia and Justin made a commitment to work on their marriage and began engaging in collaborative conversations to design the life *they* wanted to live.

They recognized they needed a place of their own. While living with Sophia's sister allowed them to save money, doing so compromised their ability to truly begin their life together as a married couple. They decided that renting a place of their own, even though it meant delaying their home purchase for a couple more years, was an important step in solidifying their marriage. They found a great apartment complex and forged new friendships with several other married couples.

That was three years ago. Sophia called me the other day to let me know that she learned she was pregnant the same day that they had submitted an offer on their first home.

Sophia and Justin put in the work, the second time around, to rebuild trust, thoroughly heal from Justin's affair, and fortify their relationship. While thoughts of the affair still comes up in her mind from time to time, Sophia told me that she can much more quickly let it go. She said, *"While it's certainly not the way I envisioned our married life starting out, looking back I think it was a catalyst for creating a much stronger relationship and marriage. And I believe we'll be much more thoughtful about how we parent as well."*

## Reflection
### *Being Married and Being a Husband*

One of the key realizations Justin made during his affair recovery process was that he hadn't previously explored what it truly meant to "be a husband." If you are married or contemplating marriage, I invite you to consider what being a husband means to you. Here are a few thought-starters:

- What did you envision marriage to look like? How has your marriage stacked up against your vision?
- What scares you most about getting, being, or staying married?
- What are the three most important characteristics that you as a husband can bring to the table to help create and maintain a strong partnership?
- What are three potential stumbling blocks to maintaining a strong connection with your spouse?
- What are the top two areas to consistently fine tune in order to strengthen your partnership?
- If you were offering advice to someone newly married on being a husband, what would you tell them?

If you're working through this book together, it's important for you both to consider these questions. Invite your spouse to first answer these questions regarding how she views your role as her husband. Then she can answer them for how she views her role as your spouse. You can consider how you see her role as well in light of these questions. Feel free to elaborate or add more areas to explore as you see fit.

## Preparing for a Fresh Start

Whether you're preparing for marriage for the first time or recommitting to a fresh start with your spouse, if you haven't already done so, it can be helpful to review the in-depth questions in Chapter 8. These questions can help you both identify the influences your upbringing had on your beliefs, reactions, and responses to life. Working through them can help strengthen your foundation as a couple as they offer you the opportunity to deepen your understanding of yourselves and each other.

**Many couples create a ritual celebration, like a renewal of vows, to commemorate their recommitment to their marriage and one another.** Creating a ceremony is a powerful way to acknowledge the work you have done to reset the tone for your relationship. Like January 1st of a new year, rituals of this nature offer a demarcation in time, symbolizing letting go of the past and creating a new vision for the future.

## Reflection
## Redesigning Your Relationship

Whether you are an unmarried couple who has not yet taken wedding vows or a couple who has been married for a while, taking time to design the next part of your life together is an important step. One way to do this is to consider your values, career goals, religious/spiritual beliefs, extended family, location, desire for adventure, ideas about sex and exploration, sleep patterns, need for validation and external stimulation, finances, health and well-being, physical engagement, and creative pursuits.

You can schedule a time each week to explore one or two topics together. You could each sit down with a blank piece of paper and write (or draw, or even create song lyrics) describing what you envision ongoing fulfillment would look like in each area.

Whatever you choose to do, have fun with it. This is a time for you to strengthen your connection and ability to talk about or revisit topics that can strengthen your connection now and in the future.

# PART SIX

—————————————— ■ ——————————————

# Understanding Things *from* Her Point *of* View: Supporting Your Partner's Recovery

The next part of your journey focuses on deepening your understanding of your partner's recovery process and explores ways to facilitate optimal healing for all concerned.

**The Recovery Process for Her:** The first chapter is dedicated to providing you with insight into your partner's experience, offer guidance on how you can best support her, and highlights important considerations for you to keep in mind.

**For your Spouse / SO:** The next chapter is written directly to your partner. It has been designed to assist her better manage her own recovery and increase her understanding of the emotional responses she may be experiencing. It may also be beneficial for you to review this chapter to gain further insight into her process.

**For the AP (Affair Partner):** A brief chapter is also included to help the AP pick up the pieces of her life after her affair with you. It is my hope that any woman involved in an affair with an unavailable man will pick up this book and use it to better understand and engage in her own recovery work. This includes your AP.

I am confident that this section will provide you with valuable insights into your spouse's challenges and empower you to navigate your situation more effectively. Additionally, my hope is that it will assist the women involved gain a greater understanding of themselves and actively working through their own recovery. It is important to note that the most effective healing occurs when all individuals involved in the affair triangle engage in their own recovery process.

# 14

## The Recovery Process *for* Her

■

*"Love is not a fragile, shiny thing, kept separate from the pain and misery of life. ... It is born of our willingness to learn from our mistakes. ... We dance not just with the bright, cheerful, effervescent, trusting side of our mates, but with the dark, fearful, sad, angry and defensive sides. If we aren't willing to dance with the dark side, the foundation never gets built. We never get to experience the fullness of love that we are capable of giving and receiving. ... This is the dance. It's not a perfect dance."*
—Paul Ferrini, *Dancing with the Beloved, Opening our hearts to the lessons of love*

Time and time again, I find myself sitting across from a bewildered spouse who is trying to comprehend how their life partner could have strayed from their relationship and become involved in an affair. They meticulously analyze every detail in their mind, attempting to solve a puzzle with crucial pieces missing.

*"How could he cheat on me? I just don't get it. Never in a million years would I have thought we would be struggling with this. What happened to the man I married?"*

In truth, a betrayed spouse will never be able to fully grasp what transpired and why. Often, the best she can do is to try to contextualize what happened. Her mood will fluctuate. If she still loves you, she will *want* to believe and trust in you again. However, she may also be struck by thoughts or memories of times when you were not present, prompting her to embark on a journey to uncover the "truth" about the affair—its details, timing, circumstances, and motivations.

Much like an archeological dig, the bones of the past leave clues that are carefully sifted through to try to reconstruct the story of what occurred. Some clues lie buried deep within the psyche of the relationship itself.

One of the most frequent questions that emerges from a betrayed partner is: *"Why did he have to keep lying to me?"* Nobody wants to be fooled, especially by someone they love and trust.

Partners can have a kind of sixth sense about infidelity. It can take great courage to speak their suspicions out loud. When they finally come forward to ask the questions, it may not result in the clarity they were hoping for.

Often, when initially confronted with the opportunity to come clean, the shock of potential discovery results in an even stronger cover-up. Rather than truth-telling the one who betrayed frequently digs a deeper ditch.

---

**If she is asking the question, she either strongly suspects or already knows the answer.**

---

## From Her Perspective

**"First of all, if you learn a simple trick, Scout, you'll get along a lot better with all kinds of folks. You never really understand a person until you consider things from his point of view . . . until you climb into his skin and walk around in it." Atticus Finch**

—*To Kill a Mockingbird*, Harper Lee

You may find throughout the recovery process that your partner can move from calm to distraught in a nanosecond. Sometimes she may seem perfectly fine, and you may assume things are okay; then, BOOM, it hits. The littlest thing can trigger a seismic wave. She may hear a song that triggers a memory or recall a time when she questioned your whereabouts or feelings she had that she ignored, and her emotions flip. Anger. Rage. Sadness. Silence. Tears.

## Working Through Grief and Trauma

For some women, shifts from one state to another will be fierce. You will definitely know when she is hitting a tough emotion. Others may work through their sorrow and discontent in silence. Regardless of her outer expression, know that during this time your woman is grieving the loss of the relationship and trust she thought she had. And she will be working through the trauma associated with the betrayal by someone she knew and deeply loved.

Grief comes in waves. And the vast majority of affairs involve intense grief. She will likely be grieving the loss of the marriage she thought she had. She may also be grieving the potential loss of security, as she faces the idea of losing you as she considers what life would look like on her own.

One client told me, *"I had this wonderful, idealized picture of who I thought 'we' were as a couple. I was proud to go out with him and interact with our friends. Now I don't know who we will be at the end of this, and I can't be sure if I will fit into what's left."*

As you rebuild your relationship, your juxtaposition to one another will be changing. Even if you become healthier, change is still occurring. As most change management consultants will tell you, any type of change is challenging. Leaving the comfort of the familiar and your anticipated future can trigger a deep sense of loss and grief.

You may be familiar with the Elisabeth Kübler-Ross stages of grief, which include denial, anger, bargaining, depression, and acceptance. There are many other grief models out there, but they all include these general emotions and processes. Accepting and managing these emotions is imperative to moving through the recovery process.

Closely related to grief is trauma. As a reminder, the word *trauma,* which we reviewed in depth in Chapter 8, originates from a Greek word meaning "to wound or pierce." Its original meaning referred to an external wound, but its later definition was expanded to a "wound inflicted not upon the body but upon the mind."[23]

*Merriam-Webster's Collegiate Dictionary* defines trauma as:

- "A deeply distressing or disturbing experience"
- "Emotional shock following a stressful event or a physical injury, which may be associated with physical shock and sometimes leads to long-term neurosis"

In essence, trauma is an experience that causes deep distress, disturbs your sense of well-being and leaves a mark that never gets completely erased. A traumatic occurrence in the present triggers a cascade of traumatic experiences, large and small, from the past. If your partner has previously experienced abuse—emotional or physical—or had a previous partner or parent who was unfaithful, her pain over your infidelity will be multiplied. Current trauma stacks on top of prior traumas.

---

## "Trauma changes not only what we think, and what we think about, but also changes our very capacity to think."
—Bessel van der Kolk, *The Body Keeps the Score*

---

Being traumatized by a loved one creates inner confusion. As we discussed earlier in the book, some people tend to **move toward connection** when scared or threatened. A movement toward someone is activated by a deep desire to connect, coupled with an intense fear of abandonment or disconnection, which intensifies this need.

Other people tend to distance themselves to find a greater sense of inner calm or peace. **Movement away** is triggered by the need to self-protect, and by distrust in a partner's ability to provide safety. This behavior is activated by a fear that *getting too close will hurt more* or that they will become engulfed in what the other person needs or wants, thus losing themselves.

During the infidelity recovery process, you will most likely experience your spouse sometimes moving toward you and other times pulling away. Both movements will be triggered by fear and fluctuations in her emotional state.

When the shock of the affair hits your partner, and when you come face-to-face with her pain and disappointment, you may feel a heightened willingness to do anything to relieve the pain. This is a vulnerable time when it is difficult for either of you to focus on anything else.

No one wants to believe their actions have brought about trauma to another, especially someone they love. But unfortunately, infidelity inflicts trauma. I am sharing this not to make you feel worse than you most likely already do, but rather to help you better understand the depth of her pain, her changing moods, and why full recovery takes time.

While you can contribute to her healing process, some aspects are hers alone to work through. She will need to recover her sense of self, fortify her self-worth, and reclaim her confidence. Your SO needs to decide what she wants (which may or may not be the relationship), and reclaim her power, passion, and purpose.

One of the most difficult aspects of your partner's recovery is her tendency to spin out inside of her head. A betrayed partner's thoughts can grow, multiply, and expand pretty darn fast. Before you know it, she may be in a full-blown meltdown. She may either totally shut you out or unleash a fire-breathing rage monster that will burn everything in its wake, including you. Healing is not a straight line. It includes many ups and downs. The ability to stay with it, and not run from it, is critical to recovery.

When outbursts or withdrawals occur, you may feel like things are hopeless, or that maybe your relationship will never go back to the way it was. The truth is it *will* never go back to the way it was. However, what is possible as you work through your affair is that the two of you can lay the foundation for a more mindful connection. In this "new" relationship, you will talk about things instead of sweeping them under the rug, which paves the way for a stronger and more authentic connection.

How is that level of improvement possible? 1) Potential loss can level up your sense of urgency. 2) You are focusing on your relationship and discussing things in ways you may have not done before. 3) Things once put on the back burner are now taking center stage. 4) You are taking a more introspective look at yourself and making more mindful choices.

Full recovery is like cleaning out your garage, tossing out what you don't need and taking care to organize what is most important. Thorough affair recovery can not only save your relationship but provide you with the tools to make it better.

# The Hardest Parts for Her

**"Discussions are better than arguments, because an argument is designed to find out who is right, and a discussion is designed to find out what is right."**

—Alan Stein, Jr., motivational speaker

Many people assume the toughest part of infidelity recovery is getting past the idea or image of a partner engaging in sexual activities with someone else. While that is tough to swallow, hearing that a partner said, "I love you," to another person can be even tougher. The idea of your partner falling in love with someone else is often more difficult to recover from than just thinking about a sexual connection. Sometimes the most problematic aspects can be the lies told before discovery, the denial when questioned, or the feeling of being fooled by someone you loved and trusted.

Here are some of the primary struggles your partner will most likely be experiencing:

**She will be grappling with how you gave a part of yourself to another person**. A precious part. Your spouse is imagining you courting her, wooing her, desiring her, and wanting to spend time with her. These are the things every woman craves in her relationship. We each long to be wanted, and she now envisions someone else as the object of your attention and desire. Your wife will most likely experience both jealousy and envy as she is:

- **Jealous** (and afraid) that she was being replaced by someone else.
- **Envious** of the things the AP was getting that she may not have been receiving from you.

These two emotions can trigger both sadness and anger. Remember that underneath the anger is sorrow.

**She will blame herself and question her adequacy as a relational partner.** No matter how confident and self-assured she may seem on the outside, deep inside, she will be looking for what she may have done *wrong*. She may also be wondering, *"What's wrong with me? Am I not good enough? Can I ever be good enough?"*

**If the person you have connected with is her friend or a family member, the betrayal factor is at least doubled.** This is the kind of thing that strains families, destroys friendships, and makes the recovery process even more intense. Not only has she lost her trust in you, but she has also lost her trust in someone else who mattered to her. I have seen betrayals occur with a best friend, the wife of someone in a couple's inner circle, her cousin, or even her sister.

**She may be fearing it will happen again, or that your marriage will not work out— and that she will need to prepare for a life alone.** While sorting through the details of the affair and maintaining the day-to-day aspects of the family, she may feel like she needs to keep one foot out the door in case your relationship doesn't get restored. This can trigger abandonment fears as well as insecurities about how she will manage her life, the finances, or cope as a single parent.

**She may feel unsure where to go for support—desperately needing to talk to others while not wanting to reveal too many details.** She may want to be sensitive to your feelings too, not exposing you to friends and family whose opinion of you may change if they found out. She may even feel her own shame, as she may feel it reflects on her role as a wife or choice in a partner. Her healing does involve her being able to talk this through with someone. You can't heal from betrayal in isolation or alone.

**If your partner has shared your betrayal with her family and/or friends, it is possible that it could make her more hesitant to move forward.** Friends who have supported your partner during this difficult time may not have the same positive opinion of you. Reconnecting with you might lead to negative reactions from them. Ultimately, your partner will need to find a way to communicate with them from a place of strength, believing that your commitment to repairing the relationship is genuine and can stand the test of time.

The more you can give her room while still showing her—through your words and actions—that you are not going anywhere, that you love her, and that she matters, the more quickly and thoroughly you can begin rebuilding trust and recreating your *new normal* as a couple. The steps you take to renew your relationship and rebuild your wife's trust are not to be taken lightly.

---

**While you cannot unbreak the broken promises, you can strengthen your commitment to her by making new promises that you consistently keep.**

---

---
## Reflection
---

What is the toughest part of working through the affair for you? What do you imagine is the toughest part for her? If you don't know, ask.

## Some Additional Dos and Don'ts with Your Partner

In an earlier chapter, we reviewed some **Emergency Dos and Don'ts**. The "dos and don'ts" list is expanded here to guide your recovery beyond the "emergency" phase:

**Don't become defensive. Do take 100 percent of the responsibility for your actions.** Remember, even if there were problems at home, *you* are the one who betrayed your SO and the commitment you made. Becoming defensive or deflecting doesn't help either of you heal.

**Don't lie to her. Do be thoughtful with your responses—even to the little things.** Remember, you are rebuilding trust. Lying or telling half-truths undermines what you are working to rebuild. You will be repeatedly tested with this. Take your time responding. Don't immediately jump in with an answer to try to shut down a conversation. Even little lies do great damage in the long run.

**Don't let your impatience or anger get the best of you. Do take a time-out as needed.** Yes, you certainly may grow tired of all the questioning and just want to put this all behind you, but healing takes time. The more thoroughly you work through things now, the greater the chance of keeping your relationship intact and weathering future storms. That doesn't mean she gets to beat you up with her words. When discussions get heated, take time and space to regroup.

**Don't reread or let her read old emails or texts from your AP. Do be prepared to grant her greater access to your phone and other media.** Information access is a tough topic for both parties to discuss. Know that you will be subject to additional scrutiny for a time. Your partner wants to know the truth and examine what she may have missed. She may want carte blanche access to all things *yours*.

I help my couples make a distinction between past, current, and future correspondence. To move forward, at least for a while, you may need to give her the ability to check to ensure there are no current communications with your AP.

I don't advise, however, for either of you to read steamy past texts or emails. Like discussing the details of physical intimacy, reading intimate correspondence between you and the AP just creates more heartache. (If there have been sexy connections in writing, hopefully these aren't things you have saved.)

Some women fight me on wanting to read old messages, stating that unless they can "know everything," they cannot move forward. I advise against grave-digging. We are trying to put the past to rest, not excavate it in ways that breathe new life into it. Enough information needs to be shared to help a couple heal but not so much that it keeps the wound festering. Each of you will have to give something up in service to healing.

One woman told me her rule of thumb for what details she wanted to know of her husband's affair: *"I only asked questions I truly wanted to know the answers to. Initially I had a lot of questions, but as I got answers, I realized that I didn't really want to know everything. So, I started asking only the questions I was prepared to face head-on."*

While the needs of each individual and couple may vary, it is important to discuss and create an agreement on what and how information is shared. If you are working with a counselor or coach, this is a great topic to have them help you both sort through.

**Don't think you can only apologize once and be done with it. Do apologize—often.** Let her know how sorry you are that you betrayed and hurt her and that you know how much you've disappointed her. As much as you probably want to put the details behind you, this repeated willingness to express your contrition will help her heal. You will need to do this at various times throughout the recovery process. Remember, the more earnest you are with your apology, the greater its impact. (Chapter 25 walks you through the process of creating and delivering a heartfelt apology.)

Many women have told me that the one thing they let their guy know at the beginning was: *"If you ever cheat, we're done."* Now that the thing she feared most has happened, her world is crushed. Even if there were struggles in the relationship, a woman is typically shocked upon discovering her man has been unfaithful. To heal, forgive, and rebuild trust, she must ultimately come to terms with what occurred, reflect on her own life, and find inner peace.

Chances are that your SO may have picked up this book for you. If so, she may have already read this section. If not, you may suggest that she read it. You can use it as a discussion tool to discover which parts fit for her and which ones she struggles with.

I hope the chapters in this section are shedding some additional light on the healing process for you both.

# Secrets, Lies, and the Fear of Discovery

**"The impetus for most marital lies does not stem from the wish to deceive, but rather from the wish to keep the relationship as it is."**

—*Tell Me No Lies, How to Stop Lying to Your Partner and Yourself,*
Ellyn Bader, PhD, and Peter Pearson, PhD

Lies. From little "white" ones to big ugly ones, we tell them all the time. Why do we lie, especially to those we care about? In their book *Tell Me No Lies,*[24] couples therapists Ellyn Bader and Peter Pearson take a deep dive into the lies people tell in close relationships. They argue that people predominantly lie in order to keep things the way they are. We lie to try to keep our relationship from being disrupted.

At the core of it, we lie to avoid dealing with uncomfortable situations. We lie to avoid admitting we did something wrong or admitting that we engaged in behavior that we promised we wouldn't. We lie when we feel ashamed. We lie when we don't want someone we care about to think less of us. We lie to avoid letting someone down or hurting their feelings. In the case of betrayal, people lie to avoid exposing their secrets—to keep a partner from getting too close to the truth. Lying is an attempt to cover the shame at the center of betrayal and to avoid the potential pain exposure would bring.

In the end though, lies don't just disappear. Even if the person being lied to never finds out or has their suspicions confirmed, lies linger in the energy field between two people, weaving themselves into the fabric of the relationship itself. Intimacy suffers in the wake of deception.

The next story offers a deeper look at the ways in which fear of discovery plays into denial.

# Denial: Laura and John's Story

Laura and John had been married for twenty-two years. Laura suspected that John was having an affair. Instead of staying silent and wondering, she decided to ask. When she confronted him about her suspicions, instead of coming clean, John denied involvement with his AP.

**Let's hear what Laura had to say about what was going on before and during her discovery of John's affair.**

*"I just knew something was going on. I could tell that John was hiding something. Finally, I got the courage to ask him straight up: Are you cheating on me? Not only did he deny it, but he became angry.*

*"'How could you think that?' he said to me. 'You know how hard I'm working to support our family. Do you think I would do that to you? To our marriage? What kind of a man do you think I am?' Then he pounded his fist on the table, stomped upstairs, and slammed the bedroom door.*

*"Immediately, I froze…swallowed everything I was going to say. John doesn't get angry a lot, but when he does, it shuts me down. I think he knows that. Maybe that's his way of shutting me up, of avoiding the topic altogether. Well, it worked. I certainly wasn't going to go chasing after him when he was in that frame of mind.*

*"I began to wonder if maybe I was just making it all up in my mind. The truth is I didn't want to believe he could be that guy. And yet I knew something was off, but I just buttoned it all up…tried to shut it down in my mind and ignore what I was feeling. I told myself maybe things would get better. And they did…for a time. John began making more of an effort and coming home on time. I thought maybe it had been my imagination. Maybe he was just stressed at work. Maybe everything would be okay.…"*

In truth, John was having an affair. So why not come clean when Laura accused him? Surely, he knew she knew. What was he thinking?

**Let's hear what John had to say about his denial.**

*"Last week Laura came up to me, without any warning, and asked if I was having an affair. Just came right out and asked. I was shocked. I had tried to be careful—to separate work and home. I didn't want her to know. Ever.*

*"I had been thinking that it all needed to stop. But before I even had the chance to stop it, she asked. I just couldn't tell her. I couldn't hurt her like that. I felt so ashamed. So, what did I do? Well, I got angry with her for even bringing it up. There was no way I could face her. I wasn't ready to sit there and listen to all the questions I knew she would ask. I just wanted to shut it all down, to shut her down. So, I lied. Straight to her face. I lied. I accused her of being out of her mind. Then I walked out of the room and hoped she didn't follow."*

John and Laura's situation is not unusual. Denial is a frequent response to being confronted by a spouse regarding an affair. Lying can be an instant reaction to avoid dealing with a challenge that will disrupt the relational connection. It could be that the person having the affair isn't completely sure what to do. In their mind, lying may buy time to sort things out.

Affairs are secretive behaviors. No one wants to be labeled as *that guy.* So, when confronted with an affair, quite often the first response is denial. As in the case of Laura and John, the shock of discovery often threatens the protective barrier around the betrayal. The shame and fear of exposure is so great that rather than telling the truth, the person having the affair will once again thicken their armor of defensiveness—fortifying the wall of protection around their secrets.

It is also not uncommon for the questions a partner asks to be met with indignation and anger, which drives a couple further apart. A betrayer can quickly shut down a conversation to shut off all questions and shield himself from exposure to the weight of his shame. Underneath the anger, once again, is a deep fear of being caught.

## FEAR ERECTS A WALL THAT SAYS, *"NO VISITORS ALLOWED."*

After coming close to having their cover blown, the person engaging in an affair may also apply the brakes, often resulting in a breakup or pause with the AP. Afterwards, things at home can seem better for a time.

But several factors can cause a slip back into connection with the AP. This can happen when:

1) Underlying personal or relational challenges are not addressed.

2) The addictive grip of the affair itself pulls the betrayer back into connection.

3) Whatever needs the affair filled aren't uncovered and worked through.

4) Efforts on the part of the AP to reconnect are too strong to resist.

**Let's continue with Laura's account of their story.**

*"When John got so angry, it caused me to question myself. Maybe this was all just my imagination. He was so adamant and angry. Would John really cheat on me? I continued to wrestle with the idea. After his outburst, things felt a little better, but I just couldn't shake the feeling that something was off. The first couple of weeks after our*

*fight, his behavior did change. John made an effort to come home on time each night and seemed more attentive. Then, gradually, the old behavior came back, and he started up with the work excuses again.*

"*I began doing a rewind, thinking back to the times he stayed late or worked on Saturdays. There was even one time he told me he was going to a weekend trade show. Usually, he sends his coworker to those, but in February he said he needed to go in person.*

"*I knew in my heart I wasn't crazy. Something had changed. I could feel it. And there were signs. When John would come home late, he would say he was working on a dead-line, but he frequently had alcohol on his breath.*

"*Sometimes he would admit to having a drink, saying he stopped off for happy hour on the way home with some of 'the guys.' Work was an easy excuse. Still, something just didn't add up. I could feel it in my bones.*

"*Then one evening after a night out with 'the guys,' he fell asleep on the couch, and I decided to check his phone. There it was in black and white: She had texted to make sure he made it home okay. She talked about what a great time she'd had. And then, the scariest thing of all, she ended the text with Love You.*

"*Love you! Holy crap! Not only was he having an affair, but they were throwing out the 'L' word. Well, at least she was.*

"*All this time, he was lying straight to my face. He made me feel like I was the crazy one! And he just covered things up with his lies. My husband. The effin' liar.*"

At this point, Laura began to sob.

"*How could he do this to me? To us. If he loves someone else, he just needs to tell me. I don't want to be with someone who doesn't want to be with me. What did I do wrong?*"

In looking at Laura and John's situation, what stands out for you? Are you surprised at John's strong pushback or to hear Laura questioning herself?

As we've explored, a betrayed woman frequently questions herself. She will replay the situations over and over in her head—trying to figure out the what, where, when, and how things happened. When you are confronted and deny what happened, she will scrutinize things even more closely. Deception hits hard, like a double whammy on top of the pain of an affair. Deceiving and denying add a heavier weight to the recovery process.

---

## Reflection
### *Deception and Incomplete Truths*

- Where do you tend to lie, deny, or not tell the full truth? What were/are you protecting yourself or the other party from? What have you been trying to avoid confronting or feeling?

- How has not telling the truth, telling incomplete truths, or dancing around honesty, impacted your relationship and your life?

- When have you been lied to or later learned that someone wasn't telling you the full truth? How did that impact your relationship with that person? Your ability to trust them?

- What are your thoughts moving forward?

In Chapter 22, you will have the opportunity to learn about Rick's affair journey. Through recovery, he became aware of his tendency to embellish, avoid, and tell incomplete truths within his relationship and his life. He used his recovery process to strengthen his integrity, leadership skills, and foster a deeper belief in himself.

The chapter that follows has been written for your spouse/partner. It has been designed to provide her with a deeper understanding of her own emotions and reactions to what has happened. I encourage you to share this with her when it feels right to do so.

# 15

## For Your Spouse/Significant Other

———————————————————■———————————————————

*"You open your heart knowing that there's a chance it may be broken one day, and in opening your heart, you experience a love and joy that you never dreamed possible. You find that being vulnerable is the only way to allow your heart to feel true pleasure that's so real it scares you."*

—Bob Marley, songwriter, musician

If you are a woman who has been betrayed, this chapter has been created specifically for you. Perhaps you are the one who picked up this book for the man in your life who has been unfaithful. Or maybe he has been reading it and invited you to read this chapter. Regardless of how you found your way here, I hope the ideas presented will help bring greater understanding and healing to your heart, soul, and relationship (whether or not the two of you choose to stay together.)

If you have not yet done so, I invite you to visit Laura's story in the previous chapter. The story ends with Laura questioning herself and wondering what she may have *done wrong* to set the stage for her husband's affair. Here is a recap of the ending of that story where Laura begins to question herself.

"How could he do this to me? To us. If he loves someone else, he just needs to tell me. I don't want to be with someone who doesn't want to be with me. What did I do wrong?"

Have you ever questioned yourself and wondered what you may have done wrong?

Here are a few statements expressed by women wrestling with affair recovery. See if you relate to any of them:

☐ *I'm a wreck. I'm torn between wanting to know more and being afraid of what I may uncover.*

☐ *I find myself obsessing about the other woman—what he saw in her, what he spent on her, where he took her. Sometimes I feel like I'm on a scavenger hunt to find out everything I can about his affair and the person he was involved with.*

☐ *I keep speculating on what was missing in our relationship that caused him to look elsewhere.*

☐ *Sometimes I blame myself or feel like I failed.*

☐ *I'm having trouble getting past all the lies he has told and wonder what he may still be keeping from me.*

☐ *I've been tempted to reach out to the other woman.*

☐ *The other woman has reached out to me, and I'm wondering if I should connect with her to hear what she has to say.*

☐ *I'm asking myself:*
   o *Is it possible to love someone and engage in an affair with someone else?*
   o *Can I ever trust him again?*
   o *Can I forgive and move past this?*
   o *Does he still love me?*
   o *Can I ever really love him in the same way again?*
   o *Will our relationship ever be the same?*
   o *Can I ever heal from this?*

All these statements have been expressed by women in your position. Affairs turn relationships upside down and frequently cause women to doubt themselves.
One thing that I would like to make perfectly clear up front is:

## Your man's affair is not your fault. Period.

Even if there are things that you look back on and you wish you had done differently in your relationship—even if you have regrets—he is the one who stepped out of the relationship. You are not to blame for his choices.

## While the affair is not your fault, solid recovery will require effort from both of you.

Throughout this section, I will be challenging you to take a good, hard look at what you want, need, and are willing to accept as you move forward. It is also helpful to more deeply consider what your *normal* really was before your partner turned toward someone else. What was working? What wasn't? What did you let slide in service to keeping the peace? What would you like life to look like moving forward? What do you want? What do you need to do differently? These are all questions to consider as you step more fully into the recovery process for yourself and your relationship.

# Don't Get Stuck in Regret

As we look back on our lives, each of us can identify things we wish we would have done differently. Don't let yourself get caught up in self-blame or regret or trapped by the *what ifs* running around inside your brain. Be careful of the tendency to beat yourself up for what you didn't see, or what you may have noticed that you ignored. Similarly, don't beat yourself up for what you didn't do, especially when you were balancing many other things or didn't know what your partner was up to. You will have an opportunity to take responsibility for things in the relationship that you can change, but staying paralyzed by shame over anything you missed isn't productive to your recovery.

When you find yourself venturing into the land of blame, self-blame, or regret, there are several strategies to shake off the negative thinking and regroup. You can refer to Chapter 21, *Defining and Navigating Your Emotions,* for a more in-depth look at working through challenging thoughts and emotions.

Four of the most common questions I hear from women whose men have strayed are as follows:

1. *Will I ever be able to forgive him?*
2. *Will I ever be able to trust him (or anyone I'm in love with) again?*

3. *How can I trust myself again? Trust my intuition? Trust that my mind is not playing tricks on me?*

4. *What can I do to make sure I'm never, ever fooled or cheated on again?*

The quick answer to the first two questions is *yes*. And deep forgiveness and regaining trust take time. Self-trust is another critical component to rebuild that involves taking a deeper look at what you may have been ignoring or not willing to confront in the past. We will dive into ways to help you strengthen trust in yourself, your partner, and your ability to set self-supportive boundaries as we continue.

# Forgiveness

Forgiveness occurs in layers. While you may want to forgive and may even say, *"I forgive you,"* true forgiveness is a multi-layered process that builds over time. The importance of forgiveness is emphasized in every religious/spiritual tradition, and it is a value held by most people, regardless of their religious affiliation or lack thereof. It is such an important component of recovery that we have dedicated an entire chapter to making amends and forgiveness. When you are ready to take a deeper look, you can visit Chapter 26.

# Trust

Rebuilding trust requires a strong commitment to yourself and your relationship. It requires a willingness to address areas of discontent you may have been ignoring, ways in which you have been neglecting yourself, and areas within your relationship that you would like to improve. All of this is possible—not necessarily easy, but possible for sure. Through this process, you will be building your resilience and ability to set self-supportive boundaries, and rebuilding trust with your partner and within yourself. Rebuilding trust requires time and commitment from you both.

One of the biggest stumbling blocks that I hear women wrestling with is: *Why did he have to keep lying to me?* Many women struggle as much with the lying as they do with the affair itself. Rebuilding trust involves making a solid commitment to telling one another (and yourself) the truth. So, what gets in the way? Let's take a look.

# Truth-Telling

Most of us embrace truth-telling as a virtue. We teach our kids to tell the truth. Yet all of us lie from time to time. Why? People tend to tell small lies to avoid uncomfortable conversations. Maybe a lie is told to spare someone's feelings. In couples work, I hear complaints about lies of omission or making a commitment to things in the moment to avoid a potential argument or trigger of a partner's discontent. Misleading someone is a form of lying.

Part of the recovery work for your man is to examine those places in his life where he tends to either not be fully truthful, say yes too quickly just to keep the peace, or avoid talking about things that may be uncomfortable to address. While these areas of concern are not nearly as hurtful as the lies told to maintain a secret liaison, they are areas where a couple's connection can begin to slip out of alignment. Through this recovery process, your man is reflecting on what gets in the way of making and honoring commitments and telling the truth. (For a more in-depth look into affairs and deception, you may refer to John and Laura's story in Chapter 14, *Secrets, Lies, and the Fear of Discovery*.)

## Reflection
### *Truth Telling*

While this work focuses on rebuilding a trust broken by the actions of your partner, this is also a powerful time to look at your own relationship with and commitment to truth-telling. You may find areas where you tend to avoid sharing what's important to you. Here are a few prompts to help you explore.

- How are you at making and honoring commitments? How about your commitments to yourself?
- In what situations do you find yourself telling half-truths or withholding to avoid an argument?
- Where do you need to set better boundaries, rather than agreeing simply to keep the peace?
- What do you tend to avoid talking about?
- How do you tend to respond when your spouse says, "No. Not Yet. Let me think about that, and I'll get back to you"?

As you work toward rebuilding your relationship—with yourself and your spouse—pay attention to the areas in which you may be compromising yourself, or your values. Trust is rebuilt by looking at any relational dynamics that have veered out of alignment.

We will dive into relational repair in more depth in upcoming chapters. Since this chapter is for and about you, let's continue diving into what you most likely will be experiencing and how you can work through it.

# Feelings

Your feelings, especially at the beginning of discovery and recovery from your partner's affair, can quickly surge up and down like a roller coaster ride you can't easily exit. You may find yourself feeling content one minute, in a puddle the next, or standing face-to-face with an inner rage monster who is ready to torch anything in her path. See if any of these statements apply:

- You tend to replay things in your head over and over, trying to figure out what you may have missed.

- You beat yourself up for not asking more questions, for not listening to your intuition, or for not being "smart enough" to avoid being blindsided.

- Your anger is sometimes directed at yourself, your partner, or the AP. You may find yourself even angrier with the AP than you are with him! After all, if she hadn't shown up, maybe life would still be normal.

- Maybe you just don't want to deal with all of this. You may find yourself moving into pseudo-forgiveness to avoid conflict and the anxiety of talking about something you would rather just forget. (I call it pseudo-forgiveness, because deep forgiveness takes time.) Some women I've worked with want to immediately move on and not talk about things with anyone. But if you shorten—or shortcut—the process of recovery, the likelihood of recurrence in the future is far greater.

It would be nice to just rewind, right?

If you find yourself moving into denial and avoidance, I strongly advise you to reach out for help. Some people feel so much shame about their partner's affair that they don't talk to anyone about it. Remember, his affair is not your fault. And it is not your shame to carry.

Should your partner try to coerce you into keeping his secret and not sharing it with *anyone*, know that this isn't healthy either. He doesn't have the right to silence you. Efforts to keep you totally silent speak volumes about your relational dynamic. This is an important time to consider what you want and need.

That being said, I also don't advise broadcasting this very intimate betrayal to the world. Sometimes a woman finds herself so enraged upon finding out that she talks to everyone she can—her friends, relatives, her partner's friends, his colleagues, his boss, their kids, and their community. One woman told me about going to the veterinarian to have her cat put down. *"Before I knew it, I was telling the front desk receptionist that I didn't know if my husband would be there for the euthanasia because he was having an affair. What was I thinking? I think I was just so traumatized that I couldn't hide it."* While I'm not suggesting you hide out, I am cautioning you to be selective in who you speak with—for your own sake, and because anything you say cannot be unsaid.

---

## Reflection
### *Sharing about the Affair*

If you are uncertain whether to share with a specific person, consider your motives for discussing the affair with them:

- Are you wanting to reach out to this individual for comfort?

- Are you sharing to get back at your man, to let people know that he's *really* not a good guy after all? Because you want him to feel pain as well? To make sure he feels sufficient shame and embarrassment?

- Is this someone who tends to be gossipy and may share what happened with other people?

  - OR –

- Is this a trusted friend that you feel can give you objective advice and honor your requests for privacy?

- Is this someone who will have your back no matter what? Who will provide sound wisdom and comfort? Who will listen and empathize, not demonize?

It can also be comforting to reach out to a professional who will help you sort through these decisions—while also letting you process in a neutral, confidential environment. Keeping things bottled up inside compromises physical, emotional, and spiritual well-being.

If you have a good friend who will be there for you no matter what, without judgment, that may be the best first person to share your raw feelings with. From there, you can decide who else to tell—or not tell. Ultimately, you both may decide that it is in the best interest of your relationship to let your wider circle of friends and family know. Good friends can be supportive during the healing process.

Remember, your feelings will spontaneously rise and fall in reaction to situations, thoughts, and triggers, some of which are rooted in past experiences. It is not your job to analyze, fix, defend, or neutralize anyone's feelings, including your own. Feelings are neither right nor wrong. They are simply responses to thoughts and situations. As our feelings are acknowledged (first internally, and then by sharing them with those we trust), we feel seen and heard. An acknowledgment can be as simple as noticing, *"I feel sad…and so angry right now,"* or *"I'm so frustrated with this project."* Or it can be a partner noticing you are off and asking, *"Are you okay? You seem a little sad today,"* or *"It feels like something is off. Do you want to talk about it?"* Or even, *"How can I help?"* When we are acknowledged, we feel accepted. This helps release us from a negative spiral and allows us to express a fuller range of who we are.

While we will do a deep dive into how feelings and emotions work in Chapter 21, *Defining and Navigating Emotions*, since you will be rolling through quite a few different emotional responses, I thought it would be helpful to review key feelings you will likely be moving in and out of.

# Grief

## You are grieving the loss of the relationship you thought you had and the future you had envisioned for the two of you.

Grief may show up at the most inopportune moments—at the grocery store when buying his favorite coffee, when "your song" pops up on the radio, when a friend who doesn't yet *know* about the affair asks about your weekend, or even when listening to an impactful podcast or TED Talk. Feelings of grief can hit without any provocation at all. Sometimes its timing sucks!

One of my clients likened affair grief to grieving over death, only worse because the person you are grieving about is still alive! When someone dies, they don't choose to exit your life. When your partner has an affair, it can feel like a personal, intentional abandonment of your relationship—even if they didn't intend it to be so. While this may sound dramatic, in truth, you are grieving a little death: the death of what was and what you envisioned your relationship to look like, or how it used to be. You may even be grieving the image of who you thought he was, and what you thought he was—and wasn't—capable of.

While it is true that you have lost your idealization of this relationship, what is also true is that something brand new can be resurrected in its place. Hanging onto that belief can help lessen the chaos in your mind and assist in your recovery. This is true even if you decide to leave the relationship.

Many times, people moving through the grief of something traumatic, like an affair, dive more deeply into their own spiritual or religious traditions for comfort. Prayer can soothe the wounds of the heart. Spending some time with your grief doesn't mean it needs to swallow you whole.

# Sadness

*"Sadness is but a wall between two gardens. Heavy hearts, like heavy clouds in the sky, are best relieved by the letting of a little water."*

—Kahlil Gibran, *The Prophet*

Sometimes tears erupt out of nowhere, even in people who don't consider themselves criers. The pain of betrayal can very quickly activate the waterworks, even in men.

*"Will I ever get over this pain? It hurts. It really, really hurts."*

I have heard versions of this quote time and time again from the partners of people who have strayed. Sometimes it's hard to get out of bed in the morning, focus on work or family, or connect with friends. Sometimes you just want to pull the covers up over your head and sleep the pain away.

Pay attention to your body and your emotions. Make sure that you get the help you need. Some ideas to lessen the sadness are meditation, running, working out. With extreme sadness or depression, it can be difficult to even consider these options. If your sadness becomes so overwhelming that you find it difficult to function, please reach out to a medical professional. They may temporarily prescribe an antidepressant to help you stabilize.

Over time, the pain *will* lessen. The most important thing is for you to take care of yourself. As one woman told me, *"Sixteen years ago when I discovered my husband's affair, there were days I thought it would kill me. My pain was so intense. But now I can't imagine not experiencing the growth that event catalyzed. While I still wish it hadn't happened, I'm grateful for how much I learned about myself in the process. I'm in a much better place today."*

Working with someone to help you work through the pain and associated emotions that arise is also highly advisable. It can be very challenging to work through this on your own. There is no shame in reaching out for help, as we have discussed.

# Anxiety

**"Our anxiety does not come from thinking about the future, but from wanting to control it."**

—*The Prophet,* Kahlil Gibran, philosopher, poet

Yes, anxiety is an emotion. It is something we feel in our bodies and experience in our minds. There are two distinct types of anxiety: mental and physical.

**Mental anxiety, also known as ruminating thoughts:** Fearful thoughts about the future. Fear for a loved one's safety. Fear of loss. These are some of the symptoms of an anxious mind. Mental anxiety comes from worrying about what may or may not happen, and these thoughts can arise when someone acts in a way that is incongruent with previous patterns. For example, a husband who is typically home at 6:00 p.m. begins changing his routine to "get caught up at work." A break in his typical pattern can evoke concern. When we don't have an outlet to express our concerns, or when expressed concerns result in arguments, it can exacerbate our mental anxiety.

**Physical anxiety, also known as stress response**: Rapid breathing. Accelerated heart rate. Shaking. Hand or jaw clenching. These are some of the physical sensations of anxiety that your body is attempting to work through. Bodily stress is activated by the release of chemicals like adrenaline and cortisol. Headaches, muscle pain, back pain, tension in the neck and shoulders, exhaustion, and digestive issues can all be bodily manifestations of unresolved stress. While our thoughts can lead to physical sensations of anxiety, situations can also trigger anxious responses that bypass our thinking brain. This is why manifestations of physical anxiety can seemingly appear out of nowhere—such as in the case of a panic attack.

Anxiety can eat away at your peace of mind. EFT (Emotional Freedom Technique) also known simply as *tapping* is a powerful tool that can be used to help calm anxiety. This technique involves gently tapping on specific bodily meridian points while verbalizing your anxious thoughts and adding a calming thought immediately afterwards. *"Even though I can't seem to get these fearful thoughts out of my mind, and I feel so stuck, I am totally willing to accept myself exactly as I am. I am okay. I am working through things. I am willing to trust myself."* The more you dive into EFT the more effective it can be. There are various protocols available online that walk you through the process.[14] If you have more interest and exploring the EFT protocol you can check out *The Tapping Solution: A revolutionary system for stress free livin* by Nick Ortner who also runs an annual tapping summit to teach people how to use this tool more effectively.

# Anger

**"Anger is just anger. It isn't good. It isn't bad. It just is. What you do with it is what matters. It's like anything else. You can use it to build or to destroy. You just have to make the choice."**

—Jim Butcher, *White Night*

We talked about sadness and grief. So how about anger? What happens when anger becomes so all-consuming it hijacks your ability to focus on anything else? How do you manage your anger without it torching everything in sight?

Quite a few of the women I work with struggle to manage, communicate, and even allow themselves to feel anger. This is especially true for women who are in a relationship with strong, dominant men. But it's important to know the consequences of *not* expressing your emotions. Unexpressed and unprocessed emotions can build up. Build-ups result in feelings of powerlessness, which can lead to blow-ups or disinterest in the relationship.

I have witnessed individuals swallowing their voices to avoid conflict, pretending like they are okay when they're not. While sometimes you need to let things go in service to giving someone the benefit of the doubt, if you find yourself frequently not sharing because you don't want to *rock the boat* or you think your feelings may not matter, I encourage you to take a deeper look.

---
# Reflection
## *Your Relationship with Anger*
---

How you work through anger depends a great deal on what was modeled during in your childhood, teen years, and prior relationships. Here are a few questions to think about regarding your relationship with anger.

- How have the men around you—your dad, brother, past or current partner—managed their anger?

- How about the women around you—your mom, aunts? Female friends?

- How did you manage anger as a child? Were you told not to be angry? Was your anger met with greater anger? Compassion? Did someone help you work through your anger in healthy ways?

- What is your relationship with anger now?
  - Is anger something you are afraid of? Do you fear yours? Someone else's?

Another's anger can shut you down. You can fear reprisal for expressing your anger. This can be confusing, and it can prevent you from feeling comfortable with anger. But anger doesn't just vanish when you decide to ignore it. It's either swallowed and festers inside, or it is released and expressed in healthy or unhealthy ways.

**Hurt lies beneath anger.** While some people bury their anger, others have an easier time expressing anger than hurt, so they react with rage when they feel slighted. Beneath that hurt typically lies feelings of powerlessness, which feed into anger and its subsets: hate and rage.

---
# Reflection
## *Hiding Out vs. Speaking Your Truth*
---

Over time, the tendency to avoid challenging conversations impacts your relational bond. This type of avoidance often results in diminishing sexual desire as well. If you fit this profile, part of your journey is to get more deeply in touch with your wants, needs, and desires; then practice owning them.

- What are you not sharing in service to "keeping the peace"?

- If you could let your partner know anything without triggering anger or reprisal, what would you say?

- Where do you tend to shrink, or feel "less than" (for example: at home, with parental figures, with your kids)?
- Where do you tend to stand up and speak your truth (for example: at work, during a PTO meeting, with your kids, during a presentation, in a podcast interview)?

As you reflect on your responses, is there anything that surprised you? Do you notice any patterns?

To grow stronger in the ability to express your desires and truths in any relationship, look at the places where you have already cultivated your voice, the places where you feel more solid and likely to express what is true for you. This gives you a framework that you can reference to help you better get in touch with what you want at home. You can activate that same "muscle" to express yourself with your partner.

These questions can provide some great discussion starters with your partner or a professional. If you choose to discuss these topics with your partner without anyone to help mediate, make sure you both are in a positive frame of mind before engaging. You may suggest that your partner explores the questions and writes out his answers prior to discussing.

Chapter 24, *Courageous Conversations*, offers a comprehensive framework to help you navigate and address difficult topics with greater confidence and effectiveness.

# Hate and Rage

*"I just hate her [the AP]. I know that sounds horrible. And I hate even hearing myself say it. Hate is such an ugly word. And yet, I can't help thinking if it wasn't for her, we wouldn't be in this predicament. I blame her. She knew he was married, and that didn't stop her. How do I keep this hate from eating me alive?"*

Hate is a tough one. No one wants to feel hate toward another human being. Whether you only know of this person or have personally met, it is easy to project your feelings of disappointment and anger onto her. It may sound strange, but projecting your ugly feelings onto her in your mind can be a safety valve to release some of the negativity you feel toward your partner.

Hate and anger can trigger a rage that hits fast and furious and overpower your sense of reason. The urge to yell, break, or smash something can arise before you are even consciously aware that it is happening. Like anger, rage is an emotion that needs to be released so that you don't have to carry it inside. It is easier to channel anger *before* it develops into rage. You just need to be sure you direct hatred and anger toward *something*, not someone. Screaming into a pillow or punching a punching bag can help with this release. Engaging in physical activities like running, working out, and playing pickleball or tennis are proactive ways to fortify yourself against a build-up of anger.

As with any emotion, giving yourself a little time to be present with and work through the lesser emotions on the anger spectrum can help you process them before they become overpowering or move into rage. This can set the stage for a calmer discussion.

That being said, it is important to remember that we are all human beings. There will be instances where partners express their anger towards each other. This can be an indicator of the seriousness of a challenge that may have previously been overlooked or downplayed. It is crucial to be mindful if a pattern emerges where it appears that anger is the only way to capture a partner's attention.

# Cultivating Self-Trust

An experience of betrayal not only shakes your trust in your partner, it can also shake your trust in yourself.

When we are young, we learn about trust through experiences with our caregivers and through observing what is modeled to us. As we grow, we integrate what we have witnessed into how we see ourselves. Through these interactions with peers, some of us cultivate a solid ense of self-trust. Others learn that they need to shrink to be accepted or not trigger a negative response from their caregivers. Sometimes the need for self-protection causes a person to push others away to avoid conflict.

Each of us wants to be loved and accepted. We learn to mold ourselves into what we believe others want in an effort to garner love and attention from those important to us. While this behavior can be observed in both men and women, it is more common for women to adapt themselves to the needs of those around them. Many women I have worked with express feeling like they have lost their sense of self. Some may have structured their lives around their children's needs, while others may cling so tightly to a partner that they lose their own identity. Self-neglect is often a learned pattern, possibly influenced by witnessing their mother prioritize others over herself. Some women may try to cope through shopping or consuming extra alcohol during social gatherings. While these actions may provide temporary relief, they often serve as a distraction from addressing underlying emotional needs.

**Affair recovery provides an opportunity to rediscover what is important to you that you may have lost sight of along the way.**

## Reflection
### *Self-Care*

The following questions are designed to help you take a deeper look at your vision for your life, relationship, expectations, and self-care.

- List three things you loved to do when you were younger, either in high school, college, or both.
- List three things you loved doing with your partner when you first connected.
- What is one thing you miss about your younger self?
- What activities do you find yourself engaging in to self-soothe? (Hint: This could be an activity that you find difficult to stop, such as shopping, eating, exercise, scrolling through social media, or alcohol/drug use.)
- What did you dream of doing or being when you were younger?
- What did you envision your life to look like when you got married (or first engaged in a serious relationship with your partner)?
  - What elements are part of your current relationship?
  - What pieces are missing that you wish were there now?
- What did you envision your life to look like with children (if applicable)?
  - What do you see yourself doing/engaging in once the children are in college, or are out on their own?
  - What are you modeling for your kids when it comes to self-care?
  - What are you modeling to your kids about adult relationships?

- ○ What are two values you would like to instill in your children?
- How have your expectations of what you wanted changed over time?
- Let's say you had a do-over ticket and could go back and redo one thing in your life. Take a moment and consider that possibility, then answer the following questions:
  - ○ What would you choose to do over?
  - ○ Why did you choose this one thing?
  - ○ How would you redo it?
  - ○ What would be different in your life now?
- What is one thing that you would be willing to begin or re-engage with that could create greater satisfaction in your life now?

Taking time to explore and write out your answers can provide you with a window into wants, needs, and desires that have gone underground. While it may not be feasible to engage in some of these activities now, there may be other ways to capture the essence of what those experiences brought to your world and infuse your life to infuse it with more joy and fulfillment.

This can be a great exercise to explore with your partner. If you choose to do this as a couple, each of you needs to take time to do the exercise solo first, writing things down. Then set up a time to discuss. I would suggest that you decide which pieces you wish to share. It is okay if you don't want to share everything. You may discover ideas that you wish to explore with a professional first to help you dive in a little deeper.

Affair recovery is part self-recovery and part relational recovery. Hopefully, this chapter has provided you with some ideas on ways in which you can come back into greater alignment with yourself.

The following chapter has been written for the AP. While it could be painful for you as the recovering spouse to have this chapter included, the greatest opportunity for recovery after an affair is when all three people engage in the healing process. You may even gain some insight from reading the following chapter. If it is too challenging for you, please skip it; you can always come back to it at a later time if you choose. Everyone's healing journey is their own. Know that I wish you well as you discern what is best for you and your relationship.

# 16

# For *the* AP (Affair Partner)

---■---

*"I was born when you kissed me. I died when you left me.*
*I lived a few weeks while you loved me."*
—Humphrey Bogart, actor

As mentioned in the previous chapter, optimal healing from infidelity occurs when each person involved in the affair triangle engages in their own healing. I have therefore written this brief chapter for the AP.

## To the Affair Partner

So, you've fallen in love with a married (or otherwise unavailable) man, or at least fallen into an intense connection with him. And that dreaded day that you feared would one day come is here. He has let you know that he needs to end things with you to focus on making things right with his spouse.

Here are some challenges you may be wrestling with. Check all that apply to you:

☐ *I tend to fall for unavailable men.*

☐ *I felt(/feel) that I needed to end things but wasn't sure how.*

☐ *I don't understand why we can't still be "friends" or share important things that occur in our lives.*

☐ *Even though he was married, I thought/fantasized we might end up together.*

☐ *I didn't know he was married when we first connected and struggled to set boundaries once I found out.*

☐ *I fell in love with him and am devastated that he's ending things.*

☐ *I feel misled and don't want to let him off the hook for his actions.*

☐ *I'm tempted to reach out to his wife and let her know my side of the story.*

☐ *I don't feel I really did anything wrong because we weren't being physically intimate.*

☐ *I feel a sense of powerlessness in the face of it all and want to reclaim my life.*

☐ *I need help letting go, moving on, and recovering myself.*

☐ *The affair served as a great distraction from other life challenges I was experiencing in my life or in my own marriage.*

Whether you knew from the beginning, or discovered it later, somewhere along the way you found out the man you were connecting with was married or deeply involved with another, and whatever drew you to him was so compelling that you chose to stay anyway. Even if you pulled away from time to time, something seemed to keep drawing you back to him. You never dreamed you would be the *other woman,* yet here you are struggling to regain your integrity, dignity, and self-respect. Even if no one knew about your liaison, you knew that you were crossing a line that you never imagined you would cross (or cross again.)

You may be someone who was cheated on in the past. You may be someone who has frequently found herself drawn to unavailable men. You may have thought you could just play it cool and not get overly emotionally involved. You may be someone who felt so connected with this particular man that you had fantasies about him leaving his partner for you. Or maybe you stayed because the chemistry was so strong that it overrode reason.

Different internal and external situations draw a woman into forging relationships with unavailable men. Perhaps somewhere along the way, you began to feel that the two of you could be *really good* together. Maybe it felt like you *were* really good together. Even if you never thought you would find yourself in this position, part of you fell into the allure, the fantasy, the adrenaline rush of secrecy, and into the arms of someone who wasn't fully yours to fall for.

Somehow you found a way to compartmentalize this relationship and justify your behavior. Do any of these statements made to affair partners by men sound familiar?

☐ *"My wife doesn't get me like you do. You really understand me."*

☐ *"We aren't even sleeping together. We haven't slept together in a long time. We sleep in separate rooms."*

☐ *"We are living separate lives."*

☐ *"I'm so attracted to you. We have such strong chemistry."*

☐ *"I like who I am when I'm with you."*

☐ *"I've never felt this way before."*

Maybe it felt like your connection wasn't just physical, it may have also been emotional. Perhaps it was intellectual. Maybe he was a great mentor. Maybe it felt like you looked at the world the same way. Perhaps you said to yourself, *He really gets me. I really get him. We can talk about anything.*

Perhaps you fantasized that the two of you would one day establish a full life together. Perhaps, even if he told you he would never leave his wife, you still dreamt that maybe after the kids were grown, you would be able to build a life together.

Or perhaps you are someone who was/is not 100 percent available to be in a relationship, and the connection with someone else who was only partially available worked well at the beginning. You were under no illusions that the two of you would become a public couple, and that was perfectly fine for you. Maybe your life at home was far less than ideal, and this connection provided a respite. Perhaps you are married, and your husband doesn't support your dreams. Maybe your partner has been wrestling with drugs or alcohol. Maybe you have been living like roommates.

Regardless of what drew you into this connection, when a man informs you that he is sincerely *done*, as tough as that may be for you to hear, and as much as it hurts, it is critical for your health and well-being, as well as his, that you honor his decision. It's imperative for you to know when it's time to let go and move on.

Yes, it's tough. Yes, it hurts. And it's important to give yourself time to grieve and work through the pain of losing someone you truly care(d) about and a relationship that filled specific needs. Now is the time for you to engage in some significant self-care and begin the process of healing and rebuilding your life. (The previous chapter written for the spouse offers some ideas that may be helpful for you as well.)

One of the most important things right now is for you to recover your dignity and self-respect. This begins inside you. Affair recovery can be a powerful time to re-evaluate your life and choices. Your challenge is to tap into your resilience and channel the energy you have been giving to this relationship back into your own wants, needs, and desires.

While *ripping off the band-aid* may be excruciatingly painful at first, cutting off all contact with him will help you stay the course and heal more quickly. Ultimately the madness in your head will slow down. Until then, you need to be careful not to set yourself up as a prisoner of hope—waiting just in case he might change his mind.

Just like his spouse, your emotions can quickly roller coaster from grief to rage to deep sadness. You may feel misled. You may want to retaliate, tell his wife, and make sure he is suffering too, or you may just feel a seemingly inconsolable sadness.

**I will tell you this:** Every man I have worked with has experienced his own version of hell working through the aftermath of his affair. If this man has been engaging with you, there is something that this connection provided that was strong enough to cause him to deceive his wife, break his vows, and make time for you. Unless this man is a sociopath or deeply narcissistic, the idea of hurting you both hurts him as well.

If you have read earlier portions of this book, you will have heard how most men don't set out to hurt anyone. While knowing this doesn't take away the pain, I hope it provides you with a small amount of comfort as you work through grieving and recovering yourself.

## WORKPLACE AFFAIRS

Recovery can be especially difficult if you work together, if he is your boss (or vice versa), or if he is a neighbor or family friend. If the breakup of your affair is a public one, that is if it has come to light that you were engaging with this man, you may be facing the consequence of being the subject of gossip or a potential move—in your career or at home.

People involved in a work setting believe they are keeping things secret. The truth is, others typically assume, judge, and often figure out what's going on before any type of confirmation. It is difficult to hide an obvious attraction to someone, especially if you are sleeping together.

Years ago when I was in the corporate world and an affair was discovered between a male boss and a female coworker, it was not uncommon to walk into work one day and find the female employee gone. Even though it was assumed she walked away with a nice severance package, it felt wrong that the woman was dismissed while the man kept his job. It was a rare occurrence to have the reverse occur. In those instances where she was there and he was gone, everyone assumed she reported the affair.

Work discovery is difficult. As the *other woman*, you are walking around with a scarlet letter pinned to your chest. We have a very strong moralistic code that an affair betrays, and many people will hold you in contempt. No one understands the circumstances surrounding your particular affair. Historically, unless the guy is seen as someone with a huge ego or that people perceive as a predator, the woman involved is generally judged more harshly.

## So, What Do You Do Now?

As indicated earlier, this is a time for you to recover and rediscover yourself. If you work with or for him, or vice versa, you should strongly consider making a change. Emotions will be running high. To see each other frequently simply isn't wise, no matter how strong your resolve is to stay away.

While each situation is different, it is important that at a minimum you create some distance between the two of you. Resist the impulse to reach out to him. Reach-outs can rekindle relationships, and benign communication attempts can result in lengthening your healing process. Resist the urge to text or call, especially after a couple of drinks.

**Enlist the help of a friend.** Find a friend who agrees to be your "sponsor," that is the person you will reach out to instead of him when you feel your resolve weakening. Set this up in advance so that when you experience a strong desire to connect, you already have your sponsor in place. You will experience weak moments. Just like any break-up, this hurts. If you were blindsided by the suddenness of his departure, you may feel the need to seek a closure that may be impossible to orchestrate. Instead, you must find healthy ways to work through your upset, longing, sadness, and grief, and find a way to bring closure to yourself.

**Create a no social checking commitment and calendar it.** Checking social media can be like a drug, the more you check, the more you want to check and the greater the difficulty in letting go. A strategy to reinforce a commitment to stay away from social media is to set your calendar for seven days at a time. No checking social media. No making inquiries about him to people you both know, and of course no contact Making it through the first seven days hopefully gives you confidence that you don't need to check up on him. Afterwards, try calendaring fourteen days, then thirty. The more time you stay away from all media, the easier it gets.

There may be things you are angry about, promises made that won't be kept. Maybe you feel misled or played. You may be inclined to reach out to his partner to tell her the "real story," thinking that there are things she has a right to know. **I caution you very strongly not to reach out to his primary partner.** Like you, she is going through her own version of hell. She has decisions to make and emotions to sort through, and it is not up to you to interfere with her healing and grieving process. The two of them are figuring out how to repair their relationship. And as difficult as that may be for you to fathom, you need to give them the space to do so.

It is also possible that you could hear things from her that you may struggle to reconcile or heal from. Secrecy plays a big role in maintaining separate lives. And often when someone is caught in an affair, they may say things to one person that they would never say to the other. This is your healing journey. You don't need to complicate it by connecting with his spouse.

It is important to keep your dignity intact. Give yourself some space at work and at home. Journaling, doing some self-reflection, and reviewing specific sections in this book may help you better understand the nuances of your particular affair. You may want to talk with a therapist or coach who understands self-recovery. If you can get away, plan a trip with a friend to help you get some fresh air.

## If You are the One Choosing to Leave

Sometimes, it is the affair partner who decides to end the relationship. If this is the case for you, the same principles apply. The difference is that you are the one definitively choosing to end things. It's important to communicate kindly and firmly to your partner that you have made the decision to end the affair, are committed to reshaping your life, and that he needs to respect your choice.

Chapter 11, *Closing the Door—How to Clearly and Respectfully End Your Affair*, guides you through the steps to cleanly and effectively end the relationship. While the chapter is written with the opposite scenario in mind, the process for ending an affair remains the same regardless of who initiates the decision.

## Reflection
### *Taking Stock of Your Life*

It is important to take stock of what was going on in your life before the affair. Consider the steps you need to take to reclaim your life now that the affair has ended. There are probably things you weren't facing or were putting on the back burner that must be reclaimed. It is time to dust yourself off, face what you need to face, and make choices about the future you want to create for yourself.

Here are some questions for you to consider. I suggest you take some time to think about and write out your answers.

- What were your biggest challenges and struggles that may have set the stage for you to be more vulnerable to engaging in an affair?
- What did this man uniquely bring into your world that was so compelling that you connected with him even if/when you found out he had another partner?
- What did this relationship activate (or bring alive) inside of you?
- What do you need to do to safeguard yourself from reaching out to connect with him?
- What steps do you need to take to truly let him go?
- Do you have a pattern of choosing unavailable relational partners? If so, do you recall a time in your childhood or past when a primary caregiver or close loved one was unavailable to you? How can you become more available to yourself—finding healthier avenues to fulfill some of this longing?
- Who can be there for you in a non-judgmental way to help you recover yourself?
- What do you need to attend to that you have been avoiding in service of connecting with this man?
- What do you want for your life now?
- If you are married, I invite you to explore other parts of this book that have been designed to explore the inner workings of your relationship.

- What do you need to face at home that you may have been ignoring or avoiding?

When we stray from our values, we tend to be pretty hard on ourselves. There is an exercise on **Self-Forgiveness** in Chapter 26 that can help with your healing process. Taking a step back to examine who you are, what you want, and what has gotten in the way of your values and goals allows you to consciously envision a path forward.

## One Last Reminder for Everyone

You have the power to realign your life in ways that support your wants, needs, desires, and values. The most impactful way to live life and make self-supportive decisions is to recognize that within each moment, you have a choice. What you choose in the present begins carving the path for your future.

This is your one sweet, precious life as *you*. How are you going to choose to live it? Who are you going to choose to live it with? And what do you need in order to feel vibrant and alive—while knowing that *you matter*?

The next section examines relational dynamics, including how we connect, love, and discover each other and ourselves through our relationships.

# PART SEVEN

--- ■ ---

# Rebuilding Your Foundation:
## *The Healing Power of Love,*
## *Like, and Learning*

*"We see our relationship as a work in progress.*
*There are times when we wonder how we can possibly stay*
*together. And there are times when we wonder how we could*
*possibly live without the presence of the other person in our life.*
*This is the dance. It's not a perfect dance."*
—Paul Ferrini, *Dancing with the Beloved, Opening our Hearts to the Lessons of Love*

Creating a dynamic and thriving relational connection isn't something we learned about in school, and for many of us, it wasn't well-modeled at home. This section is a valuable read for anyone wanting to take a deeper look at relational dynamics and their capacity to challenge, teach, and help us heal. It can be read at any time.

**If you're the one who has betrayed**, your partner needs to see that your commitment to doing the work isn't dependent upon whether or not she is willing to join you. Ideally, she will join once she is ready. While some women join their partners in relational repair work right away, others wait for their partners to begin the process. Either way, she must see that you're serious about making things work, not just agreeing to things to shut down her upset in the moment.

The stronger your resolve and the more consistently you demonstrate commitment to your partner, the fewer potholes you'll need to navigate as you work toward rebuilding trust. Remember, your objective is to build a strong, safe foundation upon which this relationship can be rebuilt.

**If you're the one who has been betrayed**, taking a step back to look at relational dynamics can help foster greater understanding and set the stage for you to design what you would like to create for your relationship and life moving forward.

In this section, we will take a look at:

**The Need for Love and Connection:**

- **Love:** How we define it, idealize it, and the impact of saying, "I love you."
- **Like:** The importance of liking the person you love, and ways to explore and rebuild your like.

**Relationship Stages:** The hallmark of the three stages relationships go through.

**Sex and Intimacy:** Sex is one aspect of relational connection. We will take a deeper look at how sex plays out in relationships and ways to explore wants, needs, and desires.

**Communicating with your children about the affair:** Some basic dos and don'ts.

# 17

## The Need *for* Love *and* Connection

---

*"To be fully seen by somebody, then, and be loved anyhow—
this is a human offering that can border on miraculous."*
—Elizabeth Gilbert, *Committed: A Skeptic Makes Peace with Marriage*

### What's Love Got to Do with It?

*"Did you love her?"* his wife whispered so softly it was barely audible. Then, *"Did you tell her you loved her?"*

A frequent assumption made when working through the aftermath of an affair is the belief that: *"If you loved her, then you certainly can't truly love me."* Or, *"You can't possibly love me and put our entire relationship at risk at the same time."* Or, *"You knew an affair would wreck me and potentially ruin us, and you did it anyway. You must not love me."*

Each of us wants to feel loved and know that the people we are closest to have our best interests at heart. Seeing a text where someone you love has used the *L word* with another, even if they say they didn't *really* mean it, can sting more than the affair itself.

We each have an idealized image of what we believe love *should* look like and how the person who loves us will show up. Deep disappointments, like infidelity, shatter that image. Unfortunately, life doesn't take a prescribed course, no matter how much we may want it to. We're imperfect beings traveling through life with our own set of wants, needs, and woundings. When life takes an unexpected turn, especially when we are the ones behind the wheel, it is critical to regroup, examine what there is to learn, apologize, forgive ourselves, and commit to choosing more mindfully in the future.

The million-dollar question that arises time and time again is this:

**Can someone love one person and engage in an affair with another?**

While it can be difficult for the betrayed partner to believe, having an affair doesn't necessarily mean you didn't/don't love your partner. It does mean you lost sight of something of value within yourself and/or between the two of you. The truth is you *can* love one person and still feel a spark of connection with someone else that can slide into an affair. This happens more frequently when career and relational challenge are avoided rather than discussed and couples begin losing sight of each other's needs, wants and desires.

## How Do Couples Lose Sight of Each Other's Needs?

The day-to-day activities and pressures of life can become all-consuming. Prioritizing couple-time can easily take a back seat to other demands. This can result in partners feeling taken for granted, discontent, and disconnected.

Instead of facing feelings of disconnection partners can throw their attention into other obligations and activities, such as work, the kids, or even charitable causes. Have you ever found yourself focusing more of your time and attention on work, kids, or other activities instead of facing feelings of emptiness and disconnection? If so, you are not alone.

Having intimate conversations about discontent and loneliness isn't typically at the top of anyone's list. These conversations involve a willingness to be vulnerable and talk about things that aren't so easy to discuss. It can seem easier in the moment to turn to something or someone else rather than face the emptiness you may be feeling within your relationship or within yourself.

As previously mentioned, living with someone doesn't safeguard you from feeling lonely or a bit empty at times. It isn't unusual for people in a relationship to experience some measure of loneliness that they may not know how to resolve. Left undisturbed, your relationship can become more transactional than transformational. Over time a couple can lose faith in their ability to connect and even question whether they are still "in love" with their partner. This can result in that all-too-common, heartbreaking phrase we heard in Joe and Carol's story, "I *love you*, but I'm not sure I'm *in love* with you."

Sometimes a nagging discontent occurs when you feel that you have achieved a certain measure of success but still find yourself feeling empty inside. Other times it can arise when you feel like the life you are living isn't the life you thought you would be living at a given age or life stage.

As we have discussed, many factors can contribute to feelings of alienation or internal discontent, which can make you more vulnerable to the attention of someone outside your primary relationship.

Let's dive a little more deeply into the nuances of what it means to love and be loved.

## Love and Shadow

Love is a core human need. As we have explored, how you were and were not loved in the past impacts the way you love and let yourself be loved in the present. At some point in your life, you have probably been both captured by and disappointed in love.

The intimate relationships you form offer opportunities for learning, growth, and healing. Opening your heart to someone unlocks everything inside—not just the good stuff. Fierce, passionate love reveals who you are and taps into where you have been. Past woundings, disappointments, desire, needs, wants, and hope for new possibilities all live inside the heart and loving someone stirs them all.

Social researcher, author, and storyteller Brené Brown dives into topics like love, vulnerability, shame, and what it means to be a "whole-hearted" human being. Brown uses her research as the backdrop for more fully defining the experience of cultivating love, empathy, belonging, and passion for the human experience. Brown developed a beautiful working definition of love in her book *The Gifts of Imperfection*:

*"Love: We cultivate love when we allow our most vulnerable selves to be deeply seen and known, and when we honor the spiritual connection that grows from that offering with trust, respect, kindness, and affection.*

*Love is not something we give or get; it's something that we nurture and grow—a connection that can only be cultivated between two people when it exists within each one of them. We can only love others as much as we love ourselves.*

*Shame, blame, disrespect, betrayal, and the withholding of affection damage the roots from which love grows. Love can only survive these injuries if they are acknowledged, healed, and rare."*

Opening ourselves up to "allow our most vulnerable selves to be deeply seen and known" by another person is a profoundly vulnerable experience. It can be soul-stirring, scary, transformative, and healing. That is both the challenge and joy of loving someone.

---

### Love either shrinks or grows in direct proportion to what we do, say, and think, how we express or shrink back from it, and how we either open ourselves up to love or shut ourselves off from receiving it.

---

Love requires nurturing, care, and attention, to grow and expand. It takes great courage and intentionality to love well and create the environment to "nurture and grow" love and to discover the places inside that fear being intimately known by another. We all have them!

Swiss psychoanalyst Carl Jung refers to those hidden, suppressed, and fearful places inside as our shadow.

**"Our shadow self remains the great burden of self-knowledge, the disruptive element that does not want to be known."**

*—Meeting the Shadow: The Hidden Power of the Dark Side of Human Nature,* edited by Connie Zweig and Jeremiah Abrams

Our shadow serves as a repository for the parts of ourselves we have labeled as unacceptable including memories of traumatic experiences that we have buried in order to function without being emotionally overwhelmed and in the hopes of being seen as lovable. It lurks beneath the surface of conscious awareness manifesting in indirect (shadowed) ways, such as overreacting to small misunderstandings or within the attributes projected onto others.

Unresolved issues and unacknowledged desires lurking in your shadow can intensify the need for validation. Sometimes this need can heighten interest in work as increased validation is received from "winning" or "closing the deal". It can also result in greater susceptibility to attention from someone outside your primary relationship.

Shadowed aspects can be difficult to readily identify as they burrow themselves deep within the unconscious. When you find yourself intensely triggered by a current experience, or a quality that really bothers you in someone else, chances are you are tapping into some shadowed aspect within yourself.

Addressing the impact of the shadow on relationships involves uncovering, recognizing, and accepting your own hidden aspects, learning how they influence your behavior, and taking responsibility for your actions when they go off course.

Through engaging in this work, you have the opportunity to excavate and make peace with the parts you have buried and determine how you want to love and be loved moving forward. It takes courage to love well, to risk being seen and known, and to confront and make peace with your own shadow.

## Expanding the Definition of Love

I would like to expand Brown's definition of love to include *acceptance.* One of the most challenging things in a relationship is to accept someone as they are, and as they are not, including the ways they may be growing and changing. Acceptance is one of the greatest gifts we can offer to and receive from someone we love.

Acceptance involves a willingness to give your partner the space and grace to be who they are. It also involves giving them the benefit of the doubt instead of assuming missteps are intentional and working toward not taking things personally when a partner disappoints.

Acceptance invites a partner to bring their whole self to the table without having to walk on eggshells or hide parts of themselves that they believe you might find unacceptable or are afraid could jeopardize the relationship. As discussed, we learn to hide that within us we believe to be unlovable. The challenge is these parts do not remain hidden forever. They find indirect means of expression—overuse of substances, avoidance, passive-aggressive behavior, or affair engagement.

Let's take a look a quick look at the level of acceptance that exists within your relationship. You can answer these questions based upon your connection prior to affair discovery.

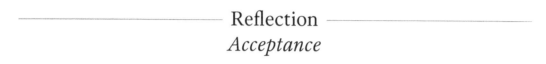

## Reflection
### *Acceptance*

- How accepted do you feel by your partner?
- How well do you accept yourself? Which aspects of yourself do you struggle with? Which aspects do you really like about yourself?
- How well do you accept your partner as they are? Which aspects of your partner do you struggle with? Which aspects of your partner do you really like?
- How accepted do you believe your partner feels by you?

This can be an insightful exercise to engage in with your partner. Part of reconnecting and healing involves engaging in meaningful discussions about things that matter. If you choose to use these questions as a discussion topic, as always, it's important that you answer the questions on your own and jot down your answers/thoughts. Then set up a time to sit down with each other to discuss.

Acceptance, love, and intimacy go hand-in-hand. Intimacy is built through heart-warming moments and expressed through actions taken that satisfy a person's unique love language.

## The Language of Love

The premise that each of us has a unique way in which we optimally feel loved was popularized in Gary Chapman's book *The 5 Love Languages*. Chapman's premise is that there are five primary ways in which we feel loved: acts of service, words of affirmation, physical touch, quality time, and gifts. We tend to demonstrate our love for other people through loving them in the ways that we prefer being loved. Challenges arise when two people's love languages don't match.

When love languages differ, it can be more challenging to recognize the ways in which our partner demonstrates their love for us. One person can feel like they are extending love and become surprised when they hear their partner isn't feeling it.

When I work with couples, we talk about how each one feels they are expressing love. People can be surprised to discover that their partner takes them into consideration more than they realize.

For example: Let's say your partner does things for you, like filling your car with gas or taking it to the car wash without being asked. Or perhaps they create meals with your favorite foods in mind. These acts of service are a way of demonstrating love. If your love language is words of affirmation, and your partner isn't letting you know the things they appreciate about you or using affirming language, you may not see their acts of service as love. Instead, your love tank may be feeling a bit empty.

It is important to know what makes your partner feel loved. When you do, you can engage in acts that speak their love language. Chapman has developed a quiz on his website to help you determine your specific love language.[15] His quiz and his book offer some great ideas that are particularly effective when love languages differ. This can be a fun way to learn about each other and work toward adapting to one another's unique language.

# The Four S's:
## *Self-Acceptance, Self-Trust, Self-Confidence, Self-Respect*

**"Loving oneself is no easy matter just because it means loving all of oneself, including the shadow where one is inferior and so socially unacceptable. The care one gives this humiliating part is also the cure."**

—James Hillman, *Meeting the Shadow: The Hidden Power of the Dark Side of Human Nature,* edited by Connie Zweig and Jeremiah Abrams

Equally as important as accepting our partner is accepting ourselves. When we are able to accept ourselves more fully, we are more inclined to move into greater acceptance of others. And, feeling acceptance from someone we care about helps us more fully accept ourselves. Both are important. True self-acceptance involves facing your own shadow, which can be tricky because it fights so hard against discovery.

**Self-acceptance and self-trust go hand-in-hand.** To trust yourself, you need to *accept* those things about you that you wish were different or wish you would have done differently. Self-trust entails making decisions that align with your deeply held values and beliefs. Self-trust is about staying true to yourself.

**Self-trust and self-acceptance lead to greater self-confidence.** At the root of self-confidence is **self-respect**. When you respect yourself you: a) trust in your value and worth, b) trust in your ability to make wise choices, and c) take responsibility for mistakes made along the way. When you respect yourself, you set up relationships built upon mutual respect.

**Embracing your value helps you set self-supportive boundaries and respect the boundaries set by others.** When done with direct kindness, setting self-supportive boundaries creates safety for all involved. Trusting yourself to set self-supportive boundaries keeps you from getting stuck in the avoidance trap, which helps to minimize relational distress.

Now we have expanded our definition of loving to include acceptance, self-acceptance, and the other three S's, let's talk about a critical relational component rarely discussed: How important is it that you *like* the person you are with? According to relationship experts John and Julie Gottman, it's pretty darn important. Let's take a look.

## Don't Underestimate the Power of *Like*

**"The determining factor in whether wives feel satisfied with the sex, romance, and passion in their marriage is, by 70 percent, the quality of the couple's friendship. For men, the determining factor is, by 70 percent, the quality of the couple's friendship. So, men and women come from the same planet after all."**

—John Gottman and Nan Silver, *The Seven Principles for Making Marriage Work*

In the relationship world, we tend to have two categories: either you're sleeping with someone (aka "in a relationship") or you're "just friends." While "just" implies that it's less desirable of a state, don't underestimate the power of friendship. Have you ever heard someone say (or even felt, yourself), *"I love them, but I don't like them very much"*? Sometimes it is easier to feel love for our spouse than it is to like them. Re-establishing friendship with your spouse is one of the cornerstones of affair recovery.

---

### When it comes to establishing a thriving marriage, in addition to loving someone, you must rebuild your *like* for them.

---

*Like* is cultivated through observing a person's actions. Their likeability is influenced by the choices we see them make in moment-by-moment interactions. Liking someone not only has to do with how the person treats you but with how you observe them treating others. How do they treat the checkout person? Waitstaff at a restaurant? The parking attendant? How do they treat the kids when they are angry? How do they treat us when angry? These seemingly little actions either move the needle forward or backward on the like-o-meter. In essence, liking is rooted in experiencing and observing respectful behavior.

Rebuilding this part of your relationship is a critical factor in re-establishing trust, getting your marriage back on track, and moving the needle from surviving to thriving.

## Reflection
### *Likeability*

- Where is the needle in the like-o-meter of your partner?
- Where was it before the affair?
- How about for yourself? How do you rate your likeability? How would your partner rate it?

Love and like are both important features of a healthy relationship. Couples who have established a strong like of each other tend to whether relational storms a bit better. The way to increase your likeability is to connect, engage, and share with each other about your dreams, goals, and day-to-day life while creating plans for the future together. Planning a trip—including discussing where to go, the desired climate, and activities that each one enjoys—can be a fun way to explore and reconnect. Even a day trip where each person takes on part of the planning, if this is something you both enjoy, can re-engage connection.

Next, we are going to dive into relationship stages to offer perspective on the movement of relationships as they evolve.

# 18

## Relationship Stages

—■—

*"I no longer believed in the idea of soul mates, or love at first sight.*
*But I was beginning to believe that a very few times in your life,*
*if you were lucky, you might meet someone who was exactly right*
*for you. Not because he was perfect, or because you were, but*
*because your combined flaws were arranged in a way that*
*allowed two separate beings to hinge together."*

—Lisa Kleypas, *Blue-Eyed Devil*

Healthy relationships grow and continue to evolve through three stages: merging, differentiation, and interdependence. Each stage offers opportunities for learning, growth, and deepening connection. The first two stages prepare a couple for the third stage of interdependence which is the most consistently mutual of the three.

It is natural for couples to encounter challenges specifically related to their progression through the first two stages. They can either become so comfortable in the merging stage that they lose their sense of adventure and impetus for growth which can result in feeling like life is on autopilot. Or, they may find themselves experiencing the frustration of the differentiation phase where they work to balance their need for independence vs. their need for connection.

The third stage of couple development revolves around interdependence. This stage evolves as relationships mature and partners recognize and acknowledge the importance of both personal and relational growth and development. Growth doesn't occur in a straight line. There will be situations that can re-activate challenges with differentiation (independence vs. freedom) such as being challenged by a partner's increasing interest in outside pursuits. And some beautiful aspects of the merging stage are important to savor as you move forward in creating a dynamic and thriving connection. The most important quality of a thriving relationship is the ability to talk about challenges as they arise.

Life offers many opportunities for growth, healing and learning. Your challenge as a couple is to use these experiences to help you continue to grow your personal and relational connection.

Let's take a deeper look.

## The Three Primary Relationship Stages

### MERGING: EMPHASIS ON WE

*I've never met anyone like you before. You are amazing. I love the way your smile lights up the room. I love spending time with you. We like so many of the same things!*

At the beginning of a relationship, partners are often idealized. The phrases above provide examples of what you might hear or say during the early merging stage of your relationship.

Here are some key indicators of the merging phase:
- Frequently wanting your partner by your side at parties/events
- Finding your partner's quirky little habits endearing (instead of annoying)
- Feeling a strong attraction to the person
- Thinking about the person frequently during the day
- Putting off other things you may want to do to spend time with your partner

During the initial courtship phase, the rush of new love takes center stage. The hall-mark of this phase is the bonding process, which occurs through spending time together and holding a positive vision of who your partner is, even when not together. Partners place a high priority on making time for each other. Each person feels desired and wanted. There emerges a sense of feeling like you have "found your person".

Remember how in Chapter 2 we discussed two primary human needs—attachment versus autonomy; connection versus freedom? **During this phase attachment tends to be the need which is satisfied most.** The merging stage is a foundational building block that helps set the stage for a couple's connection and positive attach-ment to one another.

There comes a point during the merging stage when a couple begins to feel more *comfortable* with each other. With or without children, this is the phase when two people feel like family. Even if they don't live together, they feel a sense of comfort and *at homeness* with their partner. You may have heard this referred to as "nesting."

Key indicators of the comfort substage of merging include:

- Letting down your guard with each other; feeling more relaxed in the relationship.
- The development of a stronger level of trust in the partnership
- Feeling more established as a couple and engaging more as a couple with the outside world
- Spending more time just being together, without a particular place to go, and simply enjoying each other's company.

The beginning of the merging stage is often referred to as the "honeymoon" stage which tends to be shorter lived. For some it can last up to a year; two years max. This evolves into the comfort substage which tends to be one of the longer-lasting stages. A couple can be in the comfort substage for years. Gradually, however, a couple can find themselves so comfortable that they begin feeling more like roommates than romantic partners. This is a time when one or both partners may begin feeling that they have "lost themselves".

An emerging need to engage in self-supportive activities which can include signing up for a new class, spending more time with friends, picking up an old or new hobby, are all hallmarks of the next very important stage known as differentiation.

## DIFFERENTIATION: EMPHASIS ON ME

**"Differentiation is your ability to maintain your sense of self when you are emotionally and/or physically close to others – especially as they become increasingly more important to you."**

—David Schnarch, PhD, *Passionate Couples: Sex, Love, and Intimacy in Emotionally Committed Relationships.*

As couples evolve there tends to be an increasing need to engage in personal development, time outside the relationship, with friends, work colleagues or solo experiences. As reflected in the quote above, the ability to *"maintain your sense of self"* while being deeply connected to the person/people you love, is the highest challenge of differentiation.

So, what are some of the signs of the differentiation phase? You and/or your partner can find yourselves wanting to carve out more time for independent activities. Maybe you find yourself feeling a bit *smothered.* You may also begin thinking more about what *you* want rather than focusing on your partner or your relational needs. These are all signs that you are moving into the differentiation phase of your relationship.

**During the differentiation phase the need for autonomy/ freedom and a sense of personal identity becomes paramount**. This too is an essential aspect of a couple's growth, where two people can respect one another's needs to pursue separate interests.

We have varying needs for comfort and adventure. While some aspects of adventure can be found within couples' activities, it is also important for each individual to cultivate their own sense of separate interest. Engaging with friends, community activities, the desire to learn something new or the pursuit of higher education can each help satisfy the need for personal growth, development, and differentiation.

Key indicators include:
- You notice the things about your partner that are different from you.
- The habits that you may have initially found endearing, you now find annoying.
- You find yourself desiring more alone time than usual or time with people other than your partner. Maintaining healthy friendships is important in all relational stages. If, however, you find yourself more frequently preferring time with friends and less frequently wanting time with your partner, that is a strong indicator that you have moved into the differentiation phase.

- You increasingly argue over the "little things."
- You have a renewed interest in an old hobby, or increased interest in activities that your partner doesn't particularly enjoy.

Couples can mistakenly interpret emerging needs for individual growth and learning to mean that something is *wrong*. However, this stage is a natural progression that occurs more strongly in some relationships, and with some individuals than others.

When your partner's need for independence is greater than your own, it can result in feelings of abandonment or fear that your partner may find someone or something else that is more satisfying than their relationship with you. This can trigger the need to hold on more tightly, which can result in the pursuit/withdrawal dance which is described in chapter 21. Efforts to control or dissuade a partner from outside engagement contribute to a partner's discontent, unrest, and the potential erosion of connection and intimacy.

Moving through differentiation can be tough, especially for a tightly merged couple. Staying stuck in the comfort zone, however, can contribute to a growing relational discontent which can result in a loss of aliveness, curiosity, and joy, which can trigger the thought that perhaps the only way to maintain individual identity is to leave the relationship.

**"Giving up your individuality to be together is as defeating in the long run as giving up your relationship to maintain your individuality. Either way, you end up being less of a person with less of a relationship."**

—David Schnarch, PhD, *Passionate Couples: Sex, Love, and Intimacy in Emotionally Committed Relationships.*

Feeling lost in a relationship can also occur more frequently during this stage. When a couple's merging is strong, however, it can sometimes take an unhealthy twist where the individuals feel stuck together, and then become resentful because of their dependence upon their partner. When this happens, one partner frequently begins to blame the other for their discontent.

This can also be a time when one or both people want to take a break from the relationship. Many relationships and marriages do not survive this phase. The differentiation stage is the most susceptible to affairs, as it is during this phase that partners are attempting to re-establish their independence and find their own way.

Navigating through the differentiation phase often poses the greatest challenge for couples. Sometimes instead of working through this developmental phase in ways that help create greater connection, or separating altogether, couples choose to more or less live separate lives under the same roof.

Solid coupling includes a balance of both individual pursuits and quality time together. The need for differentiation is a healthy sign of couple development. Those who successfully make it through this phase learn how to accept, adapt, and listen to each other and not hide out when things are bothering them.

## INTERDEPENDENCE: EMPHASIS ON YOU, ME, AND US

**"Every Individual and every relationship has a point at which a fundamental reorganization takes place. New behaviors and solutions appear because the system itself is changing. ... When couples realize they've been going through the natural people-growing process of marriage, they stop feeling defective and become more respectful of themselves and their relationship."**

—David Schnarch, PhD, *Passionate Couples: Sex, Love, and Intimacy in Emotionally Committed Relationships*

The prefix "inter" is defined by Merriam Webster's Collegiate dictionary as "between, among, mutually, reciprocally." Mutuality and reciprocity are two of the hallmarks of an interdependent relationship.

Couples in interdependent relationships foster each other's need for self-growth, as well as reliance upon one another. They have learned that they can turn to their partner with challenges and receive support and encouragement, rather than criticism and blame. Their dependence is mutually beneficial and healthy, not one-sided or smothering. They also trust enough in their connection to bring challenging thoughts and ideas to the table rather than *walking on eggshells* in an effort to maintain relational peace.

When we encourage our partners to do what they love, even when it differs from what we love or takes some time away from our connection, it creates greater relational health. In the long run, encouraging a partner to engage in what they are truly passionate about ends up benefiting you both.

Partners are able to acknowledge that life and their relationship is a work in progress that requires time, attention, and support on an ongoing basis. They recognize the importance of honoring their own needs as well as the needs of their partner and have greater appreciation for their ability to depend upon one another without losing their sense of self. This doesn't mean that their life is perfect, but rather that they have moved into a deeper belief and trust that they can rely upon each other to help weather the storms together, without compromising who they are.

**During the interdependent stage a couple is learning how to recognize and honor other's need for attachment—connection and their need for autonomy—freedom.** Balancing these two needs is an ongoing challenge to navigate throughout the life of their relationship.

Key indicators include:

- You are both willing to accept each other fully, without having to "walk on eggshells" around each other or hide your needs or desires to avoid conflict. You commit to discussing challenges in mutually supportive ways.
- You recognize and acknowledge that you are both doing the best you can. You give one another the "benefit of the doubt."
- You make the conscious choice to love this person and behave in a manner that demonstrates that choice.

---

## Love isn't just a feeling. It's an active choice made and demonstrated on a moment-by-moment basis.

---

- You make time for each other, recognizing that your relationship must be a priority. Creating special moments for a loved one helps them feel special, important, and desired.
- You support each other's interests and express curiosity about their endeavors.

While there tends to be a progression from one stage to another, individuals and couples move between stages depending upon various needs and the situations which present themselves. The key to best navigating individual and relational needs is to talk about them. It can sometimes be tricky to create space for both. Setting aside time for weekly discussions to talk about wants, needs, growth, and desires is a great place to start.

## Reflection
### *Your Relationship Stage*

Take a few moments to consider your relationship in relation to these stages.

- Which stage do you feel your relationship spent most of its time in just before your affair?

- Which areas can you pinpoint as most challenging?

- Can you see elements of all three stages in how you have connected in the past?

- What can you see as a possibility for your future?

A thriving relationship supports both relational and individual growth. Time needs to be carved out for a couple to connect, have fun, and engage in new experiences together. Activities that nurture individual growth and learning can also foster a couple's growth. When personal experiences and new discoveries are shared with an interested partner, intimacy is nurtured. This type of sharing helps fill the need for the Three No's: being noticed, being known, and knowing you matter.

---

**A relationship is comprised of three entities: you, me, and us. A thriving relationship makes sure all three are fed.**

---

"Your task is not to seek for love, but merely to seek and find all the barriers within yourself that you have built against it."

—Jalaluddin Rumi, philosopher, poet

# 19

## Sex *and* Intimacy

■

### SEX

*"To feel aroused is to feel alive. Having great sex is like taking in huge lungfuls of fresh air, essential to your body, essential to your health, and essential to your life."*
—Fiona Thrust, *Naked and Sexual*

### INTIMACY

*"People think that intimacy is about sex. But intimacy is about truth. When you realize you can tell someone your truth, when you can show yourself to them, when you stand in front of them and their response is, 'You're safe with me'—that's intimacy."*
—Taylor Jenkins Reid, *The Seven Husbands of Evelyn Hugo*

Sex and intimacy. While one can lead to and/or be part of the other, each can stand on its own. You can have an intimate connection without sex, and you can have sex without much intimacy. As you move forward with your relationship it is important to understand and rebuild both.

# Intimacy

**There is an intimacy that can emerge from holding space for one another without rushing to a solution.**

After an affair, uncertainty prevails. Both individuals are balancing a mixture of hope for increased connection, and fear of potential heartbreak. Trying to reconcile with a partner that you feel uncertain about can feel like sailing across an ocean without a rudder.

**The betrayed individual** may experience a fear of being caught off guard by new information. They may fear trusting too quickly, only to find out that the betraying partner is keeping secrets or still involved with the affair partner or will connect with them again in the future. They may fear that their partner won't ever fully understand the extent of their pain.

**The one who has betrayed** may fear the unpredictability of their partner's emotions. They may worry about their partner changing their mind or being unable to forgive them if they get too close. They may fear investing too much effort into rebuilding the relationship, only to have their partner ultimately leave.

These fears can lead to a pattern of taking a few steps forward and then retreating.

Rebuilding intimacy requires the ability to hold space for healing without rushing headlong into a solution. One of the most challenging things about affair recovery is that you don't know what's next. Rushing into a solution or into assumptions too quickly doesn't allow space for deeper healing and true re-establishment of relational intimacy. It's challenging to be patient, present and allow things to unfold. We tend to want to make it to the finish line. True intimacy, however, isn't about reaching a climax, but rather paying attention to the sensations, connection and joy available in the present moment. Intimacy is a gift partners give to each other.

# So, what is intimacy anyway?

**"When an individual trusts another sufficiently to expose the true self—the deepest fears, the hidden desires—a powerful intimacy is born."**

—Greer Hendricks, Sarah Pekkanen, *An Anonymous Girl*

Intimacy entails sharing the deeper aspects of oneself with another and establishing a secure space for mutual sharing. As stated in the book *The Four Intimacies* by Dr. Amy Clark and Roy Clark, "Intimacy is the crucial component that your relationship must be built upon, or your love won't sustain you when challenges arise. Nor will a relationship without intimacy enrich you."

This doesn't mean your relationship is doomed if you don't have strong intimacy, but it does mean that your intimacy levels need attention. The good news is your relationship intimacy can be fostered through physical, emotional, intellectual, and spiritual connections, as well as through shared experiences. The Clarks describe four levels of intimacy, which when developed foster a stronger relationship:

1. **Verbal Intimacy.** Listening with an intention to understand fosters verbal intimacy. In long-term relationships, the ability to reminisce about meaningful shared experiences strengthens the bond between partners. Conversely, recalling past traumatic experiences, particularly when used to criticize, blame, or shame a partner, can significantly damage a couple's intimate connection.

2. **Emotional Intimacy.** Yielding your innermost feelings to your partner in a way you don't do with anyone else builds emotional intimacy. Similarly, being receptive to your partner's emotions helps strengthen trust and fulfillment.

3. **Physical Intimacy.** This one may seem obvious, but it is about more than just sex. True intimacy comes when you understand your partner's preferences, and they understand yours. You may include non-sexual touch; as well as sexual connection that is satisfying to both partners.

4. **Spiritual Intimacy.** This level of intimacy involves sharing a connection beyond the physical realm. It could be a shared faith, or beliefs, or a focus on aspirations and dreams.

The building blocks of intimacy are presence, authenticity, vulnerability, deep listening, empathy, and touch.

Rebuilding intimacy requires desire, intentionality, commitment, and prioritization. Just like any endeavor, the stronger your desire, the more effort and focus you will dedicate to the process. Next, we will explore strengthening your intimacy through touch, followed by communication.

# Deepening Intimacy through Touch

Human touch is an important ingredient in one's sense of well-being. Studies have shown the positive impact of a *welcomed* deep, long (5 to 20 seconds) hug on a person's mental and physical well-being. Hugs of this type activate a movement from a sympathetic response (fight, flight, freeze, faint) into a parasympathetic (calm, relaxed) state. Hugs build a sense of safety and closeness as they increase the level of the hormone oxytocin (known as the cuddle hormone), which increases intimacy, strengthens the immune system, lowers blood pressure, and even increases self-esteem.[16]

Can you recall a time when you gave a deep hug to someone in distress and felt that person calm? How about receiving a hug of this nature when you were distressed? Did it help you feel soothed and safe as either the giver or receiver?

In a partnership, individuals have varying levels of touch tolerance and needs. It is crucial to be mindful of your partner's needs and your own. Differences in touch preference can lead to conflict. If this is the case in your relationship, it is important to have open discussions about comfort levels and desires.

If varying needs for touch has been a challenge in your relationship, talk about it. There are ways to fill this need that can feel less threatening if one of you is a bit touch averse. Small gestures like a hand on the shoulder or arm can foster a sense of connection. This can be particularly helpful during challenging moments or to show support during conversations. Or it is possible that your verbal and emotional intimacy need attention in order to spark a stronger desire to be physically close (see the next section on ways to strengthen your communication, which will help with this).

One of the challenges I hear from women who have been shying away from their partner's touch or from initiating touch is the concern that their partners typically expect sex to follow touch, or that their partner only touches when they want to be sexual. While touching can be a prelude to sex, an intimate connection can be built and rebuilt through touching (e.g., cuddling, hugging, handholding, kissing) without automatically culminating in sexual connection. This is important to note, especially as you are rebuilding your relationship with your spouse after an affair. She may not want to be sexual for a while. Touch, without the pressure for sex, can be a promising way to begin the trust-rebuilding process. It is important to be patient with each other as you navigate through the waters of reconnection.

Some couples have the opposite experience and jump back into a sexual connection rather quickly after an affair. As we have previously discussed, sex is one form of communication within a partnership. While physical intimacy is an important aspect of a partnership, take care to not let sexual connection overshadow other forms of communication and intimacy.

# Deepening Intimacy through Communication

Intimacy is both built and dismantled by the way you communicate. The types of communication you choose, whether light and playful, in-depth and truthful, problem-solving focused, or future-oriented, play a crucial role in fostering intimacy. By utilizing these communication styles, you can not only rebuild intimacy after an affair, but also strengthen and sustain your relationship over time. Cultivating a deeper connection through effective communication can make your bond more resilient and enduring. Remember, developing these communication habits is an ongoing process that can lead to lasting fulfillment for both partners.

**Light and playful** communication is flirty, fun, and usually involves a momentary *"I'm thinking about you"* reach out. You can initiate a fun text message during the day or send a meme or song that reminds you of your beloved. Consider things that can make her laugh, or special language or words you share together.

**Effective problem-solving communication** is crucial for nurturing a strong and healthy relationship. It entails dedicating time to have candid and open conversations about significant issues or obstacles that either of you may encounter. This form of communication enables you to collaboratively find solutions as a team or seek comfort and assistance from your partner when necessary. By proactively addressing challenges instead of avoiding them, you can foster trust, intimacy, and long-lasting connection in your relationship.

**In-depth communication** involves sharing important and often vulnerable aspects of yourself with your loved one. This can be facilitated through various activities that promote meaningful, growth-oriented discussions. You may choose to read and discuss an interesting book together, participate in a fun, spiritual, or growth-oriented class, or use card decks or games that encourage exploration. By creating a safe and supportive environment for exploration, you can foster open and honest communication and strengthen the connection with your partner. The questions in this book are also designed to spark deeper intimacy-building conversations.

**Future-building conversations** are designed to paint a picture of the future you would like to create as a couple. These conversations can include dreams, visions, wealth-building ideas, travel, individual desires, such as going back to school. or career building. Your discussions can range from fun and playful endeavors to more serious discussions about your financial future. These conversations can be pleasure-oriented and/or goal-oriented. Here are some questions to consider:

- What would you like to build as the two of you move forward, individually and together?
- What future aspirations do you have?
- What are each person's top two priorities for the next month? Year? Five years?
- What are your goals for building wealth? Retirement? Future places to live?
- Where are the two of you in sync? Where do you differ?
- How about travel? Where would your dream vacation take you? Where would you like to go in the next year? Two years? Five years?
- What are some local destinations you would love to include on your bucket list?
- What types of adventures feed your soul?

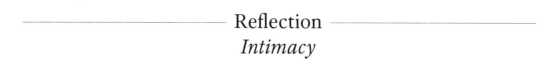

## Reflection
### *Intimacy*

Here are some questions to help you explore your comfort with intimacy and ways you can feel more connected. This can be a partner or solo endeavor.

### COMFORT, SAFETY, AND BUILDING INTIMACY

Consider your level of comfort in the following areas. If you like, you can use a rating scale of 0 to 5, with 0 being not comfortable at all, and 5 being totally comfortable. Write down some notes about what stands out for you as you explore these questions.

- How open are you to exploring new ways to deepen intimacy with your partner?
- Rate the level of intimacy with your partner in the following areas:
  o Verbal
  o Emotional
  o Physical
  o Spiritual

(If your rating is below a 3 in any category, what would help increase your level of intimacy in this area? If it is a 5, consider what stands out to make this aspect of intimacy work well.)

- Rate and rank your level of communication in each of the sub-categories discussed.
  - Light and Playful
  - Problem-Solving
  - In-Depth
  - Future-Building

Which one is easiest? Which ones do you find to be the most difficult? What are some ways that you can create a safer connection that encourages communication in each area? What are you willing to do to step-up your engagement with your partner?

- What are three things you can do to help create more intimacy in your relationship? Are there specific requests your partner has made in the past that help them feel more intimately connected to you?

- What are three things your partner has done/can do to help you feel more intimately connected?

- How do you feel about touch?
  - Is touch one of the primary ways you feel loved and cared for? How about your partner?

- I feel more connected to my partner when... (Check all that apply. Place an asterisk next to those that are the most important.)

  ☐ My partner sends me text messages throughout the day.

  ☐ My partner responds to my text messages in (kind, funny, loving, _____) ways.

  ☐ My partner calls or leaves a message during the day.

  ☐ My partner tells me he/she loves me.

  ☐ We cuddle.

  ☐ My partner touches me (rubs my shoulder, holds my hand, offers a playful touch, and/or _____).

  ☐ My partner goes out of their way to do something special for me.

  ☐ We engage in deep, meaningful conversations.

☐ We travel or plan trips.

☐ We spend time planning for our future.

☐ We engage in spiritual activities or attend services together.

☐ We spend time in nature.

☐ We engage in activities together.

☐ My partner holds eye contact when talking.

☐ My partner holds eye contact when we are sexually intimate.

☐ My partner walks into the room and I can feel their vibe; when their energy is positive, and it feels like they want to connect.

☐ My partner plans something for us (a date, an afternoon outing, _____).

☐ My partner is interested in what I have to say. I feel listened to.

☐ We engage in lively discussions about a topic of interest to one or both of us.

☐ _____ .

Be patient with one another as you rebuild intimacy and connection. Focus on creating a safe and supportive environment within which to share. Each time you engage in ways that foster connection, you build intimacy and trust.

# Sex

*"Sexuality is a vibrant force within us all. It inspires us to be more than we ever thought we could be."*

—Marilyn Monroe, actress

---

## Our sexuality is a journey of growth, learning, and transformation. It is a beautiful and complex tapestry of desires, emotions, and experiences.

---

Sexual engagement is one way of expressing and discovering who we are as individuals and within our relationships. Individuals have many notions about sex. You may think it is reserved for marriage, deeply satisfying, ecstatic, curious, perfunctory, a tension reliever, natural, a driver of male behavior, dirty, or something you feel obligated to say "yes" to if you're married. There are many factors that contribute to views on what sex is, and what is and isn't okay in your bedroom.

Next we will be taking a look at sex—what it means to you, as well as the influence it has had on your relational connections, personal development, and ways of viewing yourself and your partner. The exercises included in this portion are designed to help you consider your likes, dislikes, and preferences regarding sexual engagement and connecting with your partner. This can be a great section to work on together when you're both ready. Exploring and engaging in conversations of this nature can deepen your sexual understanding of each other and yourselves.

Keep in mind that sex may not be something your partner is currently ready to explore. If she is hesitant, don't push it. In the meantime, this reading can be helpful for you, and she can engage in it once she is ready.

# What Really Counts as Sex?

**"Sex functions in other ways, but its capacity to make us feel better quickly is arguably its primary allure, its hook par excellence. After all, doesn't just the possible promise of erotic engagement tend to push our pain more into the background?"**

—Robert Augustus Masters, *To Be a Man: A Guide to True Masculine Power*

Most of us have heard that infamous line: *"I did not have sexual relations with that woman."* Taking that as a statement of his beliefs around sex as opposed to a statement of denial, we can surmise that former president Bill Clinton's definition of *sex* did not include oral sex. While some of us may roll our eyes at that perspective, what is important to note is that we each have our specific views on sex and sexuality, including how we view sexual encounters and what constitutes fidelity and infidelity.

*Merriam-Webster's Collegiate Dictionary* defines *sex* as:
"sexually motivated phenomena or behavior; sexual intercourse"

It seems that even the dictionary is not crystal clear on the defining features of sex. According to *Merriam-Webster*, intercourse counts; but what is *"sexually motivated phenomena or behavior"*?

What's most important is how you and your partner define sexual engagement, preferences, and limits. It takes courage to fully re-engage sexually and discuss sexual needs, wants, and desires after an affair. As with other relational topics, an affair can open the door to deeper explorations and discussions regarding sex within the primary partnership—*if* managed well. As noted, it is important that you not push into this topic if your partner isn't ready, as discussions about sexual topics can provoke vulnerability, especially after infidelity.

If you are unsure whether your partner is ready to talk about sex, ask. Let them know that you would like to better understand their sexual preferences and discuss ways you can work together to create a sexual connection that is mutually meaningful and pleasurable. You can explore the questions in this chapter even if you are not currently engaging sexually. This is most likely a discussion topic to explore when you are further along in your relational recovery process.

# The Language of Sex

Sex is a distinct form of communication that is molded by the people involved. It has the potential to evolve, become routine, or grow stale over time. Sexual arousal is a multifaceted process involving a combination of thoughts, hormones, physical characteristics, desires, and our interpretation of our partner's desires. Our level of comfort with our own sexuality, body, and partner, influences sexual arousal and connectivity.

Perceptions and beliefs about sex are shaped by a multitude of factors, including past experiences, upbringing, traumas, societal influences, and personal preferences. Our thoughts, emotions, and psychological makeup all play a role in how we approach and experience sexual connection and erotic desires.

*Merriam-Webster's Collegiate Dictionary* defines *erotic* as:
"devoted to or tending to arouse sexual love or desire."

Each individual and couple have their own unique erotic blueprint, influenced by past experiences, relationship dynamics, and personal connections. Erotic desire often operates on a subconscious level and is activated by specific situations that align with our internal blueprint. Sex can be a mix of excitement, messiness, and confusion, evoking laughter, love, and feelings of closeness. It can also bring up fears related to intimacy and vulnerability.

When two people engage sexually they each bring their unique hidden needs and desires into the experience, adding to the allure of the experience. The anticipation of the unknown can heighten attention and contribute to the intensity of a new encounter.

In longer-term relationships, partners can experience an enriched sexual connection as they become increasingly more comfortable with and knowledgeable about one another. While maintaining a fulfilling sexual relationship may require a more deliberate effort as a relationship progresses, the depth of intimacy and familiarity in longer-term partnerships can allow for greater exploration and comfort in the sexual realm. However, a challenge that may arise from this deep understanding is the potential for complacency in both the relationship and the bedroom.

The dynamics of a couple's sexual connection often mirror their interactions in other aspects of the relationship. Similar to the relationship itself, the sexual bond between partners can flourish, take a backseat to other life obligations, become a source of conflict, or even serve as the primary means of connection between the couple. Emotional disturbances and disruptions in the relationship can impede the couple's desire and ability to connect physically. Conversely, collaborating closely on shared life goals and/or engaging in enlivening experiences can ignite fresh level of intimacy that can in turn fuel sexual desire.

When connection in other areas of the relationship is rocky, one or both partners may cling to sex as a way of measuring whether or not the partnership is still "okay." Using sex in this way can exert pressure on a partner to respond in a particular way to requests for sex. While engaging in sex can calm anxiety and doubt, it can also amp up anxiety if a partner fears the repercussions of what saying "no" may bring.

Be careful not to use sex as the primary determinant of whether or not you are connected, as it can exert pressure on you both, and it may even diminish desire. A partner who does something out of pressure may end up resentful and distant rather than full of bonding hormones. To get stuck on having the "perfect sex" or obsess over whether it was "good enough" for you or your partner can keep you in your head, which makes it difficult to engage and flow into the experience of physically connecting with someone you love. Additionally, a period of apathy or dissatisfaction with the sexual connection doesn't necessarily equate to a broken or doomed relationship. Sexual arousal and engagement between you and your partner can grow, especially with mutual focused attention.

**We need to rethink sex as an expression of a couple's love for one another, not a measurement of whether or not the relationship is solid.**

## Everything Begins with a Conversation

"The most powerful aphrodisiac is communication."

—Robert Augusts Masters, *To Be a Man, A Guide to True Masculine Power*

Sex can be a challenging discussion topic, especially in the face of infidelity. Discussions around sex and intimacy can be overshadowed by other aspects of affair recovery, but they are important areas of connection and potential growth to address.

When engaging in discussions about intimacy and physical connection, it is important to be mindful of your partner's readiness. Talking about sex can be a delicate journey filled with unexpected triggers. These discussions can unearth past trauma, as well as feelings of inadequacy, unworthiness, shame, excitement, curiosity, anger, and connection.

Perhaps as a couple, you have primarily felt sexually fulfilled and satisfied with your level of sex and intimacy. If so, it is important to validate that. Again, insecurity is a natural by-product of an affair. You need to reaffirm that the affair wasn't an indicator that something was amiss in the bedroom at home if that is the case for you. And this can be a great time to expand your sexual connection and talk about things that you may have been unwilling or uncomfortable discussing in the past.

If you find yourself interested in exploring sexual connection with your partner in ways that lie outside of the sexual protocols the two of you have established, it is important to talk about that as well.

**Talking comes before acting on anything outside of what has been the norm at home.**

If you are uncomfortable discussing this aspect of your relationship as a couple—or if your partner is uncomfortable but willing to try—reaching out to a professional who is well-versed in this area can help you both re-engage and explore what you would both like moving forward.

## Reflection
### *Sexual Exploration*

The following segments contain questions about sex to help explore and clarify your views and preferences. Gaining clarity about your wants, needs, and boundaries paves the way for enhanced sexual connection.

When working through this with a partner, answer the questions individually first, then schedule a time to discuss. When discussing, work through one question at a time. Determine who will be the first to share and who will be the listener. **The listener should refrain from interrupting or offering opinions.** Instead, they can nod to indicate they have heard their partner and write down any questions for later discussion. After the first partner finishes sharing, the listener should summarize what they heard and seek clarification on any questions that arose. **It's important to note that questions should aim to understand and validate, not interrogate.**

If a question triggers upset in either one of you, take a break and come back to that question later. Remind one another that this isn't about making someone right or wrong; it's about discussing ideas outside the bedroom to help free you up inside the bedroom (or wherever)!

### DEFINING YOUR COMFORT LEVEL

The questions that follow are designed to help you rate and explore your attitudes and preferences around sex, beginning with your comfort level for discussing sex with your partner. You can use the 1 to 5 scale where applicable. (If your rating is below a 3, what would help make this topic easier to discuss?)

- How comfortable or willing are you to talk with your partner about what you would enjoy sexually?
- How comfortable or willing are you to discuss or explore what your partner would enjoy sexually?

- How comfortable or willing are you to engage in discussions around sexual fantasies, and ways to stimulate greater pleasure and physical connection?

  o Is there anything in particular that stands in the way of discussing what you find pleasurable with your partner?

  o Is there something specific that you would like to discuss with your partner either now or in the future?

- If your partner lets you know they are not willing to engage in a particular sexual activity, do you accept their decision or work to convince them otherwise?

## SEXUAL INITIATION, PLANNING, AND PREFERENCES

The questions that follow are designed to help you explore your attitudes and preferences around sexual initiation and enjoyment.

- What does your partner do or say to let you know they are interested in engaging sexually? What do you do to let your partner know that you are interested?

- What is your preference around who initiates sex. Do you prefer to initiate? Do you prefer that your partner initiates? Are you open to either? Do you prefer that one of you initiates more often than the other?

- Is there a particular way that sex is initiated that most entices you?

- Do the two of you plan designated days for sexual engagement? Are your sexual encounters more spontaneous? Which would you prefer?

- Are there certain "acts" that need to be included for you to classify an interaction as "sex"? Is genital penetration required?

- Do you enjoy oral sex? Giving? Receiving? Both?

- Does kissing count as "sexual behavior"? What other behaviors count as sexual?

- How do you know when sex is finished?

- Are orgasms required for you to feel complete? Yours? Your partner's?

- Can sex be a solo activity, or does it necessitate having a partner?

- What do you feel is the purpose or greatest aspect of engaging sexually? Here are some examples: *Tension relief. To feel more connected. To express your love. To experience pleasure. To experience my partner's pleasure.*

## WHAT GETS IN THE WAY?

Next, we are going to take a look at what might sometimes get in the way of sexual engagement and enjoyment.

- If you think back to times when sex didn't work out the way you would have liked, what caused you to feel let down?
- When have you felt rejected or disappointed in sex, or attempts to connect with your partner?
- What do you wish was different in your sexual communication or connection?
- What blocks your full enjoyment of sex with your partner?
- Is it important for you to feel intimately or emotionally connected to engage sexually?
- Have you experienced sexual trauma in the past? If so, how do you feel this affects sexual engagement with your partner?

A healthy sexual connection is based upon respect and finding a balance between playfulness, spontaneity, pleasure, pleasing, exploration, and honoring boundaries. Your wants may differ from your partner's. It is important to talk about any differences in ways that invite conversation and creative solutions, rather than foster blame. It is also important to discern whether you and/or your partner are willing to explore each other's desired behaviors, or if a particular type of engagement is completely off the table.

Many people define sex by a particular conclusion, like orgasm. Setting orgasm as the defining characteristic of "successful" sex can put pressure on one or both partners, particularly as they age. This can limit sexual pleasure, intimacy, and freedom of expression. There are many ways to have sexy times that may or may not include someone reaching a climax.

## WANTS, MAYBES, AND NO WAYS

As in all aspects of relational connection, the more clarity you and your partner have around your wants and needs—including what brings you pleasure and pain and what you need to feel safe—the more you are freed up to engage in sexual conversations and experiences with one another. In essence, the more you know about yourselves, the more clearly you can articulate your wants and needs—and the more open you will be to hearing theirs.

You each have needs and likes that help make sexual connections feel more satisfying. **Next to each phrase, write an "I" next to what is most important for sex to include for you, an "O" for what you would be open to including or experimenting with, and an "N" for No, when a specific behavior is off limits.** You can place an asterisk next to the most important aspects.

- ☐ Consent—mine and my partner's
- ☐ Mental stimulation
- ☐ Ramp-up/foreplay
- ☐ Kissing
- ☐ Playfulness
- ☐ Using Sex Toys
    - ☐ Solo
    - ☐ With my partner watching
    - ☐ Together
- ☐ Being touched (where?) _____
- ☐ Vaginal penetration
- ☐ Anal penetration
- ☐ Oral-genital contact
    - ☐ Given
    - ☐ Received
- ☐ Fantasies
    - ☐ Talking about
    - ☐ Acting out
- ☐ Feeling loved
- ☐ Orgasm
- ☐ Gentleness
- ☐ Being "taken"
- ☐ Intensity (describe) _____

☐ Diversity—experimenting with different positions, places, etc.

☐ Talking dirty/provocatively

☐ _____

☐ _____

☐ _____

Take time to think about engagements that you enjoy as well as things that feel off-limits. Add to the list as warranted.

In reflecting on your needs and likes, consider the following:

- What I particularly enjoy during sex with my partner is:

  _____

- What I would like (or what I would like more of) from my partner during sex is:

  _____

- What I would like less of is:

  _____

- Something new I would like to try is:

  _____

- What I sometimes struggle with sexually is:

  _____

- One thing I wish my partner understood about my sexual needs is:

  _____

- One thing I find sexy or sexually exciting is:

  _____

Consider these items as a place to begin. Add to this list anything else that you would like to experience more of during your sexual interactions.

# The Impact of Sexual Trauma
# and Shame on Sexual Connection

Past situations and traumas can evoke a sense of confusion and shame, which can impact sexual connection. Sometimes these are topics that have been previously discussed. Other times there are encounters that have been kept hidden or situations a person may not even realize were impacting how they do and do not connect intimately or sexually with their partner.

Sexual shame, for example, can be the result of molestations or inappropriate sexual contact during childhood or teen years. The resulting confusion can be greater if those experiences were never resolved or discussed, or if they were with a relative. Sexual trauma and shame can also be the result of a difficult or confusing first encounter or a coerced or forced sexual encounter at any point in time.

The experience of abuse—sexual, emotional, or physical—creates feelings of powerlessness that, unless fully addressed, can impact future relationships. This can play out as fear of deep intimacy or too much closeness, emotional withdrawal, or ways a person does or does not like to be touched within and outside of sexual or intimate encounters.

Challenging, confusing, and abusive sexual experiences can also result in the repression of sexual desires or overly sexualized behavior and/or a heightened need for sex in order to feel okay. There also may be sexual preferences that a partner may not be willing to participate in. Sometimes it can seem less threatening to play out varying sexual preferences with someone outside of a primary relationship, which can lead to affairs.

It can be helpful to explore delicate conversations around sexual needs and past traumas with a professional. Healing is possible—both for individuals and couples. A knowledgeable professional can help you navigate through challenging discussions around trust, touch, sex, sexual trauma, and sexual shame. Sex and intimacy are topics that are frequently discussed in couples work, and they provide beautiful avenues within which couples can connect and experience their love for one another. The foundation of trust you gain (or rebuild) will be paramount to your ability to explore and experience a healthy and loving physical connection moving forward.

# The Importance of Consent

**The most important thing about engaging in any type of sexual exploration or new activity is to make sure that you receive consent from a partner before diving in.**

Early in a relationship, this may involve verbally asking what is okay and not—and always respecting those wishes, without compromise. On an ongoing basis, tune in to your partner for any changes in their boundaries—which may be communicated non-verbally or verbally. When in question, ask your partner. Consent creates freedom. When both parties agree on what they are willing to explore, a sense of safety is created. Feeling safe with a partner creates more freedom. When you know where a person's edges are in advance, you have more room to play within those edges.

**To be crystal clear, coerced consent—that is someone feeling pressured, or afraid of the repercussions saying no will bring—is not consent.**

Consent is not:

- Continuing to do something after a partner asks you to stop.
- Continuing to touch someone in a place they have indicated they don't want to be touched.
- Verbally pressuring someone to engage in or continue an activity they said they dislike or have asked you to stop.
- Trying to *wear someone down* until they give up and give in to what you want.

Another important element is that consent can be withdrawn at any time. You may find your partner willing to begin, but then partially through your sexual encounter, asking to stop.

Re-engagement after an affair can be tricky, as emotions can be triggered at any time. There may be some back and forth of boundaries early on, and it's important to communicate about and respect any changes to one person's desires. Taking time to talk and learn about each other's preferences and boundaries is something that you may have never done in this way. While conversations of this nature can be uncomfortable, they can also create breakthroughs and deepen connection. Being patient will pay off.

When your partner knows they have the freedom to choose, including the freedom to stop at any moment in time, it increases their safety in the relationship. Safety creates a foundation of trust which impacts all areas of your relationship.

# Desire Discrepancies

**"There is often minimal love in 'lovemaking' because partners don't have sex with each other; instead, they pay attention to their technique. ... Slowing down enough to make a vibrational connection – letting your partner feel you and vice versa – is not easy to do. But it's often beautiful when it happens ..."**

—David Schnarch, PhD, *Passionate Couples: Sex, Love, and Intimacy in Emotionally Committed Relationships*

Desiring and feeling desired are both important aspects of physical and emotional connection. Often a loss of desire by one or both people is indicative of struggles in other areas of the marriage. Sometimes it can be the result of physical changes or unresolved challenges that have built up resentment over time. Sometimes one person has a higher sex drive than the other.

Other disruptions could include one partner working long hours, caring for a sick family member, the birth of a child, or aging parents. Sometimes, a lack of prioritization of the relationship can also lead to disconnection. It's crucial to address these issues proactively, finding solutions that do not necessarily result in disconnection. By being adaptable and attentive to each other's needs, couples can navigate these challenges and strengthen their bond.

Sometimes the desire discrepancies are so great that they seem unsolvable. A willingness to discuss and possibly explore new ways to connect is an important first step. There are many ways to satisfy the need for sex and intimacy. Visits to medical professionals can help with physical challenges. Feeling like you have room to discuss these things with a partner who is willing to listen, without anger or blame, can help you discover ways forward, preventing the desire discrepancies from becoming a roadblock to intimacy.

A discrepancy in desire seemed to be the primary driver in our next story.

# A Different Happily Ever After:
## *Chase and Clara's Story*

For Chase, sex seemed to be the primary infidelity driver. His wife, Clara, just didn't seem to be into him anymore. They hadn't engaged sexually in over a year.

Chase grew tired of feeling rejected. He was an alive and vibrant man who didn't want to live the rest of his life without a sexual connection. Their disconnection as a couple, and his discontent as an individual, continued to grow. They simply did not seem to be able to bridge their desire gap.

### LOOKING ELSEWHERE

Ultimately Chase decided to take matters into his own hands and began looking elsewhere. He rationalized that if he could simply get his sexual needs met, it would help take the pressure off his marriage. *"Who knows, with sex off the table, maybe Clara and I might even be better together."* That's what he told himself when seeking out other women to satisfy this missing component of his marriage.

Chase enjoyed connecting with different women. They were exciting and made him feel wanted and alive. He was upfront about his needs and established a "strictly business" type of connection with each woman. By classifying it as "just sex," he convinced himself that it worked for all concerned: himself, Clara, and the women he engaged with.

For a time, it did seem to work. As he stopped pushing Clara for sex, she seemed more content. With Chase feeling more fulfilled, Clara felt less anxious. With sex off the table, however, intimacy soon followed. The two of them began drifting further apart, ultimately living relatively separate, albeit predominantly conflict-free, lives.

### SOMETHING MORE

One of the women he connected with began to grow fond of him, and he started seeing her exclusively. Ultimately their connection moved from just sex into a more emotional connection. While this isn't what Chase had set out to create, he found himself enjoying the woman's company. Sometimes instead of engaging in any type of sexual activity, they spent their time together talking. Chase found more reasons to "work late" and engage with this woman.

Over time, Chase began to feel guilty about deceiving Clara. This was not at all what he had intended. He felt like he needed to end things but wasn't exactly sure how. He went away for a weekend alone to think things through.

## CONFRONTING THE EVIDENCE

Meanwhile, Clara's Spidey sense told her something was off. Things just weren't adding up. It wasn't like Chase to stay late at work so often. And he wasn't even *trying* to connect with her sexually anymore.

Like many women who notice a shift in behavior, Clara went on a quest to discover what was behind the shift. What she discovered wasn't pretty. She found evidence that Chase had been engaging in secret liaisons with other women for over a year. The more Clara uncovered, the more her heart sank. She knew she and Chase had been disconnected, but she never thought he would explore connecting with someone else. She felt guilty for pushing him away and angry at the choices he had been making.

After gathering enough evidence, Clara confronted Chase, who came clean. He hoped he could convince Clara that he had no intention of leaving the marriage. He attempted to justify his actions, but Clara didn't want to hear his excuses. She asked him to leave immediately. He found a place to stay for a while to give them both some time to regroup.

## SPILLING THE BEANS

After Chase left, Clara was a wreck. She found herself drinking more frequently to numb the pain. About a week after Chase left, their son Zach came over to pick up some ski equipment he had left in their garage. Clara and Chase had agreed not to tell the kids until they sorted things out. However, when Zach walked into the house, he could tell something was wrong. Clara, who was emotionally distraught and under the influence of alcohol, ended up confiding in Zach about his father's indiscretions, holding nothing back.

Zach felt blindsided by his mom's story, as he had looked up to his dad as a role model and mentor. The next day Clara regretted sharing so many details with Zach, but the damage was done. Zach called his younger sister, who was still away at school, and shared much of what his mom had told him.

Since Chase and Clara had done such a great job hiding their discontent from the kids, they had no idea that the marriage was in such deep trouble. Both were devastated. Their image of the happy family they thought they had was shattered in an instant. They felt deceived by both their parents but ultimately saw their dad as the bigger offender.

Often, we assume that older kids will be less affected by parental indiscretions and break-ups. I have not found that to be the case. Many times, it is the older kids who take it the hardest, especially when they feel like they have had a "good" childhood.

The next day Zach called his dad to discuss the situation man-to-man. Chase, who was in a raw emotional state, attempted to defend his behavior, which didn't sit well with Zach. As a result, both Zach and his sister decided they too needed some space to sort things out and cut off communication with their dad. Chase truly loved his children, and their withdrawal was very painful for him.

## THE MAN IN THE MIRROR

Chase was determined to figure himself out and fix things with his family. While he wasn't sure whether he could salvage his marriage, he wanted to figure out how to help his wife feel better and reestablish a relationship with his children. After all, he thought of himself as a good dad; a good dad who made mistakes that cost him his connection with the three people who mattered the most.

He took a good look at the man in the mirror. As that man stared back at him, Chase reflected on the many things he had neglected in service to building financial success. For years, work had been his primary focus. In the company, he was "the man." People looked up to him. He had worked hard to become a leader in his field. He took great pride in what he was able to provide for his family. Somewhere along the way, however, Chase realized he had lost pieces of himself. He began to question what was next and whether all the time and effort he had put into his career was worth it.

## RETHINKING HIS INDISCRETIONS

Chase realized that what he had justified and compartmentalized had turned his world upside down. The one thing he hadn't done, however, was to have a straight-up conversation with Clara about the extent of his unhappiness before making the unilateral decision to seek pleasure elsewhere. About a year before his infidelity spree, Clara had asked him to go to counseling. He refused, saying they could work through things on their own.

Chase began to consider the possibility that he had been experiencing what is commonly referred to as a mid-life crisis. Kids grown. Not feeling as valued at home. Job didn't quite bring the "juice" it once had. Looking back, Chase realized that he hadn't been happy for quite a while. In truth, neither of them had. There were things he didn't talk to Clara about: his need for adventure, his love of travel, and his sadness that she was more satisfied staying home than exploring with him. Chase had worked hard for years, and he finally had the money, time, and freedom to explore the world, which his wife wasn't interested in doing.

Connecting with other women had become his escape. It allowed him to live in a fantasy world for a few moments at a time. The problem was that he began enjoying his fantasy world more than his day-to-day life. His liaisons began taking on more of a compulsive nature. Ultimately, he couldn't sustain both worlds and became less diligent about keeping them separate. He realized that he needed to shut down his outside world as it was beginning to consume him—just before Clara confronted him with her evidence.

He wouldn't have chosen to end the marriage outright, but he ended up doing so through the actions he took. He came to own the fact that there was a part of him that was relieved that Clara knew about his infidelity. It created the space for them to talk about things and allowed them both to see how different their wants and needs had become.

## THE INTERSECTION OF HUMILITY, DETERMINATION, AND DESIRE

Chase was humbled by everything that had happened to him. He was determined to rebuild his relationship with his wife and children. He began to shift his focus and create more of a work-life balance.

He was able to see that building his career had become a substitute for building his life at home. He got in touch with deeper aspirations, one of which was to mentor young people in business. He reached out to an organization to do some volunteer work with kids in need of mentoring. He decided to teach a college course on entrepreneurship at one of the local community colleges.

Clara was unwilling to put the past behind them, however. She simply couldn't get past Chase's indiscretions. Deep down, she too was lonely. With the kids gone, she wasn't feeling fulfilled. She felt like she gave everything to her family, and it was now time for her to rediscover who she was and what she wanted. She didn't feel she could do that within her marriage. She told Chase she wanted a divorce and filed papers the following week.

It took over a year, but ultimately Chase's son agreed to meet him for lunch. Chase shared with him some of the things he had been doing to create deeper fulfillment in his life. Chase gave him a no-nonsense, full apology for everything his decisions had put the family through. Shortly thereafter, Chase reconnected with his daughter as well.

He spoke to them both with a calm, humble strength they hadn't witnessed in quite a while. Chase became more genuine in all his interactions, at work and at home. He thought about his life and what would create deeper fulfillment.

## CHASE AND CLARA'S HAPPILY EVER AFTER

Eventually, Chase and Clara were able to create a cordial relationship. They discussed things about their marriage that they had swept under the rug for years. They realized that their paths had been heading in different directions for quite some time. While Chase never intended to leave his wife, it was Clara who decided she felt trapped in the marriage and wanted to carve a new path for herself. They made peace with their past. Ultimately Clara forgave Chase, and Chase forgave himself.

Over time, Chase grew a little fonder of that man in the mirror. His wasn't an easy road. Yet he stayed the course. I deeply admire his commitment, courage, and wholehearted dedication to the process. He worked diligently to rediscover meaning and purpose and live a more fulfilling life with greater integrity and humility.

While Chase and Clara didn't have their *happily ever after* fairy tale ending together, they both were able to create lives that were more in sync with who they were and what they wanted. Even though Chase and Clara did not save their marriage, they ended up saving themselves.

# Communicating with your children about the affair

As you witnessed in Chase and Clara's situation, there are definite ways not to handle talking to your children about the affair!

If you have children, you may be concerned about what they find out about the infidelity—and with good reason. Learning about an affair can be very painful to a child, if not handled with care. But it doesn't have to be disastrous—to their mental health, or to your relationship with them.

What you tell, or don't tell, your kids may depend upon their age and the situation. If you're working things out and staying together with your spouse, there may be less urgency to tell them anything. But if one of you is moving on to live with an affair partner, a version of the truth may come out sooner than later. Either way, it's better to be proactive with how you manage any communications with your kids.

First, remember that they didn't ask for this to happen. And no matter what you say, they may be angry, hurt, or sad. That's okay. You need to give them space for their emotions and be there to guide them. They undoubtedly love both of you, and the situation is confusing. Just like us, they don't like unpleasant change, and learning about any strife in your relationship could trigger a fear response in them.

I can't advise you on exactly what you say, since that will vary tremendously based on your situation, but I can offer you some general guidelines for this process:

- You can't un-say anything you say, so think first before you speak.

- If other people know, realize that they may hear things through the grapevine, which is worse than hearing it from you.

- Ideally, decide as a couple on what you will tell your kids—come up with talking points that you both reinforce. This helps prevent anger and confusion if they think one of you is lying or hiding something.

- You may decide to tell your kids nothing now, and reveal some details later, once they are old enough to understand. Or you may decide this is information they never need to hear. As long as they don't find out from others, this approach is fine.

- Give your partner grace if something is said that doesn't completely align with your experience. There are always two sides to a story, and as long as the focus is on the betterment of the family dynamic, some discrepancy should be forgivable.

- **This one is most important:** Your kids want to keep loving and respecting both of you. As tempting as it may be, do your darndest not to badmouth the other parent; this actually may backfire on you as the other parent feels the need to defend himself. This is another reason why coming up with a mutually agreed upon message is helpful. As much as it may be hard to take mutual responsibility for a marriage's struggles during an affair, it can even be helpful to a child to show that "a lot of things happened that we both regret, but it's allowed us to learn and move forward in our marriage ways that are making us learn and grow stronger. You don't need to know the details, but you do need to know that we are working through things. We both love you and are committed to being on the same page with how we support and parent you."

Next, we are going to dive into the process of transformation and change and ways to clarify and reinforce you sense of strength as a man.

# PART EIGHT

---

# Embracing Transformation:
## *Cultivating Positive Change and Strengthening Your Masculine Core*

*"We cannot become what we want by remaining where we are."*
—Max Depree, *Leadership is an Art*

Creating and sustaining change doesn't stand a chance without desire, commitment, tenacity, and patience. Throughout this work, you have heard stories about men and women choosing to make changes to better support themselves and their relationships. In this section, we will be exploring the following:

**The Neurobiology of Change**

- How the change process works, particularly in relation to infidelity recovery
- Ways in which your thoughts, actions, and feedback can hold you back or strengthen your capacity to implement and sustain change

**Defining and Navigating Emotions**

- How emotions are processed – through your body and mind
- The pursue-withdraw dance
- Anticipatory fear

**Exploring Masculinity: Embracing Your Power and Purpose**

- Your views on masculinity, including the messages and modeling you received while growing up male

- Ways to cultivate and strengthen your emotional awareness
- Ideas partners can implement to help support each other's desire for transformation and change

**Growing and Changing as a Couple**

- The change process in action
- Supporting your partner's desire for change

Several of the chapters in this section include exercises that you and your partner can explore and work on together when she is ready. Each time you make supportive relational choices, you reinforce your commitment. Sometimes a partner who is reluctant to engage will choose to jump in after she sees you're dedicated to staying the course.

# 20

# The Neurobiology *of* Change

∎

*"Partners may say they want better communication
or some other mechanical skill, but in almost all cases
what they really want is a major change in their spouse's
brain; they want a more relational person."*
—Terrence Real, *US: Getting Past You & Me to Build a More Loving Relationship*

Often, I get asked the question *"Can people really change?"* My answer is a resounding yes! **People can and do change if the force driving the desired change is stronger and more important than the comfort of remaining the same.**

The most frequently asked follow-up question is *"How?"* Or *"How can I get my partner to change?"* It is not unusual for people to enter couples work with the stated desire of changing their partner. This is particularly true when it comes to infidelity recovery.

In his book *US: Getting Past You & Me to Build a More Loving Relationship,* relational therapist Terry Real discusses moving past what he calls the "adaptive child self" into the "wise adult self." The *child self* creates adaptations to ensure its survival, maintain a sense of safety, and get its needs met. When two people form a relationship, their adaptive child selves bring their unique survival patterns to the table. The relationship then forges its own adaptive patterns rooted in the survival skills each of them has relied upon throughout their lives.

Our role as adults is to cultivate the ability to notice when these patterns arise. Then, instead of letting our adaptive patterns run the show, learn to form new ways of responding and collaborating with one another that are rooted in a deeper wisdom that we each possess as human beings. This is what Real refers to as the *wise adult self.*

As we shift from adaptive patterns into relationally wise ways of connecting within ourselves and with each other, trust begins to deepen. Trusting ourselves and our partner to respond thoughtfully rather than react quickly when triggered is an indication that we are on the road to creating stronger, more loving connections.

---

**A key strength to develop is the ability to pause when triggered instead of reacting without thinking.**

---

When you can put some space between a trigger and a reaction, you give yourself room to consider a more thoughtful and less reactive response.

## The Change Process: The Role of Desire and Fear

Regarding the change process, while you can inspire someone to change, change cannot be forced. No matter how badly you may want someone else to change, sustained change doesn't stand a chance without strong desire and buy-in from the person making the change. While coercion may activate a temporary shift, coerced change builds resentment, which interferes with relational connection.

Can you think of a time when someone tried to coerce you into doing something you really didn't want to do? Did you experience resentment? Did the changed behavior last?

Desire and fear play significant roles in driving and maintaining change. Fear of loss or a negative outcome can serve as a powerful motivator, which can override the comfort of staying the same.

Let's face it, change is uncomfortable, and it is often fear that activates behavioral change. The fear of losing something or someone significant can overshadow other considerations, creating a sense of urgency. However, without strong desire and determination, it becomes challenging to maintain the mental resilience and determination needed to sustain change.

Fear can also serve as a warning sign so that we can recognize a risk that triggers desire for a better outcome, resulting in behavioral changes. For example:

- A racing heart could lead to tests that prompt exercise and a better diet; *the fear of a heart attack drives change.*
- A fender bender could prompt the elimination of distractions while driving; *the fear of a worse accident drives change.*
- A meeting with a boss could prompt a shift in work habits; *the fear of losing one's job drives change.*
- A fight with a spouse could prompt a different communication approach; *the fear of hurting or losing one's spouse drives change.*

The tricky thing about fear is that it can also be the thing that holds us back from making changes. Fear of failure and of confronting things we would rather not talk about can keep us stuck in maladaptive patterns that can become a way of life. This type of fear can result in avoidance or turning toward something or someone else to relieve the pressure and get unexpressed needs met.

While crises, intense emotional experiences, and fear can be formidable catalysts activating changes in behavior, the impetus for growth can also be activated through entering a new life stage such as kids leaving home, or engaging in a supportive environment or relationship that values and encourages curiosity, growth, and learning.

---

**When what someone stands to lose or gain is valued enough, and their desire is strong enough, people can and do create lasting change.**

---

# The Science of Change

Prevailing thinking until the mid-twentieth century was that adult brain chemistry was fixed and unchangeable. Genetics and early childhood experiences were thought to be hardwired into brain chemistry, which meant significant changes in later life were considered virtually impossible. In the late 1960s neuroscientists began engaging in experiments that disproved that theory. They discovered that brain chemistry is fluid, not fixed, and while the production of new brain cells slows in later adulthood, on average we are using less than 50 percent of these newbies.

New brain cells, when stimulated, join existing brain cell structures. This contributes to the integration and expansion of learning. When not engaged, these new cells die. Heightened emotional experiences, acute stress, trauma, learning, and novel experiences are all catalysts for activating *neurogenesis*, which is the scientific term for new brain cell growth. What this means is that the brain adapts to support changes in thinking and learning.

These stimulated new cells link themselves to more seasoned cells, laying the foundation for the creation of new response patterns. When reinforced through choices made, actions taken, and positive reinforcement, these emerging patterns become stronger.

## WHAT GETS IN THE WAY?

The pull of old, well-worn patterns is strong—like the dried-out mud ruts in a field that a tractor can easily slip back into. Our inner defense systems are designed to keep us safe as we progress in life. Patterns which may seem maladaptive now worked at some point to keep us out of harm's way. It is easy to trip the autopilot switch and fall back into these old grooves. It takes time and reinforcement for our brains to create and then trust new patterns as safe and viable responses to stress and perceived threats. New patterns are reinforced or negated based on choices made on a moment by moment basis.

## INTENTIONAL CHANGE

All our systems are on heightened alert when learning something new. Think back to when you first learned to drive a car. It took focused concentration to prepare for your drive. You checked your mirrors, looked around you, put the car in gear, focused on learning the rules of the road, etc. Being new to driving heightened your sense of awareness and your will to succeed. You paid attention to the movement of everyone around you. Of course, you also made some mistakes along the way. Mistake-making is part of learning something new.

The skills that are on high alert when learning something new recede into the background as you feel more confident and cultivate a greater sense of mastery. You take your foot off the brake, so to speak, as you begin feeling more comfortable driving. As your skills shift to autopilot, you no longer excite many brain cells when getting into the car. This is part of the learning and mastery process. That is why engaging in something new (like an affair) can feel so exhilarating—it fires up excitatory, hyper-focused brain chemistry.

Intentional change requires the same focus as learning something new. Desire, determination, repetition, and choices made on a moment-by-moment basis serve as the building blocks of the intentional change process. The more consistently you respond and take actions that are congruent with the change you desire to make, the more your brain chemistry "rewires" itself to create your desires. Eventually, that change becomes routine, and you don't have to focus as hard to maintain it.

Enacting positive change involves: 1) choosing to engage in actions that reinforce the desired behavior on a moment-by-moment basis, 2) course-correcting when you veer off your intended path, and 3) reconciling with those you care about when your actions disappoint or let them down.

---

**The goal in enacting change, as well as in life, isn't perfection, but rather to more consistently make choices that support what you desire, who you want to be, and how you want to show up in your relationships.**

---

## How Personal Change Impacts Your Relationship

"May my mind come alive today to the invisible geography that invites me to new frontiers, to break the dead shell of yesterdays, to risk being disturbed and changed."

*—To Bless the Space Between Us*, John O'Donohue, author, poet

Just like your inner neural network, there is a network that exists in the energy between a couple that impacts both people. Neuropsychiatrist Daniel Siegel calls this *interpersonal neurobiology,* or IPNB. Your relationship will be reshaping itself as you and your partner engage in deeper communication and try out new behaviors and ways of thinking. This is a dynamic and ongoing process. Your relational system will experience its own rewiring during the affair recovery process.

Each of your individual response systems will be activated as you move forward, and it will take conscious effort to ensure you grow through this change rather than defaulting to what is automatic (and often not helpful). If you are the one who has betrayed, an intense fear of loss can activate a survival circuitry designed to save your marriage.

If you are the one who was betrayed, your system may move into fight-or-flight mode or collapse under the weight of it all. It is also possible that the fear of losing your marriage may result in a frenetic engagement in various behaviors, such as phone checking or a review of past credit card statements, out of an intense need to know the truth, or in a desperate attempt to save the relationship or move on.

In his book *The Neurobiology of We,* Dr. Siegel discusses how brain chemistry is impacted by human relationships. How we relate to each other has a definitive impact on the neurobiological circuitry of each individual. We impact one another with how we feel, think about, and interact with our partners. When we are authentic, present, mindful, and attuned, we create space for deeper healing and growth to occur. The cool thing about relationships is that the positive changes one person makes impact the entire system. Unfortunately, the reverse is also true. Misaligned choices and negative thinking about our partner or the relationship also leave their mark.

## Your Thinking – Friend or Foe?

**"When one voice commands your whole heart, and it is raven dark, steady yourself and see that it is your own thinking that darkens your world. ... Close your eyes. Gather all the kindling about your heart to create one spark. That is all you need to nourish the flame that will cleanse the dark of its weight of festered fear ... Search and you will find a diamond-thought of light."**

—*To Bless the Space Between Us,* John O'Donohue

Your brain is a remarkable problem-solving machine, constantly seeking solutions and safeguarding you from potential threats. Sounds good, right? So, what gets in the way of your brain's effectiveness? And where does it get stuck? Let's take a look.

When your brain detects an unresolved issue, it remains actively engaged in finding a solution, even when you're not consciously focusing on it. Significant challenges persist on its radar until a satisfactory resolution is achieved. Sometimes, giving your brain the space to process complex problems can lead to breakthroughs. Have you ever experienced a sudden insight while showering or taking a walk? This process can be beneficial, like the ways in which stepping back from a work challenge can help you find a solution. However, unresolved emotional experiences can also linger until they are properly addressed. In situations involving the actions of others, like infidelity, unclear aspects may lead to persistent thoughts that are difficult to shake as your brain works to find a solution without the necessary data.

When a challenge remains unresolved for a long time, especially if it is emotionally charged and involves close relationships, thoughts tend to intensify and multiply. Ruminating thoughts can be exacerbated by past traumas, like emotional or physical abuse or abandonment, leading to obsessive thinking that may result in feelings of anxiety, depression, or anger. Your interpretation, processing, and response to these triggers and emotional experiences are greatly influenced by your self-perception and internal dialogue, which are shaped by the messages you received during your upbringing.

If you were raised in a critical environment, what you say to yourself as you are working to resolve emotional challenges will tend to be more critical. On the other hand, if you received mostly positive reinforcement, your inner voice is likely to be more positive. It's important to recognize that most of us have been exposed to a mix of both positive and critical messages throughout our lives.

How about you? How do you process mistakes, things you judge as failings, or doing things of which you are not proud?

- **Do you tend to beat yourself up?** *What the hell were you thinking, dude? OMG. I can't believe you said that. What a dumb ass. Did you see how she looked at you? She obviously hates you. You might as well hang in up right now. Why are you trying so hard? She's never going to forgive you.*

- **What if you were a little more encouraging to yourself?** *Yep. You messed up, and you've owned it. Don't give up. Sometimes it won't be easy, but you can do it. You've worked through tough things before. You've got this. Just give it your best* *shot. That's all you can do. Trust that things are going to get better. Don't make things up in your head. If you aren't sure, ask.*

- **Your self-talk can also be proactively affirming.** What you say to yourself influences how you think about and interpret situations, relationships and life. Here are a few ideas:

*I am doing what I know needs to be done. Even my worst mistakes don't define who I am. I believe in me. I am a good man and partner. I am grateful for my relationship and my life. I can make this work. I am committed. I will not let little failures throw me off course. I am moving forward in powerful ways. I am making wise choices. It may not always feel good, and that's okay. I've got this. I am learning and growing in positive ways.*

While at first this type of positive self-talk may feel a little strange, studies show that over time, shifting into more positive thought patterns improves your health and well-being and can even contribute to greater longevity.[17]

Positive thinking doesn't mean ignoring what has happened. It means giving yourself some time to think about it, reflect on It, then focus on productive solutions that don't hold you hostage to ruminating thoughts. Shifting your focus to picture the best possible outcome, not the worst, can lead to a calmer state of mind, greater resilience, and better results over time.

Psychologist Émile Coué popularized an eleven-word phrase that he recommended repeating 20 times before falling asleep. He believed this practice would train the mind to focus on the positive and release negative thoughts. The phrase is: "Every day in every way, I'm getting better and better."[18] Its rhythmic nature also makes it an excellent mantra for staying positive during activities like walking or running. You can also substitute words like "life" in place of "I'm" to reinforce the forward momentum you are working on.

## Making an Ally of Your Mind

**"You have been given the capacity to take dominion within your own consciousness and to choose the nature and direction of your thinking."**

—Mary R. Hlunick, Ph.D., H. Ronald Hulnick, Ph.D., *Remembering the Light Within, A Course in Soul-Centered Living*

In his book *Mindsight: The New Science of Personal Transformation,* Dr. Siegel discusses in great depth how brain chemistry changes and is reinforced over time as new choices are made. A key aspect of working through any challenging situation, according to Siegel, is to find the "meaning in the challenge."

Human beings are meaning-making machines. When we can discover the deeper meaning behind something, particularly in the face of challenging life circumstances, we have a greater chance of reshaping our thinking around the situation. Through this reshaping, we can make an ally of our mind (which is comprised not just of the brain, but the body, emotions, and spirit as well.)

One of the objectives of this book is to help you discover the deeper meaning of your affair, why it occurred, what purpose it fulfilled, and what you need to pay attention to moving forward. Uncovering the deeper meaning helps you gain insights that will assist you in moving toward a more self-aware and relationally oriented way of engaging with life and your partner. As you move through this process, your brain will begin to rewire itself, supporting the assimilation of new knowledge and the development of new response patterns. Over time, these patterns grow stronger through reinforcement, facilitating personal and relational growth and transformation.

Dr. Siegel discusses four conditions that strengthen new brain-firing patterns (the ways in which brain chemistry supports change). They are as follows:
1. Emotional arousal
2. Focused attention
3. Repetition
4. Novelty

Let's explore how each of these conditions apply to infidelity recovery:

**Emotional arousal:** Getting caught in an affair is a shock to the system for the betrayer, the betrayed, and the betrayal partner. Emotional arousal commands the brain's attention, triggering its emotional response center.

When your partner is confronted with the shock of your affair and you witness their pain and disappointment, it intensifies your determination to alleviate both their suffering and your own, making it challenging to focus on anything else. Your system becomes primed for change. In addition, ending something as impactful as an affair leaves your system in a heightened state of arousal, which can enhance your motivation to fix things with your partner.

**It is also important to note:** This time is also characterized by anxiety and vulnerability, which can lead to unhealthy behaviors, such as a reaching out to your affair partner, especially in moments when your SO is not as receptive as you would like her to be.

**Focused attention:** As discussed, your brain is a problem-solving machine. When the status quo has been disturbed, the brain goes into problem-solving mode. Significant challenges move us from autopilot into "all hands on deck" problem resolution mode. Working through this program effectively requires your focused attention. The more you engage in the learning and recovery process, the more you adjust your thinking and create new brain-firing patterns that support your desire for greater personal and relational growth and change.

**Repetition:** Repeating desired behaviors strengthens new pathways, moving your response system from sympathetic (all hands on deck) mode into parasympathetic (homeostasis/re-regulation) mode. The intensity of your focus on these new behaviors will recede into the background over time as they take root and become your more consistent ways of responding.

Trust is also being rebuilt through consistency. The more consistent you become in your responses, behavior, and thinking, the more you reinforce new thought patterns and demonstrate to yourself and your partner that you are, indeed, trustworthy.

**One caveat here:** As the urgency begins to calm, there can also be a tendency for old behavioral patterns to re-emerge. This can be another vulnerable time for you both. While you don't want your system to constantly run on hyper-alert mode, these new patterns must become firmly enough rooted that they serve as your "new normal"; otherwise, you are in danger of your "old normal" grabbing the wheel.)

**Novelty:** Engaging in novel activities is a great way to reinforce your desired connection, even after the desired behavior has become your *new normal*. Part of growing together as a couple involves trying new things. Novelty stimulates excitement and strengthens connection. Dr. Siegel tells us that "brains that fire together, wire together." New experiences activate emotional arousal, help satisfy the need for adventure, and create new neural connections within each of you, and between you.

**Creating a plan:** I am adding a fifth condition to Dr. Siegel's list. To sustain momentum, you need to create a collective plan of action—prioritizing logistics as well as fun. Set aside time each week to connect in positive ways, discuss finances, plan weekend getaways or big trips, and discuss what you are passionate about. Designating a specific time for each activity is important so that logistics don't bleed into relaxation time. And schedule date nights to ensure that you keep the momentum going.

By finding stimulating, creative, new ways to connect, and engaging in personal and relational discovery, you are applying brain science to establish greater connectivity with your partner and self-trust. While the motivation to change can occur in an instant, real change in behavior—and relational healing—requires commitment, determination, and creativity. It also requires patience—within yourself and with those you love and care about.

---

## Reflection

- **Change is cumulative.** New habits are strengthened over time through repetition. Like learning to walk or ride a bike, the more we practice, the better we get.

- **Trust yourself.** Remember that positive self-talk reinforces what you are building and strengthens your connection with others.

- **Keep what you want in focus.** Let your intentions guide your behavior. (Example: "I am creating a powerful marriage. I am building a stronger connection with my wife and family. I am making self-supportive choices. We are building a beautiful life together. I am showing her that I love her daily.")

- **Stay the course.** When you veer off-course, correct. Think about what you are working toward, then take one small step forward. Small steps can lead to big outcomes. Your brain chemistry will support the changes you wish to make. Consider: Does this behavior build a bridge or erect a wall between the two of you?

This quote from Mario Brito, author of *How Creativity Rules the World: The Art and Business of Turning your Ideas into Gold,* sums up this section quite nicely:

*"Doing something new and creating something of value requires experimentation. If you want to do something unique, you must be at peace with the idea that you don't know the outcome and you may (will sometimes) fail.... To succeed in new and creative fields, you must become comfortable with being uncomfortable."*

# 21

## Defining *and* Navigating Emotions

◼

*"Our emotions are not a luxury but an essential aspect
of our makeup. We have them not just for the pleasure of
feeling but because they have a crucial survival value.
They orient us, interpret the world for us, give us vital
information without which we cannot thrive. They tell
us what is dangerous and what is benign, what threatens
our existence and what will nurture our growth."*

— Gabor Maté, M.D., with Daniel Maté, *The Myth of Normal,
Trauma, Illness, and Healing in a Toxic Culture*

Emotions bypass the thinking part of your brain and activate an automatic response
in your nervous system, either amping it up, dampening it down, or stopping you in
your tracks. Here's how it works:

1. A stimulus occurs from an external event, an internal thought about an event,
   or the anticipation of an event.

2. Your body reacts. Synapses fire, and neurochemicals are released into your
   brain, organs, and bloodstream.

3. Bodily reactions either amp up, dampen down, or freeze in response to how dangerous you perceive the "threat" to be, or based on what your past tendency has been. (Bodily reactions can include elevated heart rate, shallow breathing, more blood flow to your extremities, and less blood flow to your organs.)

When your system is overtaken by an emotional reaction, it requires different interventions to re-regulate itself, depending upon the state you are in. These states can be divided into three main categories:

- **Heightened emotional states** can trigger feelings of anxiety, anger, frustration, and fear, which require a way to be discharged and released in order to achieve a calmer state. Physical activities like running or working out can help in releasing these emotions. Calming techniques such as deep breathing can also have an immediate calming effect on the brain. It's important to experiment and find what works best for you to bring greater calm to your anxious state. Engaging in practices like EFT also known as tapping, as discussed in the Anxiety section of Chapter 15, can also help your brain refocus.

- **Lower emotional states** can trigger feelings of sadness, depression, and shame. It is important to recharge these emotional states in order to re-energize. Engaging in movement or exercise, such as working out, running, yoga, or taking a brisk walk, can help bring these states back to a healthier level.

- **Frozen states** trigger immobilization. This is a safety mechanism activated when we interpret a situation as too dangerous to move, as to do so would be dangerous. (Picture a deer frozen in the headlights of an oncoming car.)

Frozen states are typically rooted in past traumatic experiences that become linked to a present situation, frequently resulting in a shutdown of a person's ability to respond. An example of this is when a child witnesses abuse of a parent and is rendered helpless, they may be apt to freeze as adults when they feel emotionally overloaded, or in the face of angry outbursts or yelling. When a freeze response is activated, an individual needs time (and space) to "thaw out" to regain the ability to function.

It can be difficult when a partner withdraws or disengages during a conversation. Withdrawal can lead to strong emotional reactions and feelings of loneliness. Simply living with someone does not guarantee protection from experiencing loneliness. In my work with couples, it is common for both individuals to express feelings of loneliness within their relationship that they struggle to address.

---

## At the heart of loneliness lies an internal feeling of disconnection or rejection.

---

When one person withdraws, it can leave the other feeling isolated and alone. This can result in feelings of rejection or abandonment, which in turn can lead to an intense reaction (yelling, angry outbursts) or cause them to counter-withdraw or anxiously pursue re-engagement. Each of these responses is designed to soothe the anxiety associated with feeling disconnected from a partner. Let's take a quick look at the underlying dynamic of how this plays out.

# Avoidance/Withdrawal/Counter-withdrawal

### AVOIDANCE

Some individuals tend to avoid any type of conflict, particularly if they were raised in environments where they felt stifled by overprotective parents or observed frequent fighting, avoidance of conflict, or parents neglecting each other's or their own needs.

### WITHDRAWAL

An individual often disengages from a conversation or another person in response to feeling overwhelmed. Withdrawal also occurs when there is a concern that further engagement may intensify the situation and result in one or both people saying things they may later regret. Can you relate to any of these situations?

- When your wife tells you she needs more attention from you, you can't wait to retreat to the other room to be alone.

- You indicate to your wife that you desire sexual intimacy, and instead of saying anything to you or responding receptively, she rolls over to sleep.

- You both know that something isn't right in your relationship, but neither of you talk about it. Instead, you go about your evening together—engaging in your typical evening routine with the kids, eating a meal, and watching TV before crashing. You have little to no verbal connection or conflict, but nothing gets solved.

While there are times when stepping back from a potential conflict can be helpful, withdrawal without talking about things only serves to create more discord. The healthy way to pull back from an intensifying situation is to agree in advance that: 1) When temperatures begin to rise, either partner can pause the conversation; and 2) You will both reconvene at another time when things are calmer.

Both of these steps are important. The first ensures that you step away before a situation gets too heated to manage, while the second step provides reassurance that a solution will be sought out in the near future. (Chapter 24, *Courageous Conversations*, discusses best practices for addressing and collaborating through challenges.)

## COUNTER-WITHDRAWAL

Turning away from someone in response to their withdrawal of affection is a counter-withdrawal behavior which is a coping mechanism enacted to protect a partner from experiencing additional pain. In this situation, both people pull away from the relationship and often quit talking altogether.

# Pursuit/Re-engagement/People-Pleasing

A partner's withdrawal can be intensely triggering, particularly when someone has grown up in a family where they experienced rejection or some form of abandonment by their caregivers. When emotions are triggered, the "rejected" partner's brain moves into protective mode and can resort to similar coping mechanisms developed in response to earlier abandonment. This can lead to unproductive behaviors.

## PURSUIT/RE-ENGAGEMENT

When one partner disengages, the other partner often pursues re-engagement. While this can be a normal and healthy response, it can also be done to an extreme degree due to the anxiety a person can feel when attention or affection is withdrawn. In this case, the anxious partner may not respect their partner's desire for space—potentially entering the room where the partner is cooling down or placing multiple phone calls in succession to reach the person when there is no answer.

**PEOPLE-PLEASING**

Another method for attempting to regain a withdrawn partner's re-engagement is known as "people-pleasing". This type of pursuit behavior involves engaging in actions designed to please or appease another person, often to the detriment of one's own needs.

When one person consistently puts their partner's needs ahead of their own, resentment builds. This contributes to fatigue, depression, and anxiety and diminishes their quality of life, happiness, and relational connection. People-pleasing is different from doing something for a partner in the spirit of love and generosity. This type of behavior is a reactive response designed to alleviate anxiety rooted in the fear of rejection, abandonment, relational loss, and loneliness.

# The Pursuit-Withdrawal Dance

Over time, pursue-withdraw can become a reactive relational pattern wherein one person cuts off communication, and the other engages in a variety of behaviors designed to re-engage the withdrawn partner. These attempts can range from increased affection and over apologizing, to intense romantic gestures including gifts, and *love bombing* designed to relieve the anxiety associated with a partner's withdrawal.

Partner re-engagement results in a rush of neurochemicals creating momentary feelings of closeness, which may increase desires and intensify sexual connection. (I imagine many of you reading this have heard about or experienced the intensity of "make-up sex.")

The challenge with the enactment of these relational patterns is that they replace authentic communication and problem-solving. When that which was at the heart of the upset is never truly resolved, it resurfaces in subsequent disagreements when the relational temperature goes back to normal. This can trigger passive-aggressive reactions.

Becoming stuck in these relational patterns makes it difficult for couples to trust each other to engage in discussions on difficult topics, particularly when the state of the relationship is a little rocky. This can result in a greater susceptibility to outside influence. Ideally people have friends, or professionals they can work with to help them break through these patterns and create stronger connections with partners.

Time and time again, I hear individuals and couples express regret that they didn't recognize and address these patterns earlier, which could have enabled them to communicate with their partner more effectively making them less vulnerable to outside influences. It's never too late to develop emotional awareness, though. Doing so can help you break free from the pursue-withdraw cycle, as well as other ineffective communication habits.

## Cultivating Emotional Awareness

Our emotional regulatory system is a function of our genetic makeup and our environment. While temperament is something we are born with, the emotional awareness we develop is influenced by how our parents and other important figures respond to our needs.

Children who grow up in households where parental figures struggle with acknowledging, accepting, and processing emotions can learn to categorize their feelings as either good or bad, leading them to suppress the "bad" ones and question their own worth for experiencing them. This can lead to challenges identifying and managing emotions as an adult.

When parents avoid certain emotions such as anger or sadness, they may unknowingly discourage their children from accepting and expressing these feelings. Phrases like "Look on the bright side" or "It's not that bad" may appear harmless, but they can invalidate a child's emotions, leading them to internalize the negative ones. This can make it challenging for them to identify and process emotions effectively as adults. Unprocessed emotions can lead to passive-aggressive behavior and an acute sensitivity to any type of criticism.

When you view your feelings as emotional responses to events in your environment or your thoughts, it becomes easier to navigate them. While you may not have control over your emotions, you can start to uncover the underlying triggers and identify them before they become overwhelming. Often, a partner can sense when their significant other is feeling off balance even before they are aware of it.

The language we use to describe our feelings also shapes our perception of ourselves and the world around us. There is a difference between saying "I am sad" and "I am experiencing sadness," or "This sadness is affecting me deeply." Although the latter may sound a little strange initially, these statements help to externalize an emotion as something you are going through, rather than defining who you are. By separating your identity from your emotions, you create a space that allows you to process them more effectively.

**"Name it to tame it."** —Dr. Dan Siegel

# Anticipatory Fear

Our emotional reactions carry messages for us. They are part of a complex regulatory system designed to keep us safe from harm. Over time, however, our system develops coping mechanisms that can become patterned ways of responding to situations we perceive as dangerous before they even happen. This is called *anticipatory fear.* Our body responds to anticipatory fear in the same way it responds to real and present danger.

Anticipatory fear is activated when we are afraid of encountering a negative response from someone who:

- Has power over us
- We seek approval from
- We fear we will react with anger, rage, or deep disappointment
- We fear will disconnect, abandon, or leave if we discuss or share something they might find upsetting

This mechanism flies below the radar of conscious awareness unless and until we work to understand it. When our emotional antenna picks up on something similar to past trauma or difficulty, old adaptation patterns become activated, coloring how we view the person and situation. This is why two people going through an experience together can perceive it quite differently. These differing perceptions lie at the root of many communication difficulties. Adaptations originally designed as protective mechanisms can ultimately interfere with healthy growth, development, and the formation of supportive relationships.

When anticipatory fear is triggered, we can be so convinced we are right that it can be difficult to listen to another's point of view. I have seen couples engage in complex arguments over very small details, each seeking to provide "evidence" that their narrative is the correct one. This often results in an incomplete communication loop where each person walks away feeling unheard, misunderstood, and alone.

When it comes to infidelity recovery, anticipatory fear can haunt both people. Each person's experience comes from a different vantage point. The **betrayer** may fear that his spouse could decide to leave at any time, or perhaps that she will expose what happened to people he doesn't want to know about the affair. The **betrayed partner** fears her partner may not be fully honest about what has happened, or that he could still be engaging with the AP or may engage with her at any point in the future. This anticipatory fear can create a tendency to avoid hot topics, which means full communication never occurs.

Incomplete communication can disrupt a couple's ability to see one another as a safe place to land. When you are unsure whether what you would like to share will be met with openness and understanding or defensiveness, anger, or criticism, eventually you may quit sharing altogether.

---

### When a couple quits talking about things that matter, the quality of their relationship can begin to quickly deteriorate.

---

"The emotion that can break your heart is sometimes the very one that heals it..."

—Nicholas Sparks, *At First Sight*

Next, we explore masculine power dynamics and messages you received while growing up about what it means to be a man.

# 22

## Exploring Masculinity:
### *Embracing Your Power, Passion, and Purpose as a Man*

———————————————— ■ ————————————————

*"The minute we become socialized as young boys to bury our feelings is the same minute when we begin to lose the capacity to connect with each other meaningfully."*
—Justin Baldoni, *Man Enough: Undefining my Masculinity*

In this chapter, we explore how messages males receive growing up impact identity-formation. We also explore what operating as an honorable man in today's world looks like to you.

Male behavior has become a more frequent topic of conversation, prompted in part by the #MeToo movement as well as the behavior of politicians, entertainers, sports figures, and various male industry leaders. We are witnessing a rise in books, articles, and podcasts about, and for, men on masculinity and overcoming many of the disempowering messages men encounter growing up.

Today's books and podcasts highlight a growing trend of men engaging in open conversations about the challenges they face in striving to embody honor and respect for themselves and those around them. These candid narratives aim to reassure other men that they are not alone in their struggles and to emphasize that the negative actions of a few individuals do not define the broader male population's attitudes, behaviors, and beliefs.

## The Shifting Landscape of Masculinity

It appears that a new concept of masculinity is emerging in today's world. I am seeing this transformation taking shape within the men I work with, as they conscientiously navigate through the societal messages they absorbed in their formative years about masculinity. These individuals are not only reflecting on how these messages have influenced their choices but are also reevaluating their perceptions of themselves, women, and other men. They are actively striving to redefine their identities and aspirations as leaders, in social interactions, and within their personal relationships.

Actor, activist, author, and entrepreneur Justin Baldoni is one such man whose writings point to the emergence of a new masculine code. Baldoni highlights how the rigid and outdated messages he received while "growing up male" have put pressure on himself and other men—affecting their ability to be the partners, men, and role models they want to be.

In his book *Man Enough: Undefining My Masculinity,* Baldoni offers an intimate look at how his boyhood experiences, industry stereotypes, and expectations serve to shape male behavior, and created insecurities and confusion about what it means to be a man. He also explores men's drive to fit in. His book offers ways to break through outdated societal stereotypes and move beyond the masks men wear to avoid risking failure in life and relationships.

Defining—or, as Baldoni suggests, *undefining*—one's manhood is a complex endeavor that entails taking an in-depth look at the ways in which social, cultural, familial, and religious messages have influenced how a man sees himself. For example, men have been conditioned to be strong protectors. This can translate into measuring manhood based on the ability to provide financially, which helps to explain why career transitions can hit men particularly hard. When male identity is wrapped up in the ability to provide, career shifts can either significantly increase or decrease a man's internal measurement of himself. As a result, downward spirals in male depression are frequently triggered by a man's job loss, layoff, need to close his company, merger, financial loss, and other changes to career status.

Another example of the popularity of this topic is the book *Power Tools for Men: A Blueprint for Healthy Masculinity.* In it, authors Leonard Szymczak and Rick Broniec tackle tough topics like patriarchy, misogyny, sex, spirituality, and breaking free from the ties that bind men—exploring outdated and ineffective models of what it means to be a man. They discuss the ways in which men have been conditioned to maintain a sense of dominance over other men, women, children, and even the planet.

This need for dominance and control can help explain why safeguarding the planet and her creatures from issues like global warming can take a backseat to the need for a competitive edge and financial reward. *"We were taught to value winning over cooperation and to never admit our weaknesses or insecurities,"* Szymczak and Broniec write, also pointing to an emerging new masculine code of ethics, morality, and relational integrity that differs from what they learned growing up.

## Men: Careers, Leadership, and Vulnerability

Historically in the business world, under the old masculine code, men were seen as more capable than women of making more sound business choices since they were not "ruled" by their emotions. Business decisions needed to be made based upon *facts*; head over heart. Vulnerability and emotions were seen as detrimental to success and financial achievement.

While women were given a pass for their emotional expression, their extra emotionality was seen as a deterrent to making sound business decisions, thereby limiting their promotion into higher level positions. Early in my corporate career in the 80's and 90's, the worst thing a woman could do was cry. We were all taught that tears could compromise our professionalism and jeopardize promotability.

These ways of thinking not only put more financial pressure on men, but they also reinforced the gendered stereotype that men lacked emotional depth. Maleness equaled stoicism. Men were supposed to be tough and fearless. Humility and vulnerability are not strengths that men and boys typically placed at the top of their list of desirable attributes. Until very recently, vulnerability in men was seen as weakness, especially in school athletics and in the business world. Men are still climbing out of the aftermath of experiencing these messages both at school and at home.

The one emotion that was more accepted in men was anger. Men as protectors and providers needed to be strong. People took advantage of the weak. Anger demonstrated strength-- vulnerability demonstrated weakness.

But in truth, everyone, including the most masculine men, have emotional needs. They were just taught to bury them. And sometimes burying them can be detrimental, or even devastating to themselves and their relationships.

One of the careers that screams *male* is being an NFL football player. Eric Hipple, former quarterback of the Detroit Lions and author of *Real Men Do Cry: A Quarterback's Inspiring Story of Tackling Depression and Surviving Suicide Loss,* tells the story of being a passenger of a vehicle his wife was driving at seventy-five miles per hour on the freeway. He couldn't cope with his own emotions after retiring from the NFL, and he had reached his breaking point. He scrawled a note to his wife on a paper napkin, opened the door, and jumped out—expecting to die. Miraculously, he survived, only to lose his own son to suicide in 2000.

As Hipple stated for a *Detroit News* article,[19] *"[As a man] it's my job to be mentally tough, so if I'm called on to run through the wall, I'll run through the wall. We're mission oriented that way."* Yet even the toughest men have real emotions that must get processed in order to be healthy and thrive. By finally addressing his emotions and tapping into professional help, Hipple was able to thrive. He's dedicated the past two decades to advocating for mental health and helping to shape male-oriented messages—allowing men to *feel*.

Leadership consultant and author Scott Carbonara shared with me his thoughts on what it means to be male in our society, and how it applies to leadership. *"Many of us were programmed from an early age to pick ourselves up and dust ourselves off when hurt. We, as men, often equate showing emotion with weakness. But as a former executive leader, I learned the opposite: emotion, when regulated, can be the force that drives our empathy, creativity, and connection. But this doesn't mean unleashing every emotion to its extreme. The best leaders are those who recognize their own vulnerability, process their emotions, and learn to treat others with the respect they deserve. This applies to both men and women equally."*

## FATHERS, SONS, AND THE DRIVE TO WIN

To this day winning is viewed as a coveted aspect of male identity that elevates a man's position on the manhood scale. This is true in sports, business, and often even relationally, where a man's status can be seen as elevated when he captures the attention of a well-sought-after woman. It can go up even higher when he can boast of having sexual relations with multiple sought-after women. While this dynamic is shifting as women become more confident in their own worth, underpinnings of this ideology still exist today. This is one of the reasons male infidelity is more readily expected and accepted than female infidelity; we see this drive as indicative of strong masculinity. The ability to draw in a woman, even when it is taboo, is often still viewed as an inherent part of a strong male's psyche.

Fathers who grew up indoctrinated into these norms, particularly when reinforced by their own fathers, tend to be tough on sons. This is due to the impact their upbringing had on them and the belief that being tough can help protect their sons from being bullied by other males. Fathers can also live vicariously through their sons and often view their sons' "successes and failures" as a reflection of their own. A son's success can offer great pride to a father instilling a conscious and unconscious desire to "make Dad proud." This desire is a frequent underlying driver of male behavior well into adulthood. The father/son interplay helps shape a man's beliefs, self-esteem, and ways of relating to women.

We have previously spoken about parental role modeling. Both positive and negative messages become integrated into views on oneself, and relational interaction. As we have seen, a father's infidelity can influence the ways in which a boy views manhood and serve as an unconscious factor in choices he makes in adulthood—either to reject or unconsciously conform to what Dad has modeled.

Embracing new ways of being, thinking, and relating to one another and ourselves takes great courage and a willingness to explore other points of view in nonjudgmental ways. Self-exploration requires the courage to face unresolved challenges and pain.

# Shadow and Pain

"Pain, as I've come to learn, is either a teacher and guide for us men, or our owner. ... when you ignore the pain, you also ignore the wisdom and intelligence your pain has to offer. ... Ignored pain becomes the driving force behind a man's decline and descent into the abyss ..."

—Connor Beaton, author, founder of *ManTalks*

In *Men's Work: A Practical Guide to Face Your Darkness, End Self-Sabotage, and Find Freedom,* author Connor Beaton takes a look at the ways in which a man's inability to reconcile the pain he has felt, and the pain he has caused others, diminishes the quality of his life and relationships. His shadow work takes each man on a deep dive into the center of himself. As we discussed in Chapter 17, uncovering what is lurking in the shadow of your unconscious increases self-awareness and contributes to establishing a more authentic relational connection.

Like Baldoni, Beaton explores masculinity and the impact of growing up male, using his own story as a backdrop. He posits that inherent in the reigning masculine code is a kind of heroic silence where to be seen as strong, men bury what can make them look or feel weak. *"Within all men is a hidden man. An unseen men. A man who, at some point in in his life, bought into the narrative that suppression equals strength and survival."*

He argues that the way out is of this cultural conditioning for men is to unbury what has been buried and find the strength hidden within the pain, which when ignored surfaces in undesirable ways. Unresolved pain can trigger anger, unhealthy outbursts, relational disconnection, and result in engaging in self-soothing behavior that is out of alignment with a man's true nature, values, and beliefs, such as addictions and affairs.

The work you are engaging in within these pages offers you an opportunity to do exactly that, address some of the things that have been buried in the deep recesses of your own unconscious.

*"The shadow, especially within male culture, has become a storehouse of repressed, hidden, and rejected pain. This pain lies in wait and strikes when a man least wants it to – bringing up insecurities and sabotage when he most desires courage and bravery."*

# The Masks of Masculinity

Right now, you are being presented with an opportunity to pause and take a deeper look at the masks of masculinity you have been conditioned to wear that have both served you and thwarted your development. Defining—or, as Baldoni shares, "undefining"—your masculinity requires soul searching. This can initially trigger sparks of doubt and insecurity, but the journey is worth it.

This could be the perfect time to not only recover from infidelity but to better define who you are as a man. Exploring the messages you received growing up can offer insight into choices you made that don't align with who you are or what you want to create in the world. This awareness has the power to impact your choices in all areas of your life, including your relationship.

I encourage you to take some time to consider your natural talents as well as what you have worked hard to achieve. Embrace your strengths and explore your areas of vulnerability.

The following set of reflection questions focus on the messages you received growing up and your views on masculinity and manhood. The second round of questions, at the end of this chapter, help prepare you to create what you desire for the future.

## Reflection
### *Questions: Messages and Role Models*

**Exploring Masculinity (Part 1)**

- What kind of messages did you receive growing up about what it means to "be a man"?
  - Which behaviors brought positive acknowledgment by others, and which were criticized?
- Were you taught to hide your emotions or given a message that "boys don't cry"?
  - If so, how did that impact you as a child, teen, or even adult?
- How have your experiences and the way you see yourself as a man impacted your relationships with women, now and in the past?
- What role has sex played in validating or invalidating your masculinity?

- Has it ever felt like capturing the attention of more than one woman served to boost your rating on the manhood scale, internally or externally? (Saying yes doesn't mean that you have no regrets. It is simply an indication of potential societal norms upon your decision.)

- What have you done or not done to fit into a familial, cultural, or socially defined role of manhood?

- Who were/are your male role models? How did/do they influence you?
  - Were they strong businessmen? Stay-at-home dads?
  - How did they treat women?
  - Were they good at building things?
  - What skills or ideas did they teach you?
  - What activities did you share during your time with them?

- Was there a particular man or men who you thought highly of and did not personally know—such as an athlete, actor, or politician?

- What are the characteristics that stand out in the man/men you most admire? Which of these characteristics do you successfully emulate?

- In what areas do you feel strong and confident? In what areas would you like to improve?

- What does success look like to you in your career? Relationship? Life?

In the story that follows, you will hear about a man named Rick who used infidelity recovery as a way to take a deeper look at himself—including who he had become, and who he wanted to be as a man.

## Using Your Affair as a Catalyst for Personal Change: *The Story of Rick, Carla, and Gracie*

Rick was a highly intelligent, creative business consultant. He was a strategic thinker, and the guy companies would hire when they needed to quickly turn things around. He prided himself on his ability to quickly assess environments and people—cutting the fat, redefining goals, and repositioning a company for success. Rick knew what to say and how to say it. He was a catalyst for change, and he knew how to sell. He was seen as *the man*.

During an out-of-town meeting with a prospective new client, Rick encountered Gracie. Gracie worked for the company Rick was courting. Ultimately, he found himself not only courting the business but courting Gracie as well.

Gracie was a vibrant woman with a flair for business and a deep passion for the company Rick was engaging with. In his drive to impress her, Rick omitted the fact that he was married. He never said he *wasn't* married; he just didn't wear his ring. Since she didn't ask, he didn't tell.

Rick would argue that he had no intention of sleeping with Gracie. While he found her engaging and lively, he predominantly viewed her as a strategic business partner who could help him land the deal. He thought he would have a better shot presenting himself as a single guy with a little flirting on the side, and he convinced himself that he could handle a little flirtation without crossing the line.

The two engaged in several strategic planning sessions, most of which were over the phone. Rick ended up landing the deal. When he flew in to meet with the partners and begin working his magic, he invited Gracie out for dinner and drinks afterward to celebrate "their win." Their celebration worked its way into his hotel room, where a few more drinks led to Rick and Gracie spending a passionate night together.

Rick came home and was greeted by a suspicious Carla. Carla felt something was off—probably because this wasn't his first rodeo. His first time being unfaithful occurred shortly after they started seriously dating. Since they were newly dating, Rick didn't view this connection as "cheating," but Carla certainly did. He swore it would never happen again.

Now he and Carla were married, and he had broken that promise to her as well as his marriage commitment. He didn't want Carla to know what had happened; he was afraid she would leave if she found out. After his first indiscretion, Carla had told Rick she would leave him if he ever slept with another woman again. So this time, Rick became indignant and angry at Carla's accusations, quickly denying everything. In his eyes, he was lying to save his marriage.

Suspicious women rarely give up. Carla was determined to learn what she believed in her gut to be true and ultimately uncovered enough irrefutable evidence to substantiate her case. Faced with Carla's evidence and pleading for the truth, Rick confessed his indiscretion. At Carla's insistence, he also let Gracie know that he was married. His recovery was rocky as he had two unhappy women on his hands.

## RICK'S RECOVERY WORK

Rick used his situation as a catalyst to begin examining how he was functioning, both in his marriage and his business. Rick's look in the mirror revealed an uncomfortable tendency he had developed to embellish the truth and lie by omission. He came face-to-face with the messages he had received growing up and how he formed his definition of manhood. Our work together involved looking at what was underneath his tendency to engage in deception, even to himself.

Although Rick wholeheartedly dove into his recovery, determined to prove to Carla and himself that he could be a better man, she didn't make the process easy. She was steadfast in keeping Rick at arm's length after discovering his affair. The thing that bothered her most was all the lying Rick had done to cover up what happened. Carla pointed out other ways in which Rick tended to lie about little things. She told herself, *"This is not the type of man I want to be with."* And she told him she didn't want to live with a man she couldn't trust to be honest, even when it might be difficult to walk away.

Confronted with Carla's doubts, Rick began taking a deeper look at the ways in which he tended to lie or *embellish the truth* in other areas of his life.

He told me, *"It's not that I consider myself someone who typically lies, but I've begun paying attention to the many ways in which I either don't tell the whole truth or avoid situations that may lead to uncomfortable conversations."*

We discovered through our work together that at the root of his lying was his unmet need for acknowledgment. His father had been one of those "man up" kinds of dads who offered very little in the way of support. Getting his dad's approval was a strong driver for Rick, which carried over into his career and his relationships. He prided himself on being "the man with the answers" and someone other people looked up to, even if it meant sacrificing his integrity a bit to get there.

He eventually realized that embellishing the truth often made him look better to others than he actually felt about himself. His lying became a way to avoid dealing with uncomfortable feelings and concerns in situations where he felt he was missing the mark. Embellishing stroked his ego and provided a short-lived dopamine pick-me-up.

## SHOWING UP

Rick decided he wanted to improve not only his primary relationship but also how he showed up in the world at large. One of the decisions he made during his self-discovery process was to commit to truth-telling as a way of life. He said: "I really want to be the guy that people can trust and look up to, the one who they can count on to tell the honest truth."

This acknowledgment brought forth a few challenging moments that tested his resolve. He wrestled with how far his truth-telling should go. For example, one of his dilemmas along the way was this: *"What do you say to a guy who is bragging and laughing with a group of guys about something that you find to be distasteful, and not reflecting who you really believe him to be? Guys comment about things. Women's body parts. Jokes about someone's ethnicity. Then we find ourselves laughing even though the joke is not all that funny. We want to feel like we're part of the team, not the one who calls someone out. Yet if you look around the room, you can read the discomfort on at least a few of the faces over these comments."*

He added this about his coworker Jim. *"Jim's jokes often focus on racial stereotypes. There are times when he takes things a bit too far. I don't think he really feels that way, but it sends the wrong message, especially to the guys under him. It doesn't represent what our company says they stand for, and I don't think it puts Jim in a good light."*

The overriding question in this situation was: *"Am I honoring my commitment to truth-telling if I say nothing?"*

Rick added: *"Jim's a jokester. He's the guy that always has a wisecrack about everything and everyone. He likes being the funny man."*

As Rick grappled with this situation in light of his commitment to truth-telling, he decided to talk to Jim in as forthcoming and diplomatic a way as possible.

The day after our session, he found an opportunity to pull Jim aside and share his concerns about Jim's reputation and the company's. During our next session, he shared, *"I told Jim that his jokes that poked fun at race and other sensitive topics made people uncomfortable...that they made me uncomfortable. And that they could paint the company in a bad light. I also said to him, 'People who don't know you could conclude that you're racist. Not cool, especially in today's world. You don't want to be that guy.' It was a tough topic to bring up and talk about. In the end, though, Jim thanked me for sharing this perspective, which he was unaware of. Portraying those things hadn't been his intention, he said."*

*"And how was it for you afterwards?" I asked.*

*"I knew I'd done the right thing for Jim and the other guys. It's not easy to call someone out. But I think sometimes guys think they're being funny and just don't realize how they come across. It makes other people uncomfortable, but we typically just stand around and pretend that it's funny when it really isn't. I don't want to be that guy anymore. But I also don't want to be the guy who people go silent around either."*

*"Go silent? Tell me more about that," I prompted.*

*"You know, the person who walks into a conversation, and it stops. No one wants to be that guy—to feel like an outsider. I want to be a stand-up guy, not someone other guys see as too sensitive. Guys have a kind of code...a man code. It's like a club. You're either in or out. So often we're silent, not because we want to be, but because we think we need to be. No one wants to be on the outside looking in."*

While the conversation was difficult for Rick to initiate, Jim ended up taking it to heart. Rick was glad he had found the courage to talk to his friend.

## A SURPRISE BENEFIT

Rick discovered a surprising side benefit to his truth-telling commitment, and that was an increase in his confidence and a stronger core belief in himself.

Now, you may be thinking, *This guy's a mover and shaker in the corporate world, who makes impactful decisions regularly. A guy like this certainly wouldn't be lacking anything in the confidence department.* Truth be told, corporate courage and presence don't always translate into a high level of social or inner confidence. Don't get me wrong; Rick already knew how to show up at a party and be decisive in his business. That's not what I'm talking about here. The shift he needed—and began to experience—was on an inner level. Besides having the skills to operate, he was now developing a new belief in himself and connection to his deeper values for living.

Rick began to experience a growing sense of calm confidence when associating with his larger circle of friends as well. He found that some of the guys began confiding in him in ways they hadn't before. As Rick let down his mask, so did they. Conversations became more authentic all the way around. As he relaxed his "persona," he found that his unconscious need for outside acknowledgment no longer ran the show. He was finally being honest with himself and true to who he authentically was.

Carla also began noticing the change in Rick and, little by little, began trusting him again. She also began to soften her approach to dealing with her anger about the affair. She learned how to voice her needs in ways that opened their dialogue rather than shutting it down. Instead of becoming upset when Rick didn't behave the way she assumed he should, Carla became more patient. She learned how to ask for what she wanted in ways that inspired Rick to give.

Rick said, *"Through all this, I have fallen back in love with my wife. Don't get me wrong, I never stopped loving her, but I realized I had taken her for granted. Now I see where I f\*d up. I realize that we just quit talking about things that mattered. I see my part in that. I began staying at work longer and longer. Instead of talking to Carla about things, I guess I just went away....We are so much better now."*

Through the process of working through Rick's affair, the couple repaired some deep cracks in their relational foundation. Carla and Rick both learned how to better work through life's disappointments and function as partners, rather than opponents. They both committed to letting go of assumptions and vowed to turn toward each other when problems arose, rather than turning to someone else.

Men who choose to examine themselves more deeply in the wake of an affair are the ones who come out on more solid footing on the other side. There is a transformational shift available to everyone in this moment, a shift that extends past marital challenges and choices and into a deeper sense of engagement with life itself (and with oneself).

Those who don't examine themselves are apt to default to old patterns, potentially repeating the same behaviors that led to their dissatisfaction. This applies to those who stay in their marriages and reconcile, and it also applies to those who don't.

A different client who chose to divorce his wife and marry his affair partner, came to see me to work through the aftermath of his affair, new marriage, and his choices, relayed a conversation he had with his former spouse: *"You know, all of my problems followed me. I'm now in counseling seeking help with the same issues I had in our marriage. I'm sorry I didn't see that sooner and give you a chance."* In the process of leaving his former spouse for greener pastures, her husband came to the realization he had ignored his own contribution to their divorce, thereby missing a growth opportunity. He eventually chose to deal with these internal issues in his second marriage, and while the relationship was rocky for a while, they are still married today.

As you read Rick's story, I hope that you were able to envision how your current struggle could also become one of those pivotal moments in your life. Like Rick, Justin Baldoni, and Connor Beaton, perhaps you can use this time to redefine or fine-tune how you walk in the world as a man. As you begin living in greater alignment with your deeply held values and beliefs, you may even inspire your partner, your kids, and others around you to do the same.

## ———— Reflection ————
### *Questions: Navigating Your Situation*

In the initial chapters, we evaluated your motivation and readiness to participate in the process. Now, let's delve into your unique circumstances, by exploring your perspectives on masculinity and self-perception in more detail. These questions are intended to support you in gaining a deeper understanding and setting the foundation for progress in your recovery journey.

### Exploring Masculinity – Part 2

- How do you view the word *vulnerability*?
  - Is it a challenge for you to accept pieces of yourself that aren't perfect? To share your vulnerabilities with someone else?
  - Do you view vulnerability as a weakness?
- What does "humility" mean to you?
- What happens when you "know you don't know" something? Are you able to accept that and do the research to discover it, or do you tend to make something up?
- Do you embellish or omit things to impress others?
- Were you ever told to "man up"? What does that phrase evoke in you?
- How do you define the word *masculine*?
  - What does being a masculine man look like? Who do you picture when you hear the word *masculine*?

- Who can you identify that embodies healthy masculinity?
- What is your "superpower"? Are you good at reading the room? Sales? Numbers? Relationships? Strategic thinking? Making music? Truth-telling? Integrity? Fathering? Your faith?
- What is something you are proud of that you have worked hard to achieve?
- What wisdom would you like to leave to your child(ren), someone you mentor, or your spouse?
- What would you like written on your tombstone?

Regarding temptation, it is important to be honest with yourself and plan for potential challenges in advance.

## The best way to avoid slipping back into affair behavior in the future is to fortify your commitment in the present.

Trust me; your mind will play tricks on you and make it seem like the little things are no big deal. Time and time again, I have seen responding to an AP's request to "see how you are doing" or "share something" that has happened in her life become a catalyst for a recurrence of something you swore would never happen again.

In this chapter, we have reviewed stories, experiences, and questions to help you explore how you define yourself as a man, want to be seen by others, and how you want to live your life moving forward. In the next chapter, we will be looking at the ways in which couples can enact positive change.

# 23

# Growing *and* Changing *as a* Couple

---■---

*"When one advances confidently in the direction of their dreams, and endeavors to live the life they have imagined, they will meet with success unexpected in common hours."*
—Henry David Thoreau, *Walden,* or *Life in the Woods*

The truth of Thoreau's quote increases exponentially when *two people* choose to *"advance confidently in the direction of their dreams."* **The secret sauce of relational work is commitment:** commitment to yourself and commitment to supporting your partner. You saw how Rick's recovery impacted the choices he made at home and at work. Now we are going to look at how you and your partner can better support one another moving forward.

Powerful couples work provides a safe, inspiring place for people to implement change through exploring needs and wants, as well as experimenting with new behaviors. This is true for all relationships, not just working through the aftermath of an affair. It is imperative that couples create a judgment-free zone where each person can experiment with:

- Asking for what they want
- Actively listening to the needs of their partner

- Setting self-supportive boundaries

As you learned in Part 8, transformative engagement helps create new brain-firing patterns that support shifts in perspectives, which activate greater empathy, compassion, and understanding. This work offers an opportunity to dive into self-directed individual and couples healing work.

---

## Couples can build stronger trust by giving each other the benefit of the doubt instead of making assumptions.

---

To support each other's well-being and relationship, individuals can: a) practice responding instead of reacting, and b) use effective techniques to calm their nervous system and prevent negative thought patterns from taking over. With practice, both partners can recognize and address unsupportive thoughts before they become overwhelming.

By practicing techniques to stabilize your reactions, you can enhance the effectiveness of healing your relationship. You can then concentrate on these three essential areas as you work toward rebuilding your connection:

1. Focus on strengthening your primary relationship by directing your attention towards your partner and away from any external distractions.

2. Prioritize your relationship and take proactive steps to show your significant other (and yourself) that your bond is important to you.

3. Dedicate quality time to repairing any past issues, rebuilding the foundation of your relationship, and working together to create a positive present and future.

Relational healing involves recovering aspects of yourselves and your relationship. That means that the changes each of you make will impact the other. When one person in a relationship shifts, both are affected.

## The Change Process in Action

"The number one investment you can make is the investment in yourself. To achieve a greater level of success, you must be intentional in developing yourself mentally, physically, and emotionally. If you want more, you must become more.

—Alan Stein, Jr., motivational speaker, performance coach

Experts in the field of human potential indicate that it takes anywhere from 18 and 254 days to build a new habit to such an extent that it becomes automatic.[49] The more specifically you can drill down your desired change into actionable behaviors, the easier it will be to measure progress. To effectively meet your goal, you can set up a high-level objective, and then identify the actions items that demonstrate forward movement.

For example: Let's say your objective is to be "a more attentive husband." What are the actionable items you can take to demonstrate that you are moving toward that objective? Perhaps one of these could be to greet your partner when the two of you arrive home from work, before diving into phone calls or emails. That is an actionable item—in service to your overarching objective of being a more attentive husband. This type of specificity makes it far easier to know if you are succeeding in your quest.

It is important to be patient with yourself and your partner as you are setting changes into motion. You will experience both successes and failures. When you can see failures as a necessary part of the learning process, you begin cultivating greater resilience, and the ability to more easily embrace a fluid or growth mindset versus a fixed mindset.

A **fixed mindset** holds to the belief that people are pretty much set the way they are. Life and your corresponding talents are set by your genetic makeup. Things are difficult, if not impossible, to change. **A fluid or growth mindset** is based on the belief that life is about learning, and human beings can evolve and transform through choices, experiences, and determination throughout their life.

## Supporting Your Partner's Desire for Change

As we have discussed, human beings hunger for validation and are driven to solve problems. When you are met with frequent criticism and/or minimal acknowledgment of effort, you can feel defeated. In the face of defeat, effort diminishes. Essentially, you often quit trying and can internalize the idea that we are the problem. *"No matter how hard I try, I can't (make any progress, solve the problem, make my wife happy, have my husband notice me, etc.). And this makes me want to give up."*

Whether you are the one who betrayed or the one who has been betrayed, it is important for you to acknowledge the steps your partner is taking that are in alignment with the new foundation you are building.

## Acknowledgment of the things your partner is doing in service to the relationship provides the glue that helps fortify your connection.

**Effort must be rewarded.** Acknowledgment demonstrates that you are paying attention and noticing the steps being taken that are moving the needle toward the relationship you desire. Again, remember the Three No's from earlier? People want to be Known, Noticed, and to Know they Matter. Acknowledging your partner's positive changes hits at least two of the three.

By aligning your actions with your core values and beliefs, and embracing your capacity for growth and learning, you can have a powerful impact on those around you. Moving forward enables you to break free from old, unhelpful patterns that may have become ingrained. Embracing a growth mindset fosters learning, healing, and transformation, while also honoring our shared humanity.

*"Why waste time proving over and over how great you are,"* author, researcher, and psychology professor Carol Dweck writes, *"when you could be getting better? Why hide deficiencies instead of overcoming them? Why look for friends or partners who will just shore up your self-esteem instead of ones who will also challenge you to grow? And why seek out the tried and true, instead of experiences that will stretch you to even better greatness?"*

In her TED Talk, Dweck discusses the impact of mindset and belief upon enacting powerful life changes. If you would like to dive more deeply into fixed versus fluid mindset, I suggest you check out her work and TED Talk.[21] Here are examples of each type:

**A fixed mindset says:**

- *My partner will probably be unfaithful again (or drive me to be unfaithful).*
- *I can't stop my emotions from ruling my actions, just as they always have.*
- *My partner has bad habits s/he just won't change.*
- *My partner will never truly know me or "get" me.*

**A fluid or growth mindset says:**

- *My partner and I have the ability to learn how to be in a mutually fulfilling relationship.*
- *I/we can take steps to fortify our relationship against possible future infidelity.*

- *I can improve my responses to my negative emotions and learn more healthy communication techniques.*

- *I can affirm and support my partner's positive habit changes, and I learn to accept the ones that don't affect me.*

- *My partner and I have an opportunity to get to know each other better every day.*

The passion for stretching yourself and sticking to your commitments, even (or especially) when things are not going well, is the hallmark of a growth mindset. Adopting this way of thinking can help you thrive during some of your most challenging times.

───────────────── Reflection ─────────────────
## *Enacting and Supporting Change*

To create the type of relationship you desire, it's important to reflect on who you need to be and how you need to show up. Consider the changes you can make to support your vision. Following are a few questions to help stimulate your thinking (this can also be a great couples exercise):

- What qualities do you value in a relationship? How are you living these values?

- What are some ideas you can implement to be more present and available in interactions with your partner?

- What behaviors or habits do you need to improve in upon: in your communication, your acknowledgment of your partner, your patience?

- What boundaries do you need to set or strengthen to maintain healthy relationships?

- What changes, if any, do you need to make at work that are more conducive to establishing a stronger connection at home?

- What changes would you like to see your partner make?

- How open are you to collaboration? In what ways can you demonstrate your openness to mutual problem-solving or creating new strategies with your partner?

- How can you better encourage one another's visions, dreams, and goals as individuals? As a couple?

In this section, we have explored the change process—including ways to enact positive change in your life and relationship, and how emotions and feelings play into the process. In the next section, we will explore the communication process, including ways to engage in courageous conversations, how to effectively make amends, and ways to work through challenging situations.

# PART NINE

---

# Bridging Differences, Rebuilding Trust:
## *The Power of Apologies, Forgiveness and Authentic Communication*

Improving communication is one of the most frequent challenges cited by couples when diving into work with me, aside from addressing more immediate crises like infidelity.

Learning how to navigate communication style differences increases relational satisfaction and willingness to discuss areas of concern. The sooner you can create healthy dialogue around a sensitive topic, the less likely it is to build resentment and discontent.

This section covers communication styles and how to best navigate style differences. Understanding the go-to communication style for you and your partner will set the stage for more effective problem-solving, and less anticipatory fear (as discussed in Chapter 20.)

We will also be looking more deeply at the process of creating and delivering an authentic and meaningful "I'm sorry."

This section addresses each of the following:

**Courageous Conversations**
- Working through your differences
- Identifying and adjusting to differences in conflict resolution styles

**Making Amends**

- Crafting a heartfelt apology

**Forgiveness, Trust, and Reconciliation**

- The stages of forgiveness and the importance of self-forgiveness
- Rebuilding Trust

**When it might be time to leave**

# 24

# Courageous Conversations

—■—

*"Feel the fear and do it anyway."*
—Susan Jeffers, PhD, author

Effective communication is essential for nurturing strong and lasting relationships. However, many people feel apprehensive about having difficult conversations with their partners. In her book *Feel the Fear and Do It Anyway: Dynamic Techniques for Turn Fear, Indecision, and Anger into Power, Action, and Love,* Dr. Susan Jeffers explores how fear can hinder our ability to address challenging topics openly. This fear can be especially daunting when it comes to discussing matters that might disrupt a relational connection.

This chapter aims to offer a communication framework for what I call *courageous conversations.* Before engaging in challenging conversations, it is crucial to reflect on your intentions and mindset and understand your partner's approach to conflict resolution. By prioritizing honesty and active listening within this framework, individuals can communicate with greater empathy, compassion, and authenticity. Taking the time to organize your thoughts before important talks and establishing a supportive environment can foster a sense of security and pave the way for constructive and collaborative dialogues.

Let's begin by outlining some important principles for engaging in a courageous, collaborative conversation with empathy and kindness. These are essential principles that help set the stage for effective, fluid, communication that helps build/rebuild trust and connection.

## Principles for Engaging in a Courageous Conversation

**"Vulnerability is the birthplace of Love, Belonging, Joy, Empathy, Innovation, and Creativity."**

—Brené Brown

It takes great courage and vulnerability to love well, communicate authentically and kindly, listen with an open heart and refrain from judging a person's motives or intent. In *Dare to Lead: Brave Work. Tough Conversations. Whole Hearts,* author and vulnerability researcher Brené Brown discusses the ways in which the ability to be vulnerable lies at the center of courage. Engaging in courageous conversations requires the ability to make room for uncertainty, risk, and emotional exposure. These conversations are fluid, not static. You don't know what you don't know, which means you need to make room for the other person's input.

It's important to focus on being present and attentive to the person speaking. This means putting down cell phones and other distractions. Enter into the conversation with a willingness to relinquish control and the need to prove you are right, understanding that you don't have all the answers.

Here are some principles for engagement:

- Speak your authentic truth directly with kindness, allowing yourself to be vulnerable. If there is something you're not willing or ready to discuss, let your partner know instead of agreeing, telling a half-truth, or lying to avoid discomfort.

- Take responsibility for your actions and inactions and give your partner the benefit of the doubt by extending trust even without immediate proof.

- When you are the listener, avoid interrupting. Have a notepad handy to write down questions as they arise rather than interrupting. Ask clarifying questions instead of making assumptions. Be open to being influenced by the other person/people involved, including being willing to change your mind.

- If tensions rise, pause and let the other person know you need a minute to catch your breath. Take deep breaths, get a glass of water, or engage in another calming activity. Communicate with your partner if you need to step away briefly, rather than just walking away without explanation.

Your goal is to set the stage for engaging into meaningful dialogue that engenders more effective ways of connecting. The process may feel a bit overwhelming at first, but as you begin working with these principles, you will more frequently build bridges instead of erecting walls between you.

We will start by exploring communication differences that, when not properly understood, can lead to misinterpretations and misunderstandings that hinder effective communication. Understanding and navigating through these differences in communication styles is crucial for couples who aim to rebuild and maintain a strong connection after experiencing infidelity.

**We will use the acronym CPR as a tool to help you remember each of these essential communication areas**. CPR stands for **C**onflict Resolution Style, **P**rocessing Speed, **R**egulating Your State of Mind.

# Conflict Resolution Styles

The C in CPR stands for **Conflict Resolution Style**. Understanding each other's default Conflict Resolution Style is key to more effectively repairing a ruptured connection and fostering greater trust and closeness in your relationship.

It is natural for individuals to put off talking about things that may disrupt the connection with someone they care about. Sometimes couples only engage in challenging discussions when avoiding the topic becomes more painful than addressing it, or when a triggering incident increases their level of urgency. Other times it may seem like one partner is intentionally provoking a reaction by pushing the other into a conversation they would rather not have, or at an inconvenient time when emotions are running high. This behavior can be a way of seeking attention, often stemming from a feeling of distance between partners, when negative engagement may seem preferable to none at all.

Each individual and couple has a default conflict resolution style that impacts when and how they attempt to resolve relational disturbances. Let's take a look at two primary conflict resolution styles and their impact on how couples navigate challenges. While some people may switch between these styles, most have a dominant style, which tends to emerge when dealing with conflictual situations. The couple also develops a relational conflict resolution style, which is rooted in how each individual approaches conflict.

**Working things through until resolved/Anxious.** The first conflict resolution style is characterized by a strong inclination toward working through an issue until it feels fully resolved. Individuals with this style experience anxiety when conflicts are left hanging and tend to persist in a conversation until it reaches a resolution, even if it feels uncomfortable to do so. They fear that without resolving the conflict, it will continue to linger, and they won't be able to stop ruminating about it.

They tend to believe that leaving issues unresolved will result in serious consequences, such as a partner's disconnection. When their partner avoids addressing conflicts and chooses to disengage from discussions, it can evoke a strong fear of abandonment, which is the thing they fear most.

**Putting things off/Avoidant.** On the other end of the spectrum are individuals who tend to delay discussing a challenging topic for as long as possible or abruptly ending the conversation when it becomes uncomfortable or feels futile. They fear that continuing the discussion won't lead to a productive solution and that it may escalate the situation, potentially triggering overwhelming emotions or unmanageable reactions from themselves or their spouse. This fear can lead them to isolate themselves to avoid feeling attacked or triggering an angry outburst that they may struggle to control.

Their deeper fear is feeling trapped in a situation with no way out, which can cause them to shut down or turn away from the relationship, the exact thing the anxious partner fears most.

**During challenging discussions, individuals with an anxious style tend to more frequently move towards their partner when addressing challenges, while those with an avoidant style tend to withdraw from a conversation and their partner..** This can lead to significant frustration within the relationship. One partner may complain that their significant other avoids engaging when conflicts arise, while the other may feel that their partner never lets go of *the past*. The person who tends to postpone or avoid addressing issues may become weary when coupled with a partner who is driven to discuss issues until they are fully resolved.

**When both individuals in a relationship have an Anxious Conflict Resolution Style,** their discussions can become lengthy as each person strives to persuade the other that their perspective is correct. Both individuals may have a strong desire to *win* the argument.

On the other hand, **if both individuals have an Avoidant Conflict Resolution Style**, they may find themselves leaving many conflicts unresolved. They are driven to maintain harmony at all costs, which can leave conflictual issues unresolved resulting in decreased intimacy and relational discontent.

---

**Safety and intimacy are enhanced through authentically discussing things that matter, demonstrating curiosity about what's important to your partner, and listening to *learn from* them, not just to defend your position.**

---

## Reflection
### *Identifying and Adjusting to Differing Styles*

Understanding each other's go-to conflict resolution style can help you both depersonalize conflictual situations and more effectively collaborate to develop strategies to work through challenges and engage in more meaningful dialogue.

The following questions have been designed to help you identify your dominant conflict resolution style.

### ANXIOUS

- Is it difficult for you to leave a conversation unfinished?
- Do you tend to push for resolution even when it feels uncomfortable for your partner?
- Do you tend to pursue your partner even when discussions get heated, because you know you can plow your way through to the finish line?

### AVOIDANT

- Do you tend to avoid engaging in uncomfortable topics?
- Do you tend to walk away or shut down in the middle of a discussion if your partner shows any signs of upset?

- Do you tend to avoid your partner when you think they are upset by something you said or did?

Which style aligns most closely with your approach? Does your style change depending upon the discussion topic or who you are talking with? (For example: Sometimes a person's style at home may differ from their style at work.) Are there specific topics that trigger a different style? If so, what do you believe causes the shift?

Which style best fits your partner? Is their approach consistent or does it change depending upon the topic?

**What about your relational style?** Is there a push/pull between differing styles resulting in frustration and decreased intimacy? Do you both tend to avoid challenging topics, or does your relational style lean toward engaging in a heated, passionate discussion until it either ultimately wears you out, or ends up in resolution after a long and emotionally draining interaction?

Each style has underlying fears that trigger their responses. Understanding each other's underlying fears helps you both work toward creating a safer place to exchange ideas rather than doing battle.

**If your partner tends to process anxiously**, providing reassurance about safety in the relationship, even during conflicts, is crucial. They may benefit from knowing that their emotional well-being is valued, and that the relationship remains secure.

**If your partner is more avoidant,** it is important to acknowledge their need for occasional breaks during discussions to regain composure when feeling overwhelmed. Granting them space to collect their thoughts and re-center themselves can be helpful.

Regardless of each person's default style, the goal is to move towards a more collaborative approach to problem-solving, which ultimately helps build safety and increase intimacy.

# Processing Speed

The P in CPR stands for **Processing Speed.** Differences in Processing Speed frequently result in greater challenges working through difficulties. It is not uncommon for one partner to be fast-processing and solution-driven, with the other tending to be more detail-oriented, frequently requiring more information, or a lengthier discussion to feel reassured that they are making the best choice possible.

These contrasting approaches can lead to misunderstandings and misperceptions. To address this challenge, it is important for both partners to recognize and respect each other's processing speed and be willing to adjust their inherent style to find a balance between efficiency and thoroughness.

―――――――――――― Reflection ――――――――――――
## *Identifying and Adjusting to Differing Processing Speeds*

Here are some questions to help you identify your typical processing speed. Which one do you more frequently identify with? Which one seems more closely aligned with your partner's style?

### FAST PROCESSORS

- Are you a quick thinker who likes to cut to the chase in conversations or get to the bottom line?

- Do you consider yourself solution-driven, perhaps even taking pride in your ability to make quick decisions?

- Do you tend to quickly lose interest when a story includes *too much* detailed information?

- When reading a news article do you tend to skim it looking for salient points rather than reading it word for word?

- Do you sometimes feel impatient when your partner needs more information or that they ask *too many* questions?

## DETAIL ORIENTED PROCESSORS

- Do you feel uncomfortable making a decision until you have done your *homework,* to ensure that you have a thorough grasp of the topic at hand?

- Do you consider yourself thorough and someone others can trust to gather sufficient information to make the best choice possible?

- When attempting to get your point across to someone do you strive to make sure they have detailed information to support your point of view?

- When reading a news article do you tend to read every word rather than skim for key highlights?

- Have you ever been asked to shorten your explanations or *cut to the chase* when offering your perspective or telling a story?

- Does your partner ever become impatient or accuse you of asking too many questions?

Here are some ideas for more effectively addressing differences in processing speed:

## ADJUST YOUR PACING.

**Fast processors** need to slow down a bit. Present your thoughts/ideas, then give the detail-oriented person time to review things and come back to the conversation as needed. Remember, detail-driven processors can struggle to decide or respond without feeling like they have all the necessary information.

**Detail-driven processors** need to be willing to highlight their ideas as opposed to offering an in-depth analysis. Remember, fast processors can lose interest with too much detail.

Sometimes setting a designated time limit on discussions can give both parties a framework within which to operate. Fast processors may work better knowing there is a time limit. Detail-oriented processors can be compelled to streamline things to finish within the designated time frame.

## ASK OPEN ENDED QUESTIONS AND LISTEN
## TO UNDERSTAND RATHER THAN TO RESPOND.

Questions promote curiosity, particularly when they are open-ended (not yes/no). Now that doesn't mean questioning every minute detail. (Too much questioning can create frustration, particularly for fast-processing, solution-driven individuals.) But do gather the data you need to both be on the same page before diving into solutions. Asking questions in ways that help a person feel heard, invites deeper discussion, demonstrates interest, and is an art that goes hand-in-hand with effective listening. This involves a willingness to set aside preconceived notions about the situation and the speaker and focus on what they are attempting to communicate.

Questions can be divided into two basic categories: one is focused more on the person responding to the question, and the other is focused more on the person asking the question. The first is an inquiry based on curiosity. The second leans more toward seeking validation from a place of assumption. Let's take a deeper look at each.

**Curiosity Questioning:** Asking questions from a place of curiosity about the respondent's experience demonstrates an interest in the person/subject matter at hand. It invites people into a dialogue in which information and ideas are shaped through sharing. Curiosity questioning stimulates creative collaboration by allowing deeper listening. These questions generally begin with *"what."*

**Assumptive Questioning:** This tends to be more focused on the question-asker than the respondent. Assumptive questioning is frequently rooted in the need to validate a particular point of view and/or uncover evidence to support a belief/conclusion the asker believes to be true. The respondent tends to feel criticized and exhausted through this line of questioning. Assumptive questions frequently begin with *"why."*

Here are some examples illustrating the difference between *what* and *why* questions, specifically related to inquiries around the topic of infidelity.

Example:

*Why* Questions:
- Why did you (choose to)?
- Why wasn't I enough for you?
- Why didn't you talk to me first?

*What* Questions:

- What intrigued you about that?
- What were you looking for that you felt may have been missing in your life?
- What prompted you to reach out to someone else instead of talking to me first?

Generally speaking, *why* questions tend to be more accusatory. *What* questions tend to be more exploratory. **The choice of words you begin with is not a hard-and-fast rule but a guideline to creating more engagement through conversation.**

Recognize that there is no right or wrong way to process information. There are advantages to both styles. Understanding each of your styles leads to more product conversations where you can each be mindful of your partner's needs and remind them when they are sinking too deeply into their style and request that they make a change as needed.

# Regulate Your State of Mind

The R in CPR stands for **Regulating your state of mind.** Your mental and emotional state prior to entering into a conversation, as well as the overall state of the relationship, play crucial roles in the ability to engage in productive, collaborative discussions.

---

**When individuals approach discussions with a positive and open frame of mind, they are more likely to approach the conversation with empathy, understanding, and a willingness to find common ground.**

---

When your emotions are dysregulated, that is not in a calm centered place, it can be difficult to step back and see things from another's perspective or even tap into your own sense of well-being. It can be extremely difficult to climb out of a disagreement or soothe your partner when you are not feeling grounded. Sometimes dysregulation occurs because you haven't slept or eaten well, or been taking good care of yourself. Maybe you are anxious about something different, like a work situation or sick child.

Some people have a greater challenge with mood regulation than others. If you find yourself frequently becoming upset at seemingly little things, it is time to take a step back and examine what you may be struggling with or avoiding. If mood swings, or over reactivity has been an ongoing or extreme problem, speaking with a medical professional can help. Many people feel uncomfortable with the idea of taking medication to help with chemical imbalances. I will tell you that I have seen the right medication work wonders during periods of stress or ongoing challenges with depression, obsessive-thinking, and mood regulation.

Your state of mind directly affects your ability to engage with your partner. As we have previously discussed, each person's state of mind and well-being impacts the state of the relationship. Taking care of yourself sets you up in the best position to be able to effectively engage with your partner. If you are feeling "off" it is best to delay the conversation until you are in a better state of mind.

**Feeling strong and alive with someone you love elevates the energy** and increases joy and dopamine within you both. Love shared is one of the most potent drugs in the world.

**Feeling rejected by someone you love depletes dopamine and serotonin**, which has the same withdrawal symptoms, both emotionally and neurobiologically, as drug and alcohol withdrawal. Rejection induces both an emotional and neurochemical reaction.

Your objectives in re-coupling are to create more feel-good neurochemical experiences through how you connect and co-create your lives and to diminish the ways you have acted in the past that have pushed each other away.

Engaging in self-care to regulate your energy system puts you and the relationship in a better frame of mind. Here are a few mindfulness activities to consider:

**Deep breathing.** Inhale a slow deep breath. Allow it to expand your belly. Count to six. Hold for the count of four. Release your breath slowly, once again counting to six. Repeat between three and ten times. This type of breathing can help regulate your system and increase your ability to focus.

**Positive self/relational talk** can infuse a sense of hopefulness into the conversation. Consider situations when you have felt connected to your partner and have worked through challenges. Reaffirm those moments. Here are some thought starters: *We have a good foundation. We are great problem-solvers when we put our heart and mind into it. I am open to actively listening to what my partner has to say and sharing my perspective clearly and kindly. In truth we really do love each other. We've got this!*

**Meditation/prayer.** You can close your eyes, focus on your breath for three to five minutes, listen to a guided meditation in your favorite app, or offer a prayer, which can be as simple as: *I surrender to you (whomever and however you pray or to your "higher wisdom"), trusting in your healing guidance to help us both approach this conversation with an open heart, respect, and the belief in new possibilities.*

**Movement.** Go for a run, walk, or engage in your favorite workout routine to lower your body's overall tension and cortisol levels.

These are just a few suggestions. The important thing, as we discussed in *The Neurobiology of Change* (Chapter 20), is to adjust your frame of mind and work toward engaging from your *wiser adult self* as opposed to your *adaptive child self*.[22] The goal is to work toward setting the stage for greater understanding and collaboration.

## COLLABORATIVE COMMUNICATION

Collaboration offers the optimal opportunity for navigating conflict well. Collaborative conflict resolution begins with seeing the problem as being out in front of you, like an obstacle for you both to overcome, instead of between you, like a wall separating you. This way of engaging helps safeguard the relationship.

**Relationships are made up of three entities: you, me, and us.** Each needs to be valued and strengthened. Entering into discussions keeping in mind what's best for the relationship can help each person detach from feeling personally attacked. Approaching problems in this manner sets the stage for you each to be part of the solution rather than escalating the conflict.

When you see the problem as something between you, it tends to put the two of you into more of a battle-ready state, each poised to defend your position.

---

**Positioning the problem as the challenge instead of the other person, engenders a greater spirit of collaboration. There are no winners or losers when the *problem* is something you are both working to resolve.**

---

Adopting a collaborative conflict resolution style involves being open to exploring different perspectives and seeking creative solutions. It also means entering discussions with the intention of working together to find outcomes that benefit all parties. This approach fosters cooperation, understanding, and the potential for innovative problem-solving.

# Courageous Conversations Framework

We have taken a look at your CPRs—conflict resolution and processing styles, and the need to regulate your state of mind prior to engaging in potentially challenging discussions. Next, we explore a framework which can assist you in sharing your deeper struggles and uncertainties in ways that foster greater connectivity, intimacy, and overall relational well-being. We will also address the importance of listening in ways that create safety for you both to share deeper truths and reveal what you may have been afraid of, or conflicted about, sharing.

The topics of these conversations can vary, from a personal concern to relational questions, to something you want to reveal to your partner, or to proactively setting the stage for goal setting.

We will be using the acronym PIECES to describe the 6-step Courageous Conversations process:

1) Prepare.
2) Invite/Initiate.
3) Engage.
4) Collaborate.
5) Express Appreciation.
6) Set Follow-up Time.

## PREPARE

An often-overlooked step when entering into discussions on sensitive or significant topics is preparation. Taking the time to reflect on your own intentions, needs, and goals for the conversation beforehand is essential in laying the groundwork for a productive dialogue. Whether your objective is to simply be listened to, or to engage in a collaborative exchange aiming to solve a particular problem, understanding your own motivations can greatly enhance the quality of the conversation.

Here are some preparation questions:

- Are you wanting to share to garner your partner's support? Understanding? Do you just want them to listen or offer feedback?
- Are you looking for validation for your point of view?
- Are you engaging to reveal something that may be challenging for your partner to hear?
- Is this conversation being initiated to check in on the state of your relationship?
- Do you have something important that you are curious about?
- Is this a follow-up conversation to an earlier discussion? If so, have you made any new discoveries or shifted your perspective from the original conversation?
- Do you believe you already know the answer, and your conversation and questions are designed to uncover proof?
- If the respondent reveals information that you find upsetting, are you emotionally prepared to hear that?
- Is your desire to create connection and help the person feel seen and acknowledged?
- Are you open to listening to the other person's point of view?

If you are preparing to engage in a discussion about the affair, keep in mind it is not uncommon for the betrayed partner to launch into a barrage of questions when emotions are running high. Often men or women *uncovering* new information about an affair can be brutal in their delivery. This stems from their concern about being lied to and their strong desire to ferret out the *real truth*. Remember, they are feeling traumatized and probably blindsided by what has occurred. This can result in outrage when they feel things are being kept hidden.

It can be helpful to take some notes to keep yourself organized during important discussions. While you don't need to script everything, spending some time preparing can lead to clearer communication and deeper understanding.

## INVITE/INITIATE

The way you invite and begin a conversation sets the tone for the interaction. Make sure you don't jump in during a moment of distress or heightened urgency. Take your time. Set a date and place that is conducive to engaging in an open, authentic manner.

Renowned couples researchers John and Julie Gottman have conducted extensive experiments with couples. They found that by observing how a conflictual discussion is handled within the first three minutes, they can predict the state of the relationship six years later with 80 percent accuracy. This highlights the importance of starting conversations in a constructive and respectful manner, as it can have long-term implications for the relationship.

Couples in the greatest danger of breaking up, according to their research, are those who frequently begin challenging discussions with criticism, harbor negativity from past unresolved conflicts, or initiate conversations when emotions are running high. The Gottmans refer to this as a "harsh startup."

**Initiating a conversation with a calm and rational mindset greatly increases the likelihood of positive outcomes.** The Gottmans refer to this approach as a "soft startup."[23] Regulating your emotions before engaging in a conversation is a critical preparatory step that sets the stage for a productive discussion. As we have discussed, entering a conversation in a dysregulated state, such as feeling frustrated or agitated, hinders effective communication. Additionally, according to Dan Siegel's work on interpersonal neurobiology (IPNB), one person's intense state of mind can strongly impact the other person involved in the conversation. Therefore, it is important to regulate your emotions and approach the discussion with a calm and composed demeanor.

## ENGAGE

**There are two vital roles** that, when managed well, set the stage for an authentic, collaborative conversation: speaking and listening. It is important that you actively engage in each.

**When you're the speaker**, your role is to express your thoughts, feelings, and perspectives clearly and respectfully. It is important to communicate in ways that promotes understanding and encourage constructive dialogue. Remember, this is not a monologue. Even though you are the one initiating, it is important to be open to your partner's response.

**When you're the listener,** it is important to actively pay attention to your partner's words, nonverbal cues, and emotions. By listening attentively, you demonstrate respect and validate the other person's experiences and viewpoints. This helps create an environment of trust and openness.

Engaging in both speaking and listening with sincerity and empathy contributes to a productive and meaningful conversation. It allows for the exchange of ideas, the exploration of different perspectives, and the potential for finding common ground and creative solutions.

**Intention setting** is a powerful way to begin the conversation. By clearly stating your purpose for the interaction, both parties can create a safe and open space for effective communication. This approach can help ease anxiety for one partner and prevent premature disengagement for the other.

In my couples work, we typically begin by setting intentions for the session. For example, one might express their intention to fully engage in the conversation, speak their truth with respect, authenticity, and kindness, and listen with an open heart to their partner's perspective and needs. Alternatively, a simpler intention could be to be present, kind, authentic, and communicate from the heart.

**Communication is a full body experience.** Remember, we communicate not just with our words, but with our entire presence. In close relationships, you both will be assessing your partner's mood and state of mind based upon how they appear when engaging. You will be reading and interpreting their body language as well as their words. This is true for both the speaker and the listener.

As you engage, it is important to be aware of these three things:

**Tone.** Is your tone of voice defensive, critical, or angry? How you say something is as important as what you say.

**Body language.** Arms folded across your chest is an indication that you are attempting to protect yourself, or perhaps that you are closed off to what is being discussed. (Or this stance could simply indicate that you are cold!) Relaxing your body before connecting helps you both feel more open to what is about to be discussed.

**State of mind.** Entering into a conversation from a place of possibility that the two of you can work through things contributes to setting the stage for a more collaborative conversation. Are you open to hearing what the other person has to say, and the possibility of seeing things differently?

It is not uncommon to misread signals. This can happen when one partner jumps to a conclusion about what they assume their partner *really means* when their words and body language do not align. This misalignment can occur when someone is trying to present themselves differently from how they truly feel. For example, if your spouse is angry about a significant purchase you made but is attempting to hide or let go of their anger, their words may sound positive while their facial expression may tell a different story.

Sometimes, a person's irritation or frustration stems from factors unrelated to you, such as a headache or other external circumstances. It is helpful to be mindful of your own body language and avoid making assumptions about the underlying reasons behind someone else's. If you sense something is off, don't assume. Ask. *"Your words sound really positive, but your facial expression and your crossed arms makes me wonder if you are angry right now."* Or, *"You sound supportive, but I get the sense that something is off. Is there anything else going on that is troubling you?"*

As we have discussed, if one or both of you is really out of sorts, you may decide to come back to the conversation at another time. If that is what you decide, set a follow-up time to make sure an important discussions isn't avoided.

## Differing Spending Habits (Part I) *Engagement*

Let's say the two of you have differing views about how money is spent, with one of you being more of a saver, the other more spontaneous in their spending. Upon opening the credit card statement, you as the saver observe spending habits that make you feel uncomfortable. You decide this is important to discuss with your partner, as the spending is outside what you both have agreed upon.

If you begin the conversation when you are angry, hungry, or in frustrated state of mind, or shortly after a difficult work conversation, etc., you are more likely to engage in a *harsh startup* that looks something like this: *"Here we go again. Your spending is out of control. You have absolutely no regard for money. We need to talk about this."*

A better way to engage is to give yourself a little space to consider examine your upset and triggers on your own prior to engaging with your partner. Then, state your intention and discussion topic clearly and invite them into a conversation. *"I'd like to set up a time to discuss our finances, (or) how we spend and save money."* Then when you meet, initiate the conversation with a soft *startup* such as: *"I'd like to talk about this month's Visa statement. It is my intention to engage in a productive discussion in which we can collaborate on creating a solution that works for us both."*

You can then calmly state your concern.

*"It looks like the spending this month is much higher than we discussed. I'd like you to be able to buy things for yourself without feeling like I'm looking over your shoulder, and I'd also like us to build our savings. Can we brainstorm solutions to create a plan that works better for us both?"* Then give your partner the space to share their perspective.

## COLLABORATE

The *Differing Spending Habits* example demonstrates a safe start up with the speaker inviting the listener to brainstorm solutions and work to together to create a plan. This engagement style sets the stage for collaboration.

We have spent a good part of this section preparing the speaker to initiate and engage effectively. Collaborative conversations also require the presence of an actively engaged listener. The way you listen and respond either contributes to the flow of a conversation or triggers frustration which can shut off connection.

---

### When you listen to understand and learn, rather than to defend yourself or win arguments, you create an opportunity for greater intimacy and connection.

---

**Engaged listening** is an active process that involves not just your ears, but your entire being. Being an engaged listener is a gift you offer the speaker. It demonstrates interest, care, and respect. This is an active, not passive endeavor. It lets your partner know that you value what they have to say, which in turn translates into letting them know you value who they are.

Here are some questions to help you assess your most common listening style. Which of these do you learn toward, particularly when working through a more charged situation.

- When someone is talking, do you find your main goal is to defend your point of view?

- Does an urgent desire to get your point across cause you to talk over someone else?

- Is your first response more self-focused? Do you tend to hijack the conversation by talking about a time when you experienced the same thing?

**Please Note:** While swapping stories can sometimes be helpful to create common ground or break the ice, taking the attention away from the one speaking may cause them to feel like you're not really interested in what they have to say, or perhaps in who they are. It can be helpful to jot down notes so that rather than interrupting you can share your thoughts later.

People often make assumptions before someone even starts speaking. These assumptions can lead to distractions and prevent us from truly listening to what the other person is trying to communicate. When we are familiar with someone, we may fall into listening patterns like preparing to defend ourselves or assuming their intentions.

## Reflection
### *Engaged Listening*

It's important to pay attention to how you listen. Here are some questions to help you prepare you to be a more engaged listener:

- What are you inferring from the questions being asked?
- Are you assuming a particular intent?
- Are you feeling interrogated or like there is a specific agenda behind the inquiry?
- Are you trying to figure out what the Initiator wants to hear?
- Are you trying to appease? To please?
- Are you listening with an open ear, or to defend your point of view/figure out what you are going to say next?
- Are you asking clarifying questions to verify that you understand what is being asked of you?
- Are you engaging from an authentic, direct, and kind place?

As you can see, engaged listening is not a passive endeavor. Active and empathetic listening contributes to more meaningful and effective interactions.

When the speaker has finished explaining their personal or relational challenge, it is time for the two of you to reverse roles and for the listener to express their point of view. This begins with restating what you heard and perceive the speaker wants to communicate. This can begin with, *"What I heard you say was _____. Did I get that right?"* (Then the speaker acknowledges, revises, or adds to what the listener expressed.)

*"What I interpret that to mean (or what I feel about that, or what it triggers for me, or what I would like) is _____."* Sometimes the listener perceives a deeper meaning beyond the words that may or may not be accurate. Stating your assumptions aloud allows them to either be validated, invalidated, or expanded upon by the speaker.

# Differing Spending Habits (Part II) *Collaboration*

Let's expand on the *Differing spending habits* example. The segment ended with the speaker inviting the listener into brainstorming a potential plan that works for both people.

**Listener restating what they heard:** *"I hear you are struggling with last month's Visa charges, and you don't want me to think you are trying to control me. I hear that you want to collaborate to come up with a new plan. Did I get that right?"*

**Speaker:** *"Yes. I don't want you to feel controlled, and I am concerned about caring for our financial future."*

**Listener:** *"I hear your concerns about our future, and I would like to have some freedom and autonomy to make decisions without feeling like you are scrutinizing what I spend. I want you to trust that I have our family's best interests at heart."*

**Speaker:** *"Okay. I get that you don't want to feel controlled, and you want to feel like I trust you. I would love to talk about ways we can do that and also talk about ways to set aside more money to invest."*

**Listener:** *"Okay. And I would like to be more involved in decisions regarding our investments."*

## EXPRESS APPRECIATION

The last two steps are short and sweet. The first is express appreciation, which is essentially thanking your partner for carving out the time to discuss a topic important to them.

# Differing Spending Habits (Part III) *Express Appreciation*

**Listener:** *"I can see that you were really triggered by last month's Visa bill. I appreciate how you approached things and that we set aside time to discuss your concerns rather than reacting negatively when you saw the total. I know the bill was higher than usual, and I appreciate how you handled this."*

**Speaker:** *"Thank you. Me too. I feel good about our decision to discuss our overall financial picture once per quarter and looking at spending and saving on a monthly basis."*

## SET FOLLOW-UP TIME

The last letter of the PIECES method is to Set a follow-up time to touch base, complete an unfinished discussion, or, as in the case of our example, set the dates for the monthly and quarterly meetings as discussed.

It is important that both parties feel that their concerns are being taken seriously and setting a follow-up time to touch base on sensitive or unresolved topics helps each person feel important and validated.

## POTENTIAL PITFALLS

Sometimes your partner may begin a discussion in an agitated state, causing you to feel attacked and defensive. Meeting their level of agitation or attempting to prove you're right does not lead to effective resolution. Instead, consider responding in a more constructive manner. For instance, you can express your willingness to listen by saying, *"I want to hear what you have to say,"* or, *"It sounds like this is really important to you. Can we talk about it calmly, so we don't say things we might regret, or potentially get into a shouting match?"*

It is important to begin the problem-solving process by listening and asking, not yelling and telling. If the two of you are working on this material together, you can remind one another of the importance of a *soft startup*. To engage in a productive conversation, you may even need to delay the conversation until each of you is calmer.

--- Reflection ---
### *Engaged Listening Additional Tips*

- Begin with a willingness to listen with an open heart and mind. Take a few focused deep breaths. Set the intention to be present and calm. If you are feeling anxious, you another idea is to offer a quick prayer which can be as simple as, *"I am willing to be open and present to this conversation. Guide me to listen well to the underlying meaning of what my partner wants to share."*

- Demonstrate to your partner that you are listening through your body language. Sit toward them, arms and legs uncrossed. Focus on them while they are speaking, nod your head, say "okay" or some other small word to indicate you're present in your listening.

- Don't interrupt. Take notes if you have a question or want to address a particular point.

- Rather than listening to defend your point of view, listen to learn. Look for points of agreement rather than bones of contention.

- **The ABCs of listening are Always Be Curious.** Express a genuine curiosity about what your partner is sharing. Ask questions to clarify what you have heard and explore the topic more fully rather than to interrogate the one speaking.

- Here's probably the toughest of all: **be willing to be influenced by the one who is speaking to you.** Acknowledge ideas you hear that you may not have considered before. Be willing to change your mind, even just a little.

- Appreciate your partner's willingness to connect and share.

---

## When each of you leads with curiosity, kindness, and appreciation rather than judgment and fear, you become problem-solvers instead of problem-makers.

---

At this point, we have discussed the trajectory of affairs, the inner workings of relationships, how people enact and support change, and ways to courageously communicate. Next, we explore extending apologies and forgiveness in ways that build relational and self-trust.

# 25

## Making Amends

■

*"Humility leads to strength and not weakness. It is the highest form of self-respect to admit mistakes and to make amends for them."*

—John J. McCloy, attorney, diplomat, presidential advisor

Apologies are an integral part of healing. And as we have discussed, you will be called on to apologize *many* times during the relational repair process. Your spouse needs to feel your sincerity and remorse and be assured that you are truly, deeply sorry for the pain your actions have caused. As tough as this may be to hear, a part of her wants to know that you too have suffered.

Like any significant interaction, the effectiveness of an apology is directly proportional to the effort invested in it. To ensure that an apology is well-received and takes root, it must be both given and received sincerely. Effective apologies require active engagement from both sides.

## The Art of Designing and Delivering a Heartfelt Apology

**"Never ruin an apology with an excuse."** —Ben Franklin

*I'm sorry.* Some people say it so frequently that it almost loses its meaning. Others don't say it nearly enough. (I hear from some of my clients that their partner *never* says it!) An apology is about owning an infraction that has hurt someone, resulting in a disruption of the relationship between two (or more) people. In the case of major infractions, like infidelity, heartfelt apologizing is a critical component of the ongoing trust-rebuilding process.

Apologies range from a simple "I'm sorry" for a minor infraction, to a sincere, heartfelt apology for something said or done that has deeply wounded another. Apologizing is both an amends-making and relief-seeking activity. The offending party extends an apology to: 1) help shift discordant energy between themselves and the person who has been hurt, and 2) help relieve the internal tension/pain resulting from their actions.

## GIVING AN APOLOGY

Throughout the course of apologizing to your partner for the affair, you will most likely engage in a variety of different approaches, depending upon the situation. Let's explore the various approaches and types of effective and ineffective apologizing. The first three approaches tend to be more focused on the needs of the apologizer rather than the one being apologized to and are the least effective.

**1) An Excuse-Making Apology** is more of an "I'm sorry, but..." The person extending this type of apology is accepting partial responsibility for what has occurred, but by making excuses for why it happened, they are not completely owning their actions.

**Please note:** an excuse is different than an explanation. An excuse often blames the other person. An apology with an explanation is designed to help the other person understand what was going on and why you may not have honored an agreement or met their need.

An excuse-making apology may look like: *"I'm sorry I was unfaithful, but you really haven't been available for me for quite some time."*

An apology with an explanation is more like: *"I'm so sorry I turned to someone else instead of talking to you when I was stressed. Over the past few months things have felt strained between us and instead of talking to you I pulled away. I am sorry for not giving us a chance to talk things out."* This type of apology is more genuine as it focuses on the behavior of the person apologizing and expresses remorse for both actions and inactions.

**2) A Begging for Forgiveness Apology** is stimulated by the desire for relief. Begging for forgiveness typically comes after being caught engaging in behavior that has brought harm to someone who is hesitant or unwilling to reconnect. This apology is often stimulated by the desire to end the discord caused by the offending party's actions, while also seeking to alleviate internal pain.

This may look like: *"I'm so sorry.... Please, please forgive me, I can't live without you. I'm begging you. Please give me another chance. Please. Please!"*

**3) A Frustrated Apology** is enacted when someone has an impatient personality, wants to rush the process, and/or is frustrated that previous attempts have not been accepted. The apologizer is often hopeful that applying a little pressure will cause the offended party to let things go and move on.

This may look like: *"I already said I'm sorry. I can't understand why you keep bringing it up. I can't change the past. We need to put this behind us, so it doesn't keep bringing us down!"*

The final two apologies reflect sincerity. They are not simply an *"I'm sorry you feel that way"* apology, which lacks ownership, or an *"I'm sorry, but..."* apology, which negates what has been said before it. These are 100 percent responsibility-taking apologies. No excuses allowed.

## You can't transform what you don't acknowledge.

**4) An Engaged Apology** involves sincerely expressing remorse and taking full responsibility for your actions, without attempting to avoid or rush through the process. Being fully present is crucial. Looking into the person's eyes as you express genuine remorse can offer more sincerity even if it feels a bit uncomfortable. Examples of statements that can be included are: *"I deeply apologize for causing you pain. I am truly sorry for betraying your trust and creating a wedge between us."*

As you have heard many times throughout our work together, **it is important to take 100 percent responsibility** for what transpired and the choices you made. Even if the other person made the first move, even if your relationship was suffering, even if you don't know what the hell you were thinking, this is your time to take full responsibility for what happened. You are the one who stepped out. It was 100 percent your decision to get involved with someone else. Owning your indiscretions goes a long way toward the healing and trust-rebuilding process.

**5) A Wholehearted, Amends-Making Apology** is a little deeper cut than the *Engaged Apology*. It typically occurs after extensive discussions about the transgression and reflects a mutual desire for reconnection. A wholehearted apology is rooted in a genuine desire to heal the other person's heartache, acknowledge the profound remorse and sorrow caused by the offender's actions or inactions, and demonstrate tenderness and care. It requires vulnerability, openness, and humility.

Let's take a look at how the PIECES method can guide you through the process of engaging in a wholehearted apology.

# Wholehearted Apology Making

The first step for using the Courageous Conversations PIECES method to conduct a wholehearted apology is to Prepare.

### PREPARE

Delivering a heartfelt apology involves both inner and outer preparation. Inner preparation begins with self-examination. You must get real with yourself before you can get real with your partner. Here are some questions to explore in preparation for your amends-making apology. I encourage you to set aside some uninterrupted time for this activity. The more energy you give to it, the more heartfelt your apology will be. Take out your notebook/workbook and write some things down. Be honest. These answers are for your eyes only. There are three aspects to preparation:

**Self-examination**

What are you sorry for *really*?

- o That you got caught?
- o That you hurt her?
- o That you put your relationship at risk?

- o That you might lose her?
- o That you didn't talk with her first?
- o For the impact this has had on your life, work, family, community, etc.?
- Do you have remorse over connecting with this other person?
  - o (It is not uncommon for your answer to be a *qualified* yes. What this can look like is you regret the pain your actions caused, yet there are things you experienced that created connection/movement that were catalysts for growth.)
- Do you feel bad about the pain that your actions caused your partner? Okay, I realize it's highly unlikely you are going to say no to this one. Let's dive in a little deeper:
  - o How did your actions impact your spouse? Damage/hurt her? Hurt your relationship?
  - o What do you regret most?

**Partner reflection**
- What do you love about your partner? What are the qualities you admire in her?
- How does forgiving you help her?
- What do you want her to know to help bring peace to her heart? (If you aren't sure, you can ask.)

**Desire for the future**
- What would you like from your partner moving forward?
  - o Forgiveness?
  - o Another chance?
  - o To regain her trust?
  - o Her willingness to work on your relationship?

Taking time to write out your apology or jot down bullet points that are important for you to refer to if things become emotional, can help you stay on track. Coming prepared, even with a piece of paper in with your notes, demonstrates your sincerity and commitment.

In the *Neurobiology of Change* chapter, you learned about the powerful energetic connection that exists between people who are close to one another. Your thoughts and feelings towards them can either enhance or diminish your connection. Let's apply this idea to your apology preparation.

**Try this:** Close your eyes. Place your hands on your heart. Picture the face of the woman you love and in your own words tell her how sorry you are. (The more you are able to tap into your feelings the stronger the impact.)

Another tool to help with your internal preparation is to recite the words from an ancient Hawaiian prayer known as Ho'oponopono[24]: *"I'm sorry. Please forgive me. I love you. Thank you."* You may find it helpful to repeat this prayer slowly several times, allowing the words to resonate deeply within you. By doing so, you can prepare yourself for the upcoming apology conversation with her.

## INVITE

Invite her to engage in a conversation by letting her know that you have something important to discuss. Set a time and place that works best for both of you. Make sure this is a time and place with minimal possibilities for interruption, that is quiet and away from distractions.

## ENGAGE

**Identify and calm your inner and outer state.** Before connecting with your partner, assess where you are emotionally and physically. Put away all potential distractions. As a reminder, do not engage when either of you is upset or not in a calm state of mind. To do so runs the risk of triggering a negative interaction. Reschedule if the timing is off.

Remember the importance of a "soft startup." Here are a couple of ideas for ways to calm yourself before beginning:

- **Deep Breathing.** Center yourself by taking at least three long, slow, deep breaths. Picture yourself breathing in through your heart as a heartfelt apology comes from your heart, not your head. Deep breathing helps lessen anxiety.
- **Stretching.** Reach your arms above your head and clasp your hands. With your right hand, pull your left hand up just a little higher. Stretch. Then reverse the process.

**Check in.** Sit down, facing her. Verify that this is a good time for her. Ask if she is willing to listen until you have finished what you have to share. You can let her know that this could be emotional for you both so you would like her to hear you out so that you can stay on track with what you want to share. (You could provide pen and paper for her to jot down notes to minimize interruptions.)

If she begins to cry it is important to give her space to express her emotions and be compassionate and understanding. It may be helpful to have tissues nearby in case they are needed. You can ask her if she would like a hug. If she says "No," don't take it personally.

To enhance the engaged apology above, you can add something like:

*"As I look at you now, I can see the pain in your eyes, and it hurts me to know that my actions caused you such suffering. I am genuinely sorry for all the ways I have betrayed your trust—for the deceit, for not trusting in us enough to come to you before engaging with someone else. I wish there was something I could do to erase your pain. I know that healing will take time. I want you to know that I love you with all my heart. I know I eff'd up big time. I want you to know that I am committed to doing whatever it takes to rebuild the trust between us if you will let me."*

The above offers a few ideas. It is important for you to apologize in your own voice, using your own words.

## COLLABORATE

Ask if there is anything she needs from you.

Example: *"I want you to know how important you are to me, and I want to make sure that I have communicated how truly sorry I am. Is there anything else I can do at this moment to better communicate that?"*

You can ask if she is willing to accept your apology. Even if she is not ready yet, you can ask if she can envision a point in time when she may be more ready to do so and if there is anything else she needs from you to move in that direction. (Make this a light inquiry. Do not pressure her. If she is not ready, that's okay. Accepting an apology and forgiveness is a process that can take time.)

## RECEIVING AN APOLOGY – FOR THE LISTENER

Effective apologizing is a collaborative process sparked by a desire for reconciliation and a willingness to forge a new way forward. If you are the receiver, your role is engaged listening which means that you focus on what the apologizer is saying, without interruption until the apology is complete.

Once the apologizer is finished you can offer a *thank you* to acknowledge the effort and (hopefully) authenticity of what was said.

It is also important for you to pause for a moment and see if there is anything specific you wanted to hear in the apology that wasn't included. If there is something lingering it is important to acknowledge it so that it doesn't come back to haunt you later.

Here's an example: *"I appreciate your apology. I hear how sincere you are. There is something I didn't hear which is really important to me. I want to know that you are sorry for that time you got so angry with me when I asked you if you were having an affair back in March. You made me feel like I was crazy for even thinking that."*

Then the apologizer adds to the apology, saying something like, *"I am so sorry about that. I know I overreacted and lied because I just didn't want you to know. I'm sorry for how that made you feel and that I didn't come clean right then and there. I'm sorry that you had to doubt yourself."*

If that feels complete you can offer another thank-you. If you need a little more time and aren't quite there yet, you can let them know that as well.

**Note for the person being apologized to:** Acceptance of an apology doesn't mean that you are saying you are completely over what happened. It means that you are willing to honor the sincerity of the request and believe that the apologizer is genuinely remorseful for what happened. It is important for you to consider the authenticity of the person who is apologizing.

---

**An apology, like any other courageous conversation, is a dialogue not a monologue. And like forgiveness, without being both given and received, it is incomplete.**

---

## EXPRESS APPRECIATION

**Apology Giver:** Let her know that you appreciate her willingness to be present while you apologize and anything else that you are grateful for. You can also reiterate that you love her while reassuring her you intend to do everything in your power to make things right between the two of you.

**Apology Receiver:** Let the one apologizing know what stood out for you in their apology. For example: *"I appreciate your sincerity. It really felt like this came from your heart."*

## SET TIME TO FOLLOW-UP

If this feels incomplete (for example, if she says, *"I just can't feel it. I am not ready to accept your apology"*), you need to let that be okay. You cannot force things. Accept where she is and let her know you would like to follow up in the future. Apologies can take time to sink in.

If the emotional state transitions from sadness to anger or hostility, it is best to pause the conversation, regroup, and consider rescheduling if either of you is unable to re-regulate your angry emotions. It is important to recognize that her response can be unpredictable based on various factors such as how she is feeling at the time of engagement, her background, as well as her typical response to distress. It is essential to remain focused on your intended message while also being responsive to her emotional state. Again, having notes can help you stay true to the heart of your message.

For a live example of a collaborative heartfelt apology, you can refer to Justin's apology to Sophia in Chapter 13, *Making, Breaking and Keeping Promises*.

# Making Amends: Family and Friends

As we've discussed, the aftermath of an affair has a much farther reach than you probably ever imagined. It touches the lives of those close to you: families, friends, and potentially even your community.

It is essential that your amends-making extends to the core people in your life who have been impacted. This includes her family, your family, and the people who have looked up to the two of you as a couple (who know about the affair.)

While the thought of extending your amends-making to these people may feel like a daunting endeavor, it is an important step in your healing journey.

Remember, this is a vulnerable time for all concerned. Your spouse is working to regain her sense of self and determine whether she can truly forgive and rebuild her trust in you. The reactions of family and friends can significantly influence her recovery. Your spouse may hear things like, *"If my husband ever cheated on me, I'd be gone."* It is important to remember that the reactions of others stem from their own judgments, beliefs and past relational experiences. The truth is, people who have never experienced personal infidelity enacted by someone they love, have no clue how they would truly manage the situation.

Your amends-making needs to demonstrate your humility, remorse, and fervent commitment to never again so deeply hurt the person they love. Don't underestimate the value of their support. The conversations your spouse has behind the scenes can significantly enhance or thwart her recovery and your ability to move forward as a couple.

When making amends with her family you need to be prepared to face their disappointment, anger, and conflict resolution style. (See chapter 24 to review how to work with differing styles.) Some people demonstrate upset through angry outbursts, others through withdrawn silence. You can anticipate their responses based on prior interactions but be prepared for the possibility that conversations may take a different turn, particularly if they hold a deep conviction about fidelity.

While you don't need to offer a detailed explanation of what happened, you do need to take responsibility for making choices that were out of alignment with who you are as a man, and who you want to be—know you can be—as a partner. As these important people feel your remorse, regret and determination to make things better, their anger and judgment can begin to lift which helps both you and your partner garner greater support for your relational healing.

Yes, these conversations can be difficult, especially if you are someone who leans toward conflict avoidance. The hope is that you will be able to demonstrate, through your words and actions, your commitment to helping your spouse heal her heart and rebuild trust. The two of you are creating a new relational story, which ideally includes recovering from heartbreak and learning how to create a thriving relationship in the face of some very difficult challenges.

Next, we move on to forgiveness.

## Reflection
### *Engaging with Her Family*

Making amends with her family is a process that unfolds over time. Your initial meeting serves to "break the ice," where you demonstrate your remorse, acknowledge the pain your actions caused your partner and her family, and initiate the process of rebuilding trust.

It is important for you and your partner to discuss and agree upon the optimal way to engage with her family prior to engagement. You may want to review the PIECES method in Chapter 24 to prepare for this conversation. Make sure your delivery is calm and respectful. If things become heated, remember to pause, take a breath, and decide if it is best to come back to the conversation at a later date.

Prepare by considering:
- Timing and setting for the conversation.
- Your prior relationship dynamics with her family.
- Their beliefs and values regarding fidelity and relationships.
- Your key messages of remorse, commitment, and recommitment.

Decide together whether your spouse's presence would aid or hinder the conversation's healing intent. As you progress through recovery, your loved ones are able to witness firsthand the transformative power of love, dedication and commitment. They learn alongside you that healing and growth are possible, fostering stronger faith and support in your relationship, and possibly within themselves and their relationships as well.

# 26

## Forgiveness

---■---

*"It is not an easy journey to get to the place where you forgive people. But it is such a powerful place because it frees you."*
—Tyler Perry, entertainer, and philanthropist

When extending an apology, you are aiming to ease some of the pain your actions have caused, express genuine remorse, and set the stage for being forgiven. By acknowledging the impact of your behavior, expressing sincere regret, and taking responsibility, you are laying the foundation for forgiveness and potential reconciliation.

Sincere forgiveness can help release the emotional entanglement caused by past actions and calm the static between individuals. When you don't forgive, you maintain a dissonant connection with the one who has brought you harm. Even if the lack of forgiveness remains unspoken, it exists in the relational energy between two people. That being said, sometimes an offense feels too egregious to forgive, such as extreme childhood trauma or abuse. Other times a person needs more time to move into forgiveness. True forgiveness can't be coerced or pressured.

So, why do people withhold forgiveness? Forgiveness is sometimes withheld to maintain some sense of personal power over a situation in which the offended party has felt powerless. Sometimes people don't extend forgiveness out of fear that doing so lets the other person *off the hook*, in that it serves as an indication that everything is now okay, or that what happened didn't matter. In truth forgiving someone doesn't mean what happened doesn't count or matter.

What forgiveness is and isn't:

**Forgiveness is:**
A powerful decision that helps clear the toxic energy between two people.

A gift that is given to the one forgiving and the one being forgiven.

**Forgiveness is not:**
Something that should be agreed to on a whim because you feel sorry for someone else, or because someone continues to beg for it.

Something you hold over someone's head or use as a tool of manipulation to keep someone frantically doing or buying things in hopes of being forgiven.

---

**True forgiveness shifts the discordant energy between two people, even when it is done without the other person present.**

---

## Forgiveness Occurs in Layers

**"The words 'I'm Sorry' are a formal declaration of intent. Changed behavior is the actual apology."**

—Kalen Dion, author, poet, artist

Forgiveness is a multi-layered process that occurs over time. It's not a one-time occurrence. Saying the words *I forgive you* doesn't magically make things better.

**Forgiving is an active, not passive, state.** The person extending forgiveness must trust themselves first in order to begin extending trust to the one who has offended. Then they must set ground rules for how they want to be treated in the future. It can take courage to forgive something that caused you great pain.

Forgiveness is a process on a continuum that ranges from:

**Light Forgiveness** – *I am willing to forgive you enough that we can be civil with one another, but not fully engaged. I still feel hurt, and probably don't trust you at this moment. Or, I might trust you in some areas but not others.*

**Growing Forgiveness** – *I am willing to forgive you enough that we can begin to interact more. (This can be a time to engage in some light activities together.) I am beginning to trust you more, as I am seeing you take actions that align with the commitments you are making and more consistently following through on.*

**Rooted Forgiveness** – *I am feeling more comfortable and trusting that when you give me your word, you mean it. Thoughts of the past are haunting me less and less. I can see a light at the end of the tunnel. I am more confident that we are making our way through this.*

**Forgiveness as Acceptance** – *I am willing to accept that a mistake was made. I am willing to put things behind us instead of between us. I am willing to accept the sincerity of your apology(ies) and desire to make amends. I am committed to doing my best to keep the past in the past.*

**Deep (Collaborative) Forgiveness** – *I am willing to forgive you and not hold what has happened in the past over your head when differences arise. I am willing to give you the benefit of the doubt and trust in the sincerity of your desire to do things differently, show up more authentically, and talk things out instead of acting them out. And I commit to doing the same for you. I deeply forgive you.*

As with all courageous conversations, deep forgiveness is a collaborative process, requiring the engagement of both parties. It is sparked by a desire for deepening connection, a willingness to move through the past, and a commitment to forge a new path forward. This is the deepest level of engagement which occurs over time as a couple works through the challenges which led to the behavior in question.

# Self-Forgiveness

An important but less frequently discussed aspect of forgiveness is self-forgiveness. Quite often we can become stuck in a cycle of self-blame for the idea that we caused or allowed ourselves to become involved in a painful situation.

In the case of infidelity, self-forgiveness is an important process for all involved. If you are the partner of someone who had an affair, you may be saying to yourself, *But I wasn't the one who had the affair.* True. And, I have found that a betrayed person can become plagued with self-doubt in the aftermath of a partner's affair.

**Self-Forgiveness** involves taking responsibility for yourself, embracing your humanity, and setting a strong future resolve to be present, committed to truth-telling, and breaking the cycle of avoidance (where appliable.) Both of you will have things to forgive yourselves for doing or not doing.

**If you are the one who has been offended,** you might be blaming yourself for not listening to your intuition or for trusting someone's words instead of their behavior. You may regret not having the courage to engage in a discussion, ask questions, talk about difficult things, or walk away from a toxic situation soon enough. Or you may blame yourself doing something to contribute to marital conflict.

**If you are the offending party,** extending forgiveness to yourself involves a willingness to quit beating yourself up over what happened. The shame of betrayal runs deep. I have heard from many men that they don't feel they can forgive themselves until they are forgiven by their partner. Seeing someone you love experiencing pain that your actions have caused is not easy. Yet it is important to accept that you are human, and human beings are imperfect.

Your ability to forgive yourselves increases over time as your commitment grows stronger. By practicing self-compassion and understanding, you can begin to rebuild your self-respect and regain a sense of dignity.

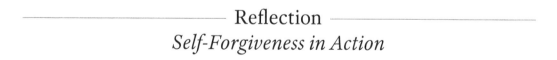

## Reflection
### *Self-Forgiveness in Action*

Here is a simple but powerful exercise that walks you through the self-forgiveness process. It includes things you can say to yourself as examples. Feel free to expand on these or create your own.

### STEP ONE
- Place one hand on your heart.
- Close your eyes and say the following, out loud or to yourself:

○ *I forgive myself for judging myself as (wrong, not good enough, or not worthy).*

○ *I forgive myself for (not expressing myself, not setting better boundaries, or not focusing on what I wanted/needed.)*

○ *I forgive myself for (not expressing my needs, believing that other people's needs took precedence over my own, not taking better care of myself, believing I was less than, believing I didn't deserve (love/respect/happiness/ kindness).*

## STEP TWO

Next, move into owning your truth. (Following are some examples. Go with your heart and speak what is positive and true about you.) With your hand still over your heart state what your wisest self knows to be true:

*The truth is I am a smart/wise person. I am fully capable of taking care of myself. Moving forward, I am willing to set self-supportive boundaries and honor my commitments.*

*The truth is I am a good person who is capable of making wise decisions that honor myself and my spouse.*

*The truth is what happened doesn't define me or diminish who I am.*

*I am releasing any fears I have into the care of (the Divine/God/My Higher Self/the Holy Spirit), trusting that I will be guided to make the wisest choices for all concerned moving forward.*

Now take three deep breaths, drop your hands to the ground, and shake them— releasing any tension into the earth. Rituals are powerful. Use/embellish this one or create your own. Like any activity you engage in, the more authentic your approach, the more effective the results.

Repeat the self-forgiveness exercise any time you need a little extra inner grace.

Next we review the trust rebuilding process.

# 27

# Rebuilding Trust

---

*"Trust is choosing to make something important to you vulnerable to the actions of someone else."*
—Charles Feltman, *The Thin Book of Trust*

Closely tied to forgiveness is trust which is critically important to continue rebuilding. When trust is high, forgiveness for small infractions occurs much more easily.

Trust is like a bank account which either builds or diminishes with the actions taken, and the assumptions made about those actions by a partner. Trust builds when you stay true to your word, treat people with respect, and set clear boundaries. Setting boundaries builds trust because it clarifies where you stand on issues. Boundary-setting also helps build self-trust. When you trust yourself, you feel more confident in your decisions and are more likely to speak up when something feels "off."

A critical, less spoken about aspect of trust is self-trust. Self-trust provides a baseline. When you trust yourself to make the *right* choices, even when faced with difficult situations, your ability to trust others increases.

Trust diminishes when you make promises you don't keep, talk down to or judge others, criticize, use harsh words, or don't set clear boundaries. Challenges with trust are often rooted in past situations that get triggered by current events.

## Trust builds over time and can be lost in an instant.

---
## Reflection
### *Trust Building*
---

The next exercises can be helpful for the two of you to work through individually and then set up a time to discuss together. If you are doing this work on your own, diving into these questions can provide insight that you can share with your partner if you choose.

- Where have I been unclear with my boundaries?
- Where do I tend to let things slide instead of speaking up (kindly and directly)?
- Where do I find myself becoming the most critical?
- Can my friends and family count on me to do what I say I'm going to do?
- Do I discuss what bothers me, or drop hints I expect others to pick up on?
- Do I become passive-aggressive when a partner doesn't get the hint or behave as I feel they should?

### PERSONAL AND PARTNER TRUST ASSESSMENT

If you are working on this together, I invite each of you to reflect upon your level of trust in your partner and yourself. Rate these questions based on your interactions **before** the affair. Use a 0 to 5 scale, with 0 being not at all, and 5 indicating that the behavior is something you have observed or feel consistently able to count on.

1) First rate yourself (adjusting the language as appropriate). 2) Rate how you see your partner. 3) Rate how you believe your partner sees you. If working on this together, complete the exercise first, and then use it to engage in a discussion.

☐ When my partner makes a commitment, they stick to it.

☐ I can count on my partner to do what they say they will do.

☐ I can talk to my partner about things that bother me without fear of reprisal (i.e., expressions of anger, frustration, or bringing it up in a critical way at a later date.)

☐ My partner treats others with respect.

☐ My partner talks respectfully to me. I feel respected by my partner.

☐ My partner is good at setting boundaries. I know where they stand on things. They will give me an honest "no" as opposed to saying "yes" and not following through.

☐ My partner affirms the things they appreciate about me. They notice and say thank you when I go out of my way for them or others.

☐ My partner encourages my growth; they support me in learning new things.

☐ My partner takes an interest in what's important to me. They express curiosity about my (work/day/endeavors/etc.).

I suggest you retain your original answers and revisit these questions on a monthly or quarterly basis to help monitor your progression. Measuring progress helps both parties recognize forward movement and areas which may need a little more work. Staying focused on the things that matter helps strengthen the level of trust in your partner, your relationship, and yourself.

**Self-Trust:** Self-trust is built by sticking to the commitments you make to yourself, authentically communicating what you want to your partner, and setting self-supportive boundaries. Taking care of your own needs in healthy ways helps strengthen your relationship.

**Relational Trust:** Relational trust is strengthened by focusing on the needs of your partner, taking the initiative to set up and engage in experiences together, appreciating each other's efforts, and setting and honoring boundaries.

Your couples work will involve cultivating new ways of connecting and re-engaging in things you did when you felt connected in the past. It's important to make space for each other's needs and place a high priority on your relational connection.

**The truth is this:** If you both want to reclaim your marriage and are willing to do the work, you will find your way through. It takes courage and commitment to move through your emotions, rebuild trust, forgive, and safeguard the future of your relationship. With grit, determination, compassion, and effort, you can find your way through and create an even stronger connection. I've seen it happen. Many times.

# 28

## When It May *be* Time *to* Leave

———————————— ■ ————————————

*"Some of us think holding on makes us strong,*
*but sometimes it is letting go."*
—Daman Zahariades, *The Art of Letting Go*

Sometimes an affair is a symptom of greater discontent that cannot be repaired. It is possible that even if you put a decent amount of work into attempting to recover your marriage, it will become clear to one or both of you that you no longer work well as marital partners. While dissolving a marriage is never easy, there is some relief in climbing out of indecision. Once a choice has been made, you are both free to move on and rebuild your lives.

Marriages can be dissolved in ways that minimize scarring. Working with an expert mediator and coach/counselor can greatly assist you in handling logistics as well as the psychological and emotional aspects of separating from someone you had pledged to spend your life with. If you have kids together, it is important to make sure they don't end up as collateral damage. It is critical to affirm to your children, repeatedly, that both parents love them, and that the separation is in no way based upon anything they did or did not do. Look for ways to reinforce this as opportunities arise and as questions come up from them.

Often a child's distress does not show up directly in questions they ask, but rather in their behavior. Pay attention to changes in your children's actions and moods as they may be warning signs that they need a little extra love and understanding. Let them know that you are available whenever they have questions or just want to talk. When it feels appropriate, you may also want to talk to your child's teacher and let them know that you are working through a separation or divorce. Invite them to reach out if they notice any changes in behavior. Alerting teachers can help them offer a little extra grace to your children. Make sure in so doing you don't say derogatory things about your spouse.

When addressing your children's questions, it's important to handle the situation with care. You can explain to them that some issues are meant for adults to work through with the help of professionals who specialize in providing guidance. This demonstrates to your children that seeking help is normal and there's no shame in it. Avoid using your children as sounding boards or involving them in obtaining information about your spouse.

Working with a counselor who focuses on children and teens can be beneficial, as well as seeking guidance from your own therapist on how to approach these sensitive topics. It's crucial to create a unified approach with your co-parent on what information will be shared with your children and how it will be communicated. Prioritize your children's well-being, even if it means setting aside challenging emotions to co-parent effectively. For more detailed guidance on discussing the affair with your children, you can refer to the end of Chapter 19.

While it isn't within the scope of this work to detail how to best recreate your life after divorce, here are some suggestions to keep in mind as you move forward.

## If You are the One Choosing to Leave

Know that your affair adds fuel to the fire of separation/divorce. Take care not to make the affair the focal point of your leaving (unless it truly was). Sometimes people fall in love with other people and want to create a life with them. If that is the case for you, I caution you to proceed as gently as possible, as being left for another person can intensify the pain.

Keep in mind that your partner may place a lot of blame on the AP for your choice to dissolve the marriage. This is particularly true if your spouse is totally blindsided by your wanting to leave. As we have discussed previously, be careful of your inclination to defend the AP, as doing so can make matters worse. Tread as lightly as possible here.

**If you are having trouble envisioning the trajectory of your life in either direction, it is best to take some time apart before jumping into a more permanent solution.** Often an affair runs its course. If you jump into a permanent solution prematurely, you run the risk of losing a marriage that may just need a little breathing room to regroup. While *temporary* separation in the face of an affair isn't easy, it may be the best option for you both. This is a time when you need to be honest with yourself. Don't jump either way if you are truly on the fence.

**If you are contemplating leaving your marriage for your affair partner**, it's important to proceed with caution and give yourself ample time to consider all aspects before making any major decisions, such as moving in together. Going through a divorce while starting a new relationship can be particularly challenging and painful.

Taking time to process the end of your marriage and experiencing life outside the shadow of your affair can be beneficial for your emotional healing and clarity. It allows you to better understand what you truly want and need in a long-term, committed relationship.

Remember, every situation is unique, and the final choice lies with you and your chosen partner. Take the time to explore different perspectives and seek support as you navigate this complex period of reflection.

## When Your Spouse Chooses to Leave

As your spouse moves into her own personal discovery, she may be the one who decides to call it quits. Once again, I suggest taking some time apart before diving into something permanent. Maybe she needs time away to clear her head, get to know herself a bit more, and decide whether she is willing to re-engage and work on the marriage. Time apart doesn't mean you are finished; it can put some much-needed space between you to determine your best course moving forward. While you can let her know how sorry you are, you cannot force her to stay if she truly wants to leave.

# When Leaving Is a Mutual Decision

Sometimes it becomes clear to you both that it is in the best interest of all concerned to part ways. Maybe sparks can't be reignited. Perhaps you have grown in different directions. If this is the case, it is possible to create an amicable path forward. This is especially important when kids are involved. Even adult children are impacted when parents decide to split. As we have discussed, the circle of people impacted by an affair is far wider than you would think. The same is true when a couple decides to move in different directions.

Regardless of who wants to call it quits, challenging emotions will surface for you both. Working with a professional can help you more amicably sort through and make more definitive choices on what's next.

In this segment, we have reviewed ways to uplevel your communication with your partner, including how to work through difficult situations, create authentic apologies, and engage in forgiveness. We have also discussed some self-examination techniques and ways to rebuild trust. Next, we dive into the power of choice and commitment.

# PART TEN

---
■
---

# Designing *your* Future:
## *Elevate your Standards. Align with your Purpose. Choose Mindfully*

*"Excellence is never an accident. It is always the result of high intention, sincere effort, and intelligent execution; it represents the wise choice of many alternatives—choice, not chance, determines your destiny."*

—Aristotle

Excellence doesn't mean being perfect. It does mean holding yourself to a higher standard by discerning well and aligning your actions with your vision and values. Making mindful choices means that you consider your commitments and the potential consequences of your actions *before* taking them.

You are being called to embrace a life and relationship that demands more from you—more presence, authenticity, mindfulness, and heart. Your mission, should you choose to accept it, is to strive for excellence in all areas of your life. Envision yourself as the man you aspire to be and take actions that reflect that vision. Be a person of honor, trustworthiness, and respect, who keeps commitments and helps others heal. This is how you cultivate trust, self-respect, and confidence while making a positive impact on those around you.

## You are shaping your future with the choices you make today.

Throughout this book you have been given a significant opportunity to redefine yourself individually and in partnership. By engaging with the material, you have likely gained deeper insights into relationship dynamics, addressed personal challenges, and developed strategies to protect your integrity. It is my hope that you now have a better grasp on maintaining fidelity, rebuilding trust, and establishing clear boundaries to safeguard your relationship from future misunderstandings.

During this final segment, we will be taking one last look at trust and then review key principles and commitments designed to help you maintain your momentum and fortify your relationship moving forward.

**There is something incredibly moving about a couple who, after a fall, steps out together hand-in-hand, determined to walk through the fire to recreate their lives together.** This is a powerful demonstration of love that can also serve as a role model for others.

# 29

## The Power *of* Commitment, Courage, *and* Trust

∎

*"Have enough courage to trust love one more time."*
—Maya Angelou, *I Know Why the Caged Bird Sings*

*The courage to trust love one more time*—this is what we have been exploring throughout our work together. It takes great courage to rebuild trust after disappointment and choose love over fear. This doesn't just apply to the one who has been betrayed; it applies to the one who has betrayed as well.

You are building the courage to trust yourselves—to trust that you will be mindful of your word and honor your commitments. Should a challenge arise that potentially compromises your commitment, you can apply that courage to trusting yourself to bring it to the table before acting on it. **Commitment and trust go hand-in-hand.**

You are also building trust as a couple—which starts by being truthful, listening open-heartedly, and saying what you mean with clarity and kindness. You are building trust that each of you will:

- Refrain from criticism and passive-aggressive ways of dealing with annoyances.
- Give each other the benefit of the doubt and embrace the belief that your partner is not intentionally undermining you.

- o This means trusting that your partner has your back and will love and care for you even when you make mistakes.
- Come back to unresolved discussions in the face of disagreements, taking a little breathing room as needed.
- Handle situations with integrity, honesty, and respect.
- Not use the past as a weapon to hurt or belittle your partner during an argument.
- Not abandon your partner when things get tough.

As we have discussed, building trust requires being mindful of your commitments, and setting supportive boundaries with kindness and grace. While a *no* can be tough to hear and deliver, trust is reinforced when the receiving party accepts it without trying to guilt or manipulate the situation to elicit a *yes*. This fosters greater honesty and safety within the relationship—which strengthens intimacy and trust.

---

## Reflection
### *The Motivation Assessment – Round Two*

Remember the **Motivation Assessment** you took at the beginning of your journey in Chapter 2? This is a great time to go back and retake that assessment, adjusting the language as needed, comparing where you were then versus now. If you don't have access to your original results, you can think back to where you were at the beginning and compare it to where you are now.

Here are a few questions to help with your review:

- What has changed in your beliefs about your relationship and your approach?
- What has stayed the same?
- How are you feeling now about your ability to rebuild and reconnect with your partner?
- What areas still need a little fine-tuning?
- What areas do you need to continue to keep in top-of-mind awareness?
- What are some key learnings you have taken away from this process?
  - o About yourself?
  - o About your partner?

Hopefully you can see the growth and expansion you have gained in working through this material. The final chapter offers some key takeaways and ideas to help reinforce what you have been building as you move into the future.

**"Love is a two-way street constantly under construction."**

—Carroll Bryant, author

# 30

# The Keys *to the* Castle:
## *Making and Honoring Commitments*

---

*"What many couples think is the hallmark of a bad relationship is actually the potential hallmark of a good one. ... If anything should be regarded as aberrant, it's the expectation that a good marriage is a serene one. ... healthy relationships are anything but smooth."*

—David Schnarch, PhD, *Passionate Couples: Sex, Love, and Intimacy in Emotionally Committed Relationships.*

---

**Rebuilding your marriage requires a strong commitment, a willingness to do things differently in service to the relationship, and the wherewithal to keep your expectations in check.**

---

We often make assumptions about what a good marriage entails. It's not uncommon for me to hear people say, *"A great relationship shouldn't be difficult."* The truth is that growth doesn't come from hanging out in your comfort zone or avoiding challenges.

Think of nurturing your relationship like building muscle. You grow stronger through effort, self-discipline and sweat. Like physical growth, effort channeled into relational growth increases mental stamina, clarity, resilience, and confidence which carries over into many other areas of your life.

Your number one job right now is to fortify the trust and understanding you are rebuilding within your relationship and yourself. Each time you move toward your partner with kindness and interest, you are rebuilding trust. Each time you avoid or move away from your partner without a commitment to return, you are creating distance which erodes trust.

Each time you make choices that align with your core values and commitments, your self-trust builds. Each time you engage in behavior that is out of alignment with what you value and have committed to, your self-trust weakens. Your ability to stay true to your values in the face of challenges is strengthened with each decision you make that supports your internal and external commitments.

In this final chapter, we review key takeaways from the book and highlight commitments that reinforce the foundation of trust and connection you are working to rebuild. These commitments are designed as affirmative statements to reinforce key learnings.

**"By daring to consistently challenge your comfort zone, you'll discover that you're becoming a person whose fear has been gradually replaced by Courage, Trust, and a positive sense of awe and wonder."**

—Mary R. Hlunick, Ph.D., H. Ronald Hulnick, Ph.D., *Remembering the Light Within, A Course in Soul-Centered Living*

# KEY #1: *Tell the Truth*

Telling lies can seem easier at times than sharing your true thoughts and feelings with kindness. However, deception leads to disconnection, even if the other person never finds out. Truth-telling is an important muscle to build. This begins with being honest with yourself. Pay attention to the situations in which you feel tempted to lie. Then pause and examine what is behind the lie or the thought of telling a half-truth. (Chapters 14 and 15 offer a deeper dive into deception and truth-telling.)

It's particularly critical not to lie about your affair. Honesty, even when it's uncomfortable, builds trust. It's okay to say, *"I don't feel comfortable talking about that."* Or,

*"I'm not ready to talk about _____."* Don't make something up to avoid the discomfort of addressing it.

**Commitment #1:** *I commit to telling the truth to my partner with kindness, clarity, and compassion, even when it may be uncomfortable to do so.*

**If you are the one who betrayed,** remember, she will be looking for evidence that she can trust you again. When you lie, even about something unrelated, you fail the trust test and take two giant steps backward on the recovery board.

**For example:** If you promise your spouse that you will let her know if the AP calls or texts you, then let her know. I have seen many people slide backward on this one. This can be tricky, because at this point, you would rather do almost anything not to trigger her disappointment and anger. Trust me on this one: is better tell her than to risk the possibility of her finding out on her own.

**If you are the one who has been betrayed**, pay attention to the areas you may be fearful of discussing or in which you are tempted to tell lies or half-truths to avoid conflict. Each person's commitment to truth-telling sets the tone for the relationship you are working to create.

# KEY #2: *Be Patient*

Learning new ways of relating takes time. You *will* both make mistakes. Mistake making is part of learning. If you are not making mistakes, you are probably not venturing very far outside of your comfort zone. Trying something new will feel uncomfortable at times. Be patient with yourself and your partner as you reinforce new behaviors, and ways of thinking and relating to one another. Take healthy risks. Patience is a key priority in your ongoing journey of learning and personal development.

**Commitment #2:** *I commit to practicing patience with myself and my partner as we embark on learning new things. I understand that making mistakes is a natural part of learning, and I will not be harsh with either of us for any missteps that occur.*

## KEY #3: *Pay Attention to Things You Tend to Automatically Say Yes To out of Obligation or Fear of Reprisal*

Relational healing can be a little complex at times. You want to create connection, and sometimes this means putting another's needs first. There is a difference, however, between engaging in an activity that you know your partner would enjoy, even if it's not your favorite, and agreeing to something that truly makes you uncomfortable to avoid potential upset.

**Commitment #3:** *I commit to setting clear, supportive boundaries and gaining the clarity I need to offer a solid yes or a clear no to requests made.*

When you allow someone to pressure you into doing something you are not comfortable with, it can lead to resentment. Resentments build over time and can trigger anxiety and the need to emotionally distance. As we have discussed, you must be able to say *"yes"* or *"no"* without fear of reprisal.

**Try This:** When you're unsure whether or not you will be able to fulfill a request, press the "pause" button. Let your partner know that you need some time to consider their request before responding. Pausing can be challenging for people who want answers now, however, giving a half-hearted *yes* to avoid a partner's potential reaction isn't healthy. You are better off experiencing a little upset by saying *no* now than a volcanic-sized eruption later by making an unfulfillable promise. Saying yes when you *really* want to say no also erodes your self-esteem and builds resentment, which can lead to a loss of intimacy and desire.

## Key #4: *Don't Push Past Your Partner's* No

Hearing *no* can feel like rejection. Give your partner the freedom to honor a request or graciously decline it. When you want something from them, don't coerce or force a yes. Giving your partner a little extra space to decide, when needed, builds connection, trust, and freedom.

**Commitment #4:** *When I make a request, I commit to giving my partner room to decide and not pressure them into a yes or push for a quick answer.*

Sometimes you may not be sure what your partner wants. When you are unclear, or they seem hesitant to offer a solid *yes* or *no*, you can ask a few clarifying questions. I caution you to be mindful of your approach. Don't make this an interrogation.

**Try This:** Here are a few supportive questions that can help you both gain greater clarity:

- *"You seem hesitant. Is there something that I can do or say to help you decide?"*
- *"Would it be helpful to discuss this a little further?"*
- *"Can we talk about this to see if we can come up with something that works for both of us?"*
- *"Do you need a little more time to think things through?"*
- *"Can we talk about this a little more? It is something really important to me, and I want to honor what works best for us both."*
- *"I'm okay with whatever you decide. No pressure."*

## KEY #5: *Pay Attention to Your Judgments, Especially Regarding Your Spouse*

Judgments can infiltrate our thoughts before we even realize they're there. As we discussed in Chapter 20, *The Neurobiology of Change*, your thoughts impact your connection with your partner. Pay attention to the critical voices in your head; recurring critical thoughts are an indication that something is not being addressed. By actively monitoring your thought system, you help prevent unsupportive thinking from becoming all-consuming and adversely affecting your relationship.

**Commitment #5:** *I commit to proactively addressing and working to transform negative thought patterns as they arise. I commit to paying attention to times when I am triggered by circumstances or negative thoughts and taking steps to address them, whether through internal reflection or open communication with my partner.*

Pay attention to your inner dialogue when your spouse responds in ways you don't expect. If you find thoughts running around in your head that you cannot seem to squelch, consider how they need to be addressed.

- Do you need to work through your thoughts on your own? To share your concerns with your spouse?
- Is there something you must resolve that is clouding your ability to listen?
- Are you willing to see your spouse as someone who has your best interests at heart, even when they *miss the mark*?

**Try This:** When intrusive thoughts arise even after you have worked toward resolution, shift your thinking. 1) Make sure there isn't something you haven't addressed that needs addressing. 2) Say to yourself, *STOP. This is not helpful or how I want to see things.* 3) Flip the thought by focusing on something more affirming/positive about the person/situation.

**Question to consider:** Am I building a bridge or erecting a wall by this (thought, action, response)?

# KEY #6: *Make Time for Self-Care*

Sometimes it can be easy to become so involved with the needs of other people and career pursuits that you can find yourself neglecting your own needs for learning, growth, and fun!

I have seen both men and women lose themselves into work, child rearing, and tending to other people's needs. When raising a family, quite often you must put others' needs above your own. But you also need to set aside quality time for yourself. Take care not to become so hyper-focused on obligations that you neglect you!

**Commitment #6:** *I commit to engaging in self-care and dedicating time to explore and participate in activities that spark my interest, and to support and encourage my partner to do the same.*

**Try this:** Creating time for you.

- Take a walk, spend time in nature, get a massage, have a spa day, share a meal with a friend, journal, make art.
- Play golf, pickleball, or tennis, or go for a bike ride, or join a sports team.
- Pick up that guitar that's been gathering dust. Play piano.
- Learn a new language.
- Engage in something uplifting. Do something that engages your soul and has nothing to do with attending to another's needs.

**Feeding your soul calms your nervous system and revitalizes your spirit.** Taking care of yourself strengthens your self-trust—which generates greater self-confidence and self-esteem. When we feel good about who we are, we frequently experience more enjoyment connecting with those we love.

# KEY #7: *Commit to Couple and Family Time*

When individuals are involved in business development, a demanding job, and/or managing a busy home life, it is common for these responsibilities to encroach upon couple and family time. With the increasing number of people working from home, transitioning out of work mode can be challenging. Establishing a clear delineation between work and home life involves setting aside dedicated time to disconnect and transition your focus from work to personal matters.

**Try This:** If you work outside the home, take time on the drive home to think through the last few remnants of the day, and then shift your focus to what you are looking forward to at home. Come into the home focused on connecting with your family. If extra work must be done in the evening, set aside a designated time for it. Whenever possible, don't allow work to bleed into family time.

If you find yourself facing a hectic day, a pressing issue, or an important upcoming event that makes it challenging to switch off work mode, communicate this with your partner. Consider allocating a period of uninterrupted couple or family time before returning to work tasks. An hours' worth of quality time can work wonders to strengthening your bond and rebuilding connection.

**Commitment #7:** *I commit to setting aside uninterrupted to time to engage with my partner on a regular basis. I commit to turning toward instead of away from my partner as challenges arise.*

Be mindful of any recurring obstacles to spending quality time together. Quality time is when you are focused and present with the person sitting in front of you. We are all busy. Intentionally setting aside uninterrupted time to interact builds connection.

**Try This:**

- Carve out specific times during your week for topical discussions on things like finances, career-building, connecting, dates, and even sex can give couples something to look forward to. If you both agree to set times for specific activities, it will help you stay focused on each other and what's important. When you schedule it, you are committing to it. Uphold that commitment.

- Pay attention to the inclination to grab your phone instead of working through a challenge or connecting at home. Social media can become a great avoidance tool.

- Carve out time in advance for engaging family and relational activities. Take turns making plans and stick with them.

Raising children is a full-time job. We often have the erroneous belief that children enhance marital connection, when in fact the opposite tends to hold. Kids are a beautiful blessing. And they take time, energy, and dedication to raise them in healthy ways. Make sure you set up time for just the two of you, as well.

# KEY #8: *ABC – Always Be Curious*

Embracing curiosity awakens your senses and fosters a deeper connection with others. By approaching interactions with a curious mind, you create opportunities for personal growth and enhanced problem-solving. Instead of assuming motives, staying curious helps maintain connection and fluid exchanges between the two of you. Curiosity engenders connection and creates space for greater understanding.

Drawing inspiration from Buddhist philosophy, you can adopt the concept of the Beginner's Mind. This practice encourages setting aside preconceived notions and approaching situations with fresh eyes and an open heart. While simple in theory, implementing the Beginner's Mind concept requires conscious effort and active listening. By listening as if for the first-time, you can enhance learning, curiosity, and connection.

**Commitment #8:** *I commit to listening and responding to my partner's interests with a curious and open heart. I am willing to embrace a more curious mindset about life and the world around me.*

**Try This:** When your partner talks to you about a problem at work or something new they have discovered:

- Listen to learn rather than to respond.

- If you don't know or are unsure, don't assume. Ask.

- A great "go-to" is to say, *"Hmm. Can you tell me more about that?"* Or, *"That sounds interesting. I would love to hear more."*

- If you have some problem-solving ideas, ask if your partner would like to hear them, or if they just want you to act as a sounding board.

# KEY #9: *Engage in Growth-Oriented Activities as Individuals and as a Couple*

**Brains that fire together, wire together.** This means that engaging in something new, be that an activity or a class, seminar, or workshop strengthens your connection. Engagement can be a solo activity that you engage in then talk about, or something you do together. Adventure fire up different parts of the brain and stimulate relational neurons.

**Promise #9:** *I commit to setting aside time to discuss ways my partner and I can explore new and interesting activities, adventures, and ways to grow. I commit to supporting my partner's interests in personal growth and development.*

**Try this:** Both of you can explore activities that you find enjoyable together. Create a list and alternate planning exciting experiences. Stay open to trying out things that interest your partner. Stay curious and embrace new experiences to broaden your horizons. Interested in cooking? Consider enrolling in a couple's cooking class. Fancy dancing? Why not sign up for dance lessons together? Let your creative juices flow! Show support as your partner delves into personal growth and ventures into new territories of learning.

# KEY #10: *Cultivate an Attitude of Gratitude*

Gratitude grows gratitude. The more consistently you appreciate and acknowledge the contributions of others, the more you will find to be grateful for.

Appreciation is a gift you offer to those around you as well as yourself. What you notice and acknowledge grows, internally and externally. A business classic I read years ago during my time as a training manager left a lasting impression upon me— Ken Blanchard's *The One Minute Manager.* For me, the biggest takeaway from the book is *"catch someone doing something right."*

So often, things that are running smoothly fly under the radar. What we tend to notice and more frequently comment on are the things that aren't going so well. Blanchard invites a shift in attention to the things that are working well, how someone is giving a little extra—be this going the extra mile on a project or showing up with a positive attitude, and then acknowledging them for it.

Another large study of 200,000 done by Boston Consulting Group showed that of multiple factors, the one thing that employees consistently want more of—even more than attractive pay—is *appreciation*.[25] It's the same in a marriage. Appreciation doesn't cost anything to give, and there are plenty of opportunities to give it. Catch someone in your household doing something well and let them know that you noticed the effort. Offering appreciation creates connection, makes people feel good, and reinforces their positive behaviors and helps set a positive vibe in your home.

**Promise #10:** *I commit to cultivating an attitude of gratitude and acknowledging and appreciating the people and world around me.*

**Try This:**
**Family:** Create a gratitude jar. Invite family members to write down things that they appreciate about another family member or an experience they are grateful for. These can be small or large things. Set aside a time to read the gratitudes aloud together. Sundays tend to be a nice time for a family day and reflection on the positive aspects of the week.

**Couple Time:** I call this exercise *Three Things*. At the end of the day before heading off to sleep, each person states three things they are grateful for that occurred during that day. (Hint: at least one needs to be about your partner.) As this becomes a nightly ritual, you will begin noticing more things you are grateful for!

## KEY & Commitment #11: *Love and Accept Each Other*

**"Until we accept our partner as the one we have chosen to dance with—until we stop lashing out and running away—we won't really know what the dance of intimacy is all about."**

—Paul Ferrini, *Dancing with the Beloved, Opening our hearts to the lessons of love*

**Love the woman she is.** Take time to see the beauty in her. Appreciate the things she is doing to help recreate your relationship and let go of the past. Rekindle your love for her by recalling and sharing past moments standout moments of connection. Loving her is the greatest gift you can give her. Love her through it all. Think of her with love. Extend loving thoughts. Hold the space for her love to return.

**Love the man he is.** Appreciate the work he is doing to make things right with you. Look for things he is doing well and acknowledge them. Think back to the man you fell in love with. He's still in there. Be willing to extend forgiveness and grace when he doesn't do it exactly right. Acknowledge his efforts. Set clear boundaries. Think of him with love and hold the space for him to love you even more deeply.

---

**Loving is a choice that can work wonders to heal wounded hearts and nurture tender souls. Loving grows love.**

---

## KEY & Commitment #12: *Choose Love over Fear*

*I commit to choosing love over fear* and to making decisions that align with that choice. I commit to talking to you when challenges arise and working together to create collaborative solutions. I commit to continuing to do my own work to ensure that I stay true to these commitments. I commit to creating a safe space for us to continue to heal and grow as individuals and within our relationship. I commit to appreciating you, and to respecting, honoring, and cherishing you and the life we are building together.

**"May you realize that the shape of your soul is unique, that you have a special destiny here, that behind the façade of your life there is something beautiful and eternal happening [within yourselves and with each other.]"**

—*To Bless the Space Between Us,* John O'Donohue, author, philosopher, poet

# 31

# Loving Courageously:
## *The End. The Beginning.*

---

*"Being deeply loved by someone gives you strength,*
*while loving someone deeply gives you courage."*

—Lao Tzu, philosopher

**It takes great courage to love well.** Whether you have read this work cover to cover, skipped to the sections that caught your interest, or landed somewhere in between, I hope you have discovered valuable insights that will guide you towards a flourishing future.

It has been an honor to support you on your journey of healing and growth. I trust that you now have a deeper understanding of yourself—your motivations and obstacles, especially in the realm of relationships. And that you have gained a greater understanding of your partner. I wish you abundant success in shaping and embracing the life you envision for yourself, both now and in the days ahead.

I will leave you with a quote by one of the earliest motivational speakers, author and radio personality **Earl Nightingale,** describing how he views success:

> ## "Success is the progressive realization of a worthwhile goal or idea."

Inherent within success is the movement toward what you want. It isn't just about getting there; it's about embracing the moments, large-and-small, as you discover and rediscover yourselves and one another.

Thank you for taking this deep walk with me into exploring new ways to recover, heal, and create a dynamic and thriving relationship with your partner, within yourself, and with those you love and care about. May you be blessed with much love, kindness, respect, understanding, acceptance, and a deep commitment to living life that is aligned with your deeply held values and beliefs.

May you walk through the world knowing that you are thoroughly and completely loved. May you be blessed with the gift of wholehearted living and loving, and may you cherish the sacred experience of walking lightly upon this earth in your unique human body, emotional makeup, and spiritual essence, expanding and growing even more fully into your unique essence, knowing that who you are and how you express yourself matters.

> ## Love is a Courageous Journey into the Unknown Recesses of the Heart.

Wishing you a lifetime of Courageous Living and Loving!

*Dr. Jeanne Michele*

# Endnotes

1   Silva, T. (2021). Straight Men's Same-Sex Behavior. *Contexts*, *20*(3), 46-51. https://doi. org/10.1177/15365042211035339

2   Notes for men engaging in an affair with another man.

As with any affair, the first step is to get in touch with your own wants, needs, and desires. Sometimes there are significant religious/belief systems that and have influenced your life choices. Did you see engaging in an affair with a man as a way to keep your marriage vow intact? Do you have a preference for engaging with men? Is this a desire that you want to continue to explore?

This is a great time for you to step back and consider your options and preferences. If you find yourself in a state of inner conflict, you may first want to visit a nonjudgmental coach/ therapist who is well versed in the area of sexual choice and identity before speaking with your spouse.

In an ideal world, you are able to communicate your preferences, and potential uncertainty, with your partner. There is not a singular way through this situation. Partners need to jointly decide what they are and are not comfortable with and make decisions accordingly.

The biggest keys to creating and maintaining a vibrant, thriving relationship when in this situation are as follows:

- Take some time to explore your personal wants, needs, desires, fantasies, and relationship ideals for your partnership and its emotional/sexual expression.
- Engage in authentic, courageous conversations with your significant other (SO) to explore your discoveries and deeply listen to theirs.
- Decide as a couple what is okay, and what is not okay within your partnership.
- Create an agreed-upon plan for your relationship.
- Respect the process by honoring your commitments, and reassessing should situations occur that cause you to be tempted or interested in making a different choice.

While I have worked with couples in this situation, addressing this type of betrayal is beyond the scope of this book. If this is something you and your partner are working through, feel free to reach out to me individually. I would be happy to serve as a resource to help you both gain the clarity you need to make the best choices possible for yourselves and your family.

3   Castleman, Michael, MA. Why Infidelity in Relationships is so Common. (2023, Sept. 17). *Psychology Today.* https://www.psychologytoday.com/us/blog/all-about-sex/202102/why-infidelity-in-relationships-is-so-common

4   L.A. Intelligence. (2021, Mar. 10). Infidelity: The Cold Hard Truth About Cheating. *LAIntilligence.com.* Infidelity: The Cold Hard Truth About Cheating (laintelligence.com)

5   Martin, Rebecca A., Christensen, Andrew, and Atkins, David. C. "Infidelity in Behavioral Couple Therapy: Outcomes over 5 years Following Therapy." *Couple and Family Psychology: Research and Practice.* Vol. 3. (2014, Nov. 1): 1-12. DOI: 10.1037cfp0000012. https://www.apa.org/pubs/journals/features/cfp-0000012.pdf

6   Zimbardo, P. (1999; 2024) The Stanford Prison Experiment. https://www.prisonexp.org

7   Siegel, D. (2021) https://DrDanSiegel.com

8   Cherry, Kendra, MS. Ed. (2014, May 2). Erikson's Stages of Development: A Closer Look at the Eight Psychosocial Stages. *Verywell Mind.* Erikson's Stages of Development (verywell-mind.com)

9   Cherry, Kendra, MS Ed. (2023, Dec. 4) Identify vs. Role Confusion in Psychosocial Development. *Verywell Mind.* Identity vs. Role Confusion in Psychosocial Development (verywellmind.com)

10  Kolaitis, G., & Olff, M. (2017). Psychotraumatology in Greece. *European Journal of Psychotraumatology*, *8*(sup4). https://doi.org/10.1080/20008198.2017.13517575

11  Elesser, Kim. (2019, Feb. 14) These 6 Surprising Office Romance Stats Should be a Wake-up Call for Organizations. *Forbes.* (These 6 Surprising Office Romance Stats Should Be A Wake-Up Call For Organizations (forbes.com)

12  "Symptoms of addiction: What to know." *Medical News Today*, updated October 12, 2021. Accessed July 11, 2024. https://www.medicalnewstoday.com/articles/323459.

13  Sanchez Cuevas, Gema, MA. (2022, Jul. 28). The Attractiveness of What is Forbidden. *ExploringYourMind.com* https://exploringyourmind.com/attractiveness-whats-forbidden/

14  Leonard, Jayne. A Guide to EFT Tapping. (2019, Sept. 26). *Medical News Today.* https://www.medicalnewstoday.com/articles/326434

15  Chapman, G. (2024) Discover Your Love Language. https://The5LoveLanguages.com

16  Kumar, Karthik, MBBS. How Do Hugs Make You Feel? Medicine.net. (Accessed June 23, 2024). https://www.medicinenet.com/how_do_hugs_make_you_feel/article.htm

17  Mayo Clinic Staff. Positive Thinking: Stop Negative Self-Talk to Reduce Stress. MayoClinic (Accessed June 24, 2024) https://www.mayoclinic.org/healthy-lifestyle/stress-management/in-depth/positive-thinking/art-2004390

18  Gershon, Livia. "The Self-Help Mantra That Got Better and Better." *JSTOR Daily*, 13 Aug. 2020, daily.jstor.org/the-self-help-mantra-that-got-better-and-better/.

19  Bouffard, Karen. (2018, Jan. 1). Ex-Lion QB Helps Men Tackle Health Stigma. *The Detroit News*. https://www.detroitnews.com/story/news/local/michigan/2018/01/01/eric-hipple-mens-mental-health/109087956/

20  Lally, P., Cornelia H. M. Van Jaarsveld, H. W. W. Potts, and J. Warde (2009, Jul. 16). *European Journal of Social Psychology, Eur. J. Psychol.* 40, 998-1009. DOI: 10.1002/3jsp.674. How are habits formed: Modelling habit formation in the real world (ispa.pt)

21  Dweck, C. (2014, Dec). The Power of Believing You Can Improve. [Video file]. TED Conferences. www.ted.com/speakers/carol_dweck

22  Real, Terrence. *Us: Getting Past You and Me to Build a More Loving Relationship*. New York: Rodale Press; Random House. 2022.

23  Lisitsa, Elle, PhD. How to Fight Smarter: Soften Your Startup. (Accessed June 23, 2024). *Gottman.com.* How to Fight Smarter: Soften Your Start-Up (gottman.com)

24  Vitale, Joe and Hew Len Ihaleakala. *Zero Limits: The Hawaiian Secret for Health, Wealth, Peace, and More.* Hoboken: Wiley & Sons, Inc. 2009.

    The story behind the Ho'oponopono prayer as detailed in the book *Zero Limits*, describes how psychologist Dr. Ihaleakala Hew Lin used this prayer to transform a hospital ward of reactive mentally ill patients. He would first read through their charts and then recite the Ho'oponopono mantra, focused on each person. Remarkably, without ever meeting the patients in person, the once violent ward began to change for the better.

25  Himelstein, Cord. (2015, Mar. 12). Base Pay vs. Recognition: What's More Important? The keys to employee happiness and motivation may not be what you think. *Entrepreneur.com.* https://www.entrepreneur.com/leadership/base-pay-vs-recognition-whats-more-important/243258

# Bibliography

## BOOKS

Angelou, Maya. *I Know Why the Caged Bird Sings.* New York: Random House, 1969

Bader, Ellen, PhD, and Dr. Peter Pearson, and Judith Schwartz, *Tell Me Know Lies: How to Stop Lying to Your Partner and Yourself in the 4 Stages of Mariage.* New York: St. Martin's Press. 2001.

Baldoni, Justin. *Man Enough: Undefining My Masculinity.* New York: HarperCollins Publishers. 2021.

Beaton, Connor. *Men's Work: A Practical Guide to Face Your Darkness, End Self-Sabotage, and Find Freedom.* Boulder: Sounds True Publishers. 2023.

Beattie, Melody. *A Co-dependent's Guide to the 12 Steps: How to Finde the Right Program for You and Apply Each of the Twelve Steps to Your Own Issues.* New York: Fireside; Simon & Schuster. 1990; 1998.

Blanchard, Ken, PhD, and Dr. Spencer Johnson, MD. *The New One Minute Manager.* New York: HarperCollins Publishers. 2015.

Boyle, Greg. *Tattoos on the Heart: The Boundless Power of Compassion.* New York: Free Press; Simon & Schuster. 2010.

Brito, Maria. *How Creativity Rules the World: The Art and Business of Turning Your Ideas into Gold.* Harper Collins Leadership; Harper Collins. Canada: 2022.

Brown, Brené. 20*The Gifts of Imperfection*: 10th ann. ed. New York: Random House; Penguin Random House Publishing. 2010; 2020

Brown, Brené. *Dare to Lead: Brave Work. Tough Conversations. Whole Hearts.* New York: Random House Publishing, 2018.

Burchard, Brendon. *The Motivation Manifesto: 9 Declarations to Claim Your Personal Power.* Hay House. Macon: 2014.

Burney, Robert. *Codependence: The Dance of Wounded Souls.* Deerfield Beach, FL: Joy to You & Me Enterprises, 1995.

Butcher, Jim. *The White Knight.* New York: Roc, 2007.

Chapman, Gary. *The 5 Love Languages: The Secret to Love that Lasts.* Chicago: Northfield Publishing. 1992; 2015.

Chapman, Gary. *Things I Wish I'd Known Before We Got Married.* Chicago: Northfield Publishing. 2010.

Chopra, Deepak. *The Seven Spiritual Laws of Success: A Pocket Guide to Fulfilling Your Dreams.* San Rafael: Amber-Allen Publishing. 1994; 2007.

Clark, Amy, PhD, and Roy Clark. *The 4 Intimacies: Unlocking the Love You Desire.* USA: Lovemaker Publishing. 2022.

Covey, Stephen M. R., *The Speed of Trust: The One Thing that Changes Everything.* New York: Free Press; Simon & Shuster. 2006; 2018.

DePree, Max. *Leadership Is an Art.* New York: Dell Publishing, 2004.

Diamond, Jed. *The Irritable Male Syndrome: Managing the 4 Key Causes of Depression and Aggression.* USA: Rodale Inc. 2004.

Feltman, Charles. *The Thin Book of Trust: An Essential Primer for Building Trust at Work.* 2nd ed. Bend: Thin Book Publishing Company. 2021.

Ferrini, Paul. *Dancing with the Beloved: Opening Our Hearts to the Lessons of Love.* USA: Paul Ferrini. 2001.

Ford, Debbie. *The Right Questions: Ten Essential Questions to Guide You to an Extraordinary Life.* New York: HarperOne, 2003.

Frankl, Victor. *Man's Search for Meaning.* Boston: Beacon Press. 1959; 2006

Gibran, Kahlil. *The Prophet.* New York: Alfred A. Knopf; Random House. 1923; 1951.

Gilbert, Elizabeth. *Committed: A skeptic makes peace with marriage* [Audiobook]. New York: Penguin Audio. 2010.

Gladwell Malcolm. *The Tipping Point: How Little Things Can Make a Big Difference.* Boston; New York, London: Little Brown and Company. 2000.

Gottman, John, PhD and Nan Silver. *The Seven Principles for Making Marriage Work; A Practical Guide from the Country's Foremost Relationship Expert.* New York: Harmony Books; Crown Publishing; Penguin Random House. 1992; 2015.

Hale, Amanda. *The Single Woman. Life, Love, and a Dash of Sass.* Nashville: Thomas Nelson; Thomas Nelson, Inc. 2013.

Hendricks, Greer, and Sarah Pekkanen. *An Anonymous Girl.* New York: St. Martin's Press, 2019.

Hipple, Eric and Dr. Gloria Horsley et al. *Real Men do Cry: A Quarterback's Story of Tackling Depression and Surviving Suicidal Loss.* USA: Quality of Life Publishing. 2008.

Hulnick, Mary, PhD. and Dr. Ron Hulnick. *Remembering the Light Within: A Course in Soul-Centered Living.* USA: Hay House. 2017.

Jackson, Phil and Hugh Delaney, *Sacred Hoops: Spiritual Lessons of a Hardwood Warrior.* New York: Hyperion; Hatchette Book Group. 1995; 2020.

Jeffers, Susan, PhD. *Feel the Fear and Do it Anyway: Dynamic Techniques for Turning Fear, Indecision and Anger, into Power, Action, and Love.* 20th ann. ed. USA: Ballantine Books. 2007.

Jung, Carl G. *Man and His Symbols.* Garden City, N.Y.: Doubleday, 1964. Keen, Sam. *Fire in the Belly: On Being a Man.* New York: Bantam Books. 1991.

Kelly, Matthew. *Life is Messy.* USA: Blue Sparrow. 2021.

Kelly, Matthew. *Perfectly Yourself. Discovering God's Dream for You.* 3rd ed. N, Palm Beach: Beacon Publishing. 2006; 2017.

Kipnis Aaron R., PhD. *Knights Without Armor: A Guide to the Inner Lives of Men.* 3rd ed. Santa Barbara: Indigo Books. 2004.

Kleypas, Lisa. *Blue-Eyed Devil.* New York: St. Martin's Press. 2008.

Kornfield, Jack. *A Path with Heart: A Guide Through the Perils and Promises of Spiritual Life.* New York: Bantam Books; Doubleday Publishing Group, Inc. 1993.

Lee, Harper. *To Kill a Mockingbird.* New York: Harper Perennial Modern Classics, 2006.

Levine, Amir, and Rachel Heller. 2010. *Attached: The New Science of Adult Attachment and How It Can Help You Find—and Keep—Love.* New York: TarcherPerigee.

Levine, Peter with Ann Frederick. *Waking the Tiger: Healing Trauma.* Berkeley: North Atlantic Books. 1997.

Masters, Robert Augustus, PhD. *To Be a Man: A Guide to True Masculine Power.* Boulder: Sounds True. 2018.

Maté, Gabor, MD. *In the Realm of Hungry Ghosts: Close Encounters with Addiction.* Berkley: North Atlantic Books. 2008; 2010.

Maté, Gabor, MD, with Daniel Maté, *The Myth of Normal: Trauma, Illness & Healing in a Toxic Culture.* New York: Avery; Penguin Random House: 2022.

Nerburn, Kent. *Letters to My Son: A Father's Wisdom on Manhood, Life and Love.* Novato: New World Library. 1994; 2014.

O'Donohue, John. *To Bless the Space Between Us: A Book of Blessings.* New York: Crown Publishing; Penguin Random House. 2001.

Ortner, Nick. *The Tapping Solution: A Revolutionary System for Stress-free Living.* Carlsbad: Hay House. 2013.

Perel, Esther. *The State of Affairs: Rethinking Infidelity.* New York: Harper. 2017.

Plank, Liz. *For the Love of Men: From Toxic to a More Mindful Masculinity*. St. Martin's Griffin; St. Martin's Press. 2019

Reid, Taylor Jenkins. *The Seven Husbands of Evelyn Hugo*. Miami: Atria Books, 2017.

Ruiz, Don Miguel. *The Four Agreements: A Practical Guide to Personal Freedom*. San Rafael, CA: Amber-Allen Publishing, 1997.

Siegel, Daniel, MD. *The Neurobiology of We: How Relationships, the Mind, and the Brain Interact to Shape Who We Are*. Boulder: Sounds True. Audible Books and Originals. 2011.

Silverstein, Shel. *The Missing Piece*. New York: Harper Collins Children's Books; Harper Collins Publishers. 1976; 2006.

Skinner, Kevin, PhD. *Treating Trauma from Sexual Betrayal: The Essential Tools for Healing*. Lindon: KSkinner Corp. 2017.

Sparks, Nicholas. *At First Sight*. New York: Grand Central Publishing, 2005.

Szymczak, Leonard and Rick Broniec. *Power Tools for Men: A Blueprint for Healthy Masculinity*. Dana Point: GPS Books. 2023.

Thoreau, Henry David. *Walden, or Life in the Woods*. Boston: Ticknor and Fields, 1854

Vitale, Joe and Hew Len Ihaleakala. *Zero Limits: The Hawaiian Secret for Health, Wealth, Peace, and More*. Hoboken: Wiley & Sons, Inc. 2009.

Wexler, David, PhD., *When Good Men Behave Badly: Change your Behavior, Change Your Relationship*. Oakland: New Harbinger Publications. 2004.

Wireland, John. *From the Core: A New Masculine Paradigm for Leading with Love, Living Your Truth, and Healing the World*. Boulder: Sounds True. 2022.

Wooden, John with Jack Tobin. *They Call Me Coach*. New York: McGraw Hill. 2003.

Youngblood, GD. *The Masculine in Relationship: A Blueprint for Inspiring the Trust, Lust, and Devotion of a Strong Woman*. San Francisco: GS Youngblood. 2019

Zahariades, Daman. *The Art of Letting Go: How to Let Go of the Past, Look Forward to the Future, and Finally Enjoy the Emotional Freedom You Deserve*. Daman Zahariades. 2022

Zweig, Connie and Jeremiah Abrams. *Meeting the Shadow: The Hidden Power of the Dark Side of Human Nature*. New York: Jeremy P. Tarcher; Penguin Books. 1991.

# ARTICLES

Baldwin, James. "As Much Truth As One Can Bear." The New York Times, January 14, 1962.

Bouffard, Karen. "Ex-Lion QB Helps Men Tackle Health Stigma," *The Detroit News*, January 1, 2018, https://www.detroitnews.com/story/news/local/michigan/2018/01/01/eric-hipple-mens-mental-health/109087956/.

Castleman, Michael, MA, "Why Infidelity in Relationships is so Common," *Psychology Today*, September 17, 2023, https://www.psychologytoday.com/us/blog/all-about-sex/202102/why-infidelity-in-relationships-is-so-common.

Cherry, Kendra, MS Ed., "Erikson's Stages of Development: A Closer Look at the Eight Psychosocial Stages," *Verywell Mind*, May 2, 2014, Erikson's Stages of Development, https://www.verywellmind.com/eriksons-stages-of-development-2795746.

Cherry, Kendra, MS Ed., "Identity vs. Role Confusion in Psychosocial Development," *Verywell Mind*, December 4, 2023, Identity vs. Role Confusion in Psychosocial Development, https://www.verywellmind.com/identity-vs-role-confusion-2795732.

Elesser, Kim. "These 6 Surprising Office Romance Stats Should be a Wake-up Call for Organizations," *Forbes*, February 14, 2019, These 6 Surprising Office Romance Stats Should Be A Wake-Up Call For Organizations, https://www.forbes.com/sites/kimelester/2019/02/14/these-6-surprising-office-romance-stats-should-be-a-wake-up-call-for-organizations/.

Himelstein, Cord. "Base Pay vs. Recognition: What's More Important? The keys to employee happiness and motivation may not be what you think," *Entrepreneur.com*, March 12, 2015, https://www.entrepreneur.com/leadership/base-pay-vs-recognition-whats-more-important/243258.

Kolaitis, G., and M. Olff. 2017. "Psychotraumatology in Greece." *European Journal of Psychotraumatology* 8, suppl. 4. https://doi.org/10.1080/20008198.2017.1351757.

Kumar, Karthik, MBBS. "How Do Hugs Make You Feel?" *MedicineNet*. Accessed June 23, 2024. https://www.medicinenet.com/how_do_hugs_make_you_feel/article.htm.

L.A. Intelligence. "Infidelity: The Cold Hard Truth About Cheating." *L.A. Intelligence*. March 10, 2021. https://laintelligence.com/infidelity-the-cold-hard-truth-about-cheating.

Lally, P., Cornelia H. M. Van Jaarsveld, H. W. W. Potts, and J. Warde. 2009. "How Are Habits Formed: Modelling Habit Formation in the Real World." *European Journal of Social Psychology* 40: 998-1009. https://doi.org/10.1002/ejsp.674. https://ispa.pt/how-are-habits-formed-modelling-habit-formation-in-the-real-world.

Leonard, Jayne. "A Guide to EFT Tapping." *Medical News Today*. September 26, 2019. https://www.medicalnewstoday.com/articles/326434.

Lisitsa, Elle, PhD. "How to Fight Smarter: Soften Your Startup." Accessed June 23, 2024. Gottman.com. https://gottman.com/how-to-fight-smarter-soften-your-start-up.

Martin, Rebecca A., Andrew Christensen, and David C. Atkins. "Infidelity in Behavioral Couple Therapy: Outcomes over 5 Years Following Therapy." *Couple and Family Psychology: Research and Practice* 3 (November 1, 2014): 1-12. https://doi.org/10.1037/cfp0000012. https://www.apa.org/pubs/journals/features/cfp-0000012.pdf.

Mayo Clinic Staff. "Positive Thinking: Stop Negative Self-Talk to Reduce Stress." Mayo Clinic. Accessed June 24, 2024. https://www.mayoclinic.org/healthy-lifestyle/stress-management/in-depth/positive-thinking/art-2004390.

Sanchez Cuevas, Gema, MA. "The Attractiveness of What is Forbidden." *Exploring Your Mind*, July 28, 2022. https://exploringyourmind.com/attractiveness-whats-forbidden/.

Silva, Tony. 2021. "Straight Men's Same-Sex Behavior." *Contexts* 20, no. 3: 46-51. https://doi.org/10.1177/15365042211035339.

## WEBSITES AND TED TALKS

Barker, Gary. (2024, February 1). *A reframing of masculinity, rooted in empathy*. TED. YouTube. Accessed Aug. 3, 2024. https://www.youtube.com/watch?v=coAopEn8Fn4

Brown, Brené. 2010. "The Power of Vulnerability." TED Conferences, March. Video, https://www.ted.com/talks/brene_brown_on_vulnerability.

Chapman, G. (2024). *Discover Your Love Language*. Accessed July 4, 2024, from https://The5LoveLanguages.com

Dweck, Carol. 2014. "The Power of Believing You Can Improve." TED Conferences, December. Video, https://www.ted.com/speakers/carol_dweck.

Dion, Kalen. "Kalen Dion Poetry." Accessed July 19, 2024. https://www.kalendionpoetry.com/about.

Mate, Gabor, and J.B. Coleman. 2024. "Conversational Intervention on Working Through Addiction and Its Associated Trauma." YouTube. Video, https://www.youtube.com/watch?v=90xi362qDRk.

Mate, Gabor, and J.B. Coleman. 2024. "How to Deal with the Pain of My Past: Dr. Gabor Will Uncover the Secrets to Engaging with the Tension." YouTube. Video, https://www.youtube.com/watch?v=90xi362qDRk.

Siegel, Daniel J. 2021. "Dr. Dan Siegel." Accessed July 19, 2024. https://DrDanSiegel.com.

Stein, Alan, Jr. n.d. "Discussions are Better than Arguments, Because an Argument is Designed to Find out Who is Right, and a Discussion is Designed to Find out What is Right." Alan Stein, Jr. Accessed July 8, 2024. https://alansteinjr.com/discussions-are-better-than-arguments/.

Zimbardo, Philip. The Stanford Prison Experiment. 1999; 2024. Accessed July 19, 2024. https://www.prisonexp.org.

## MOVIES AND QUOTES

Bogart, H. (n.d.). "*I was born when you kissed me. I died when you left me. I lived a few weeks while you loved me.*" Goodreads. Accessed July 4, 2024, from https://www.goodreads.com/author/quotes/279455.Humphrey_Bogart

Bryant, Carol. "Love is a 2-way street constantly under construction." Goodreads. Accessed June 20, 2024. URL: https://www.goodreads.com/quotes/445582-love-is-a-two-way-street-constantly-under-construction

Butcher, J. (n.d.). "*Anger is just anger. It isn't good. It isn't bad. It just is. What you do with it is what matters. It's like anything else. You can use it to build or to destroy. You just have to make the choice.*" Goodreads. Accessed July 10, 2024, from https://www.goodreads.com/quotes/214421-anger-is-just-anger-it-isn-t-good-it-isn-t-bad.

Coue, E. "*The Self-Help Mantra That Got Better and Better.*" *JSTOR Daily*. Accessed July 14, 2024. https://daily.jstor.org/the-self-help-mantra-that-got-better-and-better/.

*Jerry Maguire*. Directed by Cameron Crowe. Performed by Tom Cruise, Cuba Gooding Jr., and Renée Zellweger. Columbia Pictures, 1996.

Daly, T. (n.d.). *Tim Daly Quotes*. Goodreads. Accessed July 8, 2024, from https://www.goodreads.com/quotes/search?utf8=%E2%9C%93&q=tim+daly&commit=Search

Hillman, J. (1991). "*Loving oneself is no easy matter just because it means loving all of oneself, including the shadow where one is inferior and so socially unacceptable. The care one gives this humiliating part is also the cure.*" In C. Zweig & J. Abrams (Eds.), *Meeting the Shadow: The Hidden Power of the Dark Side of Human Nature* (p. 31). Jeremy P. Tarcher/Putnam.

Malik, Z. (n.d.). *Zayn Malik Quotes*. Goodreads. Accessed July 8, 2024, from https://www.goodreads.com/quotes/537705-there-comes-a-day-when-you-realise-turning-the-page

Marley, B. (n.d.). *Bob Marley Quotes*. Goodreads. Accessed July 10, 2024, from https://www.goodreads.com/quotes/151476-only-once-in-your-life-i-truly-believe-you-find

McCloy, John J. "*Humility Leads to Strength and note weakness.*" AZ Quotes. Accessed July 10, 2024, https://www.azquotes.com/author/23119-John_J_McCloy.

Merriam-Webster's Collegiate Dictionary. 11th ed. Springfield: Merriam-Webster, 2003. s.v. "erotic."

Merriam-Webster's Collegiate Dictionary. 11th ed. Springfield: Merriam-Webster, 2003. s.v. "sex."

Monroe, Marilyn. "Sexuality is a vibrant force within us all. It inspires us to be more than we ever thought we could be."

Perry, Tyler. "*It's not an easy journey, to get to a place where you forgive people, but it is such a powerful place, because it frees you.*" Goodreads. Accessed July 10, 2024,  Quote by Tyler Perry: "It's not an easy journey, to get to a place whe..." (goodreads.com)

Thrust, Fiona. *Naked and Sexual*. 2014. Goodreads, Accessed June 22, 2024. www.goodreads.com/book/show/23201647-naked-and-sexual

## RESOURCES AND PODCASTS

Baldoni, J. (n.d.). *The We Are Man Enough Podcast.* [YouTube]. Accessed July 4, 2024, from https://www.youtube.com/channel/UC2MbPazrSLEbgiHT3yQ4DnQ

Howes, L. (n.d.). *The School of Greatness* [Podcast]. Accessed July 4, 2024, from https://podcasts.apple.com/us/podcast/the-school-of-greatness/id596047499

The Mankind Project. (n.d.). *Men's Community for the 21st Century*. Accessed July 4, 2024, from https://TheMankindProject.org

Real, Terry. (n.d.). *The crisis of masculinity: Why men struggle to show emotion*. YouTube. Accessed Aug. 3, 2024, from https://www.youtube.com/watch?v=UGsiS2iBkZs

*Remaking Manhood: The Healthy Masculinity Podcast*. (n.d.). Podcast. Accessed July 4, 2024, from https://podcasts.apple.com/us/podcast/remaking-manhood-the-healthy-masculinity-podcast/id1559291290

# Acknowledgements
# and Heartfelt Thanks

Writing *The Infidelity Cure* has been a journey of discovery, compassion, and commitment. I am deeply grateful to all who have supported and inspired me along the way. I'd like to take a moment to acknowledge a few key individuals.

As writers, we draw inspiration from the works of others that inform and shape our own. While many of these influential sources are listed in the bibliography, I want to extend special thanks to two exceptional writers and educators whose dedication to expanding understanding and compassion for the human condition deeply resonates with me—Drs. Gabor Maté and Daniel Siegel. These men are true heroes, embodying an unwavering commitment to personal growth, lifelong learning, and inspiring positive change in the world.

To my corporate mentors, especially Ed Bayer and Steve Bloom, I offer heartfelt thanks. Your creativity, humor, and leadership were instrumental in helping me grow, sharpen my leadership skills, and confidently build my corporate career.

I am also profoundly grateful to Drs. Ron and Mary Hulnick for their extraordinary explorations in the advancement of human consciousness. Your unwavering love, respect, and commitment to creating a compassionate, judgment-free world has inspired me and countless others to learn, grow, and pursue careers in the healing professions.

For guiding me through some of the most challenging times in my life, I extend my heartfelt gratitude to Dr. Laura Pinegar. Our time together was instrumental in inspiring the pursuit of my current field and exemplifying excellence in the healing arts.

To my friends, editors, and coaches, your encouragement and belief in my ability to tackle this challenging topic have been invaluable. Diane Altomare guided me through moments of doubt and modeled writing excellence. John Seeley supported me when I felt like giving up, and Patrick's steadfast faith in me helped me to continue believing in myself.

My sincere appreciation also extends to those who helped breathe life into this work. Jocelyn Carbonara's expert editing helped shape the book's final versions, while Ian Koviak and Alan Dino Hebel of BookDesigners patiently guided this first-time author through the design process, transforming words into a work of art.

And to my mama, whose unshakable belief in me laid the foundation for my confidence, resilience, and the work I do today. Thank you for the countless hours and unwavering encouragement you invested in nurturing my curiosity and supporting me in living my dreams.

I am grateful to the spiritual forces who continue to guide and sustain me, teaching me patience and the power of silence to connect with wisdom that transcends both internal and external obstacles.

And, I am forever humbled and grateful to the courageous men and women who have inspired this work. Thank you for trusting me to accompany you on your healing journey. May your courage inspire others and demonstrate the transformative power of love, dedication, and commitment to healing hearts and changing lives.

Finally, my hope for you, dear reader, is that this work serves as a valuable resource, offering pearls of wisdom that illustrate the power of commitment, inspire hope, and ignite curiosity. May it support you in your ongoing journey of transformation, learning, and deepening love

Dr. Jeanne is currently working on her next book, *Loving Courageously*.
To stay informed about her work and upcoming projects, please visit:
drjeannemichele.com/connect

Printed in the USA
CPSIA information can be obtained
at www.ICGtesting.com
CBHW082017250924
14924CB00039B/744